A GUIDE TO ILLUSTRIOUS I

BY JULIA HOLMES

The Little Bookroom • New York

Editors: Angela Hederman and Nadia Aguiar
Book Design: Milton Glaser, Inc.

First printing: November 2004. Printed in U.S.A.

Library of Congress Cataloging-in-Publication Data.
Holmes, Julia, 1970–. One hundred New Yorkers : a
guide to illustrious lives & locations / Julia Holmes.
p. cm. ISBN 1-892145-31-6 1. Celebrities–
Homes and haunts–New York (State)–New
York–Guidebooks. 2. Historic sites–New York
(State)–New York–Guidebooks. 3. New York
(N.Y.)–Guidebooks. 4. New York (N.Y.)–Biography.
5. New York (N.Y.)–Intellectual life.
I. Title. F128.18.H635 2004
920.0747'1'0904–dc22
2004013944

Published by The Little Bookroom
1755 Broadway, Fifth floor, New York, NY 10019
(212) 293-1643 Fax (212) 333-5374
editorial@littlebookroom.com

Distributed to the trade by Publishers Group West.

Contents

Introduction

These 100 New Yorkers, illustrious and sometimes notorious, lived in New York during different periods in the city's three-hundred-and-fifty-year history. Whether they lived in New Amsterdam in the seventeenth century or in the Greenwich Village of the early twentieth, they experienced the same New York that everyone must, one invented along the way, a city particular to their ambitions, fortunes, and affinities. By following their paths, it's possible to explore the intrinsic city, often elusive behind the great wall of noise, activity, and architecture that is also New York.

Each of these 100 was deeply and permanently preoccupied with New York City. For many, like Dawn Powell and Malcolm X, the city stood for a sense of personal destiny, and they made it their home. Those who chose to leave it (Edith Wharton, Sojourner Truth) obsessed over what it lacked or what it had lost; those who lamented its rough character (Mark Twain, Sarah Bernhardt) loved it nonetheless; some despaired over its moral lassitude and its appetite for danger and novelty (Anthony Comstock); while others (Emma Goldman, Dorothy Day) devoted themselves to helping the victims of city life—immigrants, workers, poor women, and children. All of them were both frustrated and enchanted by New York. Through novels, paintings, performances, philanthropy, legislation, invention, and commerce, they strove to create a truer, bigger picture of what New York is and might be.

These New Yorkers moved to the city from all over the country and the world: from Denmark, Mexico, Russia, China, and Lebanon; from the Midwest, the Deep South, and from elsewhere in the state of New York. Some of them, like Joseph Cornell and Walt Whitman, walked thousands of miles through the city streets in obsessive pursuit of objects and impressions that captured the energetic and variable nature of the living metropolis. Others, like Henry James, lived largely off their memories of a genteel, romantic, and circumscribed city.

There are two indexes. One includes all the individuals and sites profiled. The other is an index of the connections among the 100 New Yorkers and the places in the city where their lives intersected: the fateful meeting of Elizabeth Bishop and Marianne Moore on the bench outside of the New York Public Library reading room; architect Stanford White's creation of the Washington Square Arch, which Marcel Duchamp would storm in the next century to declare a Free and Independent Republic of Greenwich Village; the midnight walks of Jacob Riis and Theodore Roosevelt through the slums of Lower Manhattan. When using this book, it is helpful to know that sites in the Bronx, Brooklyn, Queens, and Staten Island are designated by a street address, followed by neighborhood and borough; sites in Manhattan are designated by street address only.

These biographies and site descriptions are not intended to be comprehensive. Neither are these 100 New Yorkers meant to be the "Top 100" or exhaustive of the many individuals and communities that have shaped the life of the city. While the majority of them were born or later settled in New York, there are some, like Diego Rivera, who lived here only briefly. New York made a complicated and lasting impression on all of them, however, and each contributed to its artistic, political, and social climate. New York is cultivated, rambunctious, towering, cramped, generous, mysterious, and, in moments, profoundly serene. In short, it is as diverse and driven as these 100 New Yorkers, who altered the city and were altered by it, and as the millions who, either passing through or rooted in the life of the city, choose New York.

JULIA HOLMES, NEW YORK CITY

Diane Arbus

PHOTOGRAPHER 1923–1971

"All odd and splendid as freaks and
nobody able to see himself, all of us victims of
the especial shape we come in."

L ike Weegee, whom she admired, Diane Arbus focused her lens on the troubled, dark, and eccentric outer ring of city life. Photojournalistic predecessors had captured slum life, criminal life, and public spectacle, but Arbus the artist managed to implicate the viewer in new and controversial ways. Though she photographed a range of people, she became famous for her portraits of "freaks"—twins, dwarves, drug addicts, the institutionalized, the transgendered, and others, it was argued, who were less than able to protect themselves from the lens. Even when Arbus photographed apparently ordinary couples on lunch breaks or boys playing in Central Park, she made them seem "freakish" and succeeded in blurring the conventional division between normal and abnormal. The reckless, some said ruthless, chronicler of human frailty was charismatic and outgoing. Arbus grew up with her brother, the poet Howard Nemerov, in roomy, well-appointed comfort near Central Park. She was physically slight and tended to daydream. She married Allan Arbus, an employee in her family's department store, and the couple launched a fashion photography studio—he did the shooting, and Arbus did the styling. At thirty-three, Arbus tired of traditional family photos and fashion shoots and enrolled in a class with Viennese photographer Lisette Model, whose pictures often captured grotesque aspects of city life. Arbus was awarded Guggenheim Fellowships in 1963 for "Photographic studies of American rites, manners, and customs" and again in 1966. Arbus claimed that her favorite activity was to go where she had never been before. At forty-eight, she took her own life in her New York apartment.

Central Park

From Central Park South (59th Street) to Central Park North (110th Street)
and from Fifth Avenue to Central Park West (Eighth Avenue)

Arbus grew up in an apartment on Central Park West—one of her childhood bedrooms, in which she was forced to rest and convalesce during periods of fragile health, faced the park. Her brother, Howard Nemerov, recalled being taken to the park by their nannies, who admonished the children to keep on their white gloves while they played in the sandbox. One of Arbus's strongest and earliest memories was of a shantytown in the then drained reservoir. This preoccupation with unpleasant and willfully ignored aspects of the city prefigured her later expeditions in search of subjects, which yielded works such as *Jack Dracula, The Marked Man* (1961), a photo of a man tattooed from head to foot and lying in the grass in Central Park. Now a place for picnics, weekend idylls, and summer concerts, Central Park in the 1960s was a frightening prospect to many New Yorkers. Crime flourished and the presence of figures such as Jack Dracula had become emblematic to some of the city in a state of decline. Unlike many New Yorkers, who steered clear of the park, Arbus spent much time here in search of subjects.

Museum of Modern Art (MoMA)

11 West 53rd Street, between Fifth and Sixth Avenues
tel. (212) 708-9400, www.moma.org

In 1967, Arbus's photographs appeared alongside the works of fellow young photographers Lee Friedlander and Garry Winogrand (who took the photo of Arbus on page 1) in a MoMA exhibit titled "New Documents." In the year after Arbus's death, MoMA mounted a retrospective of her work—it broke attendance records for a solo photography show. That same year, she became the first American photographer to be represented at the Venice Biennale. MoMA was an important place in Arbus's life and work; she often met with other photographers and curators here, and was a regular at openings and exhibitions throughout the 1960s.

New School University

66 West 12th Street, between Fifth and Sixth Avenues
tel. (212) 229-5600, www.newschool.edu

Arbus studied at The New School under her mentor Lisette Model in 1957 and 1958. Model encouraged Arbus to develop an eye for the unusual, the unexpected, and the vulnerable. Arbus later taught for the New School at the Parsons School of Design.

Former residence

121-1/2 Charles Street, between Greenwich and Hudson Streets

Arbus lived in this converted stable from 1959 to 1968 after her marriage to Allan Arbus ended. She slept in the living room while her daughters slept in the upstairs bedroom.

Former residence of Weegee

451 West 47th Street, between Ninth and Tenth Avenues

Arbus visited a broken-down brownstone at this address in 1968. It was the last home of the crime photographer Weegee, whose work she greatly admired. Weegee, notoriously disorganized, had stuffed thousands of negatives and photographs into bags and piled them on the floor. At the invitation of Weegee's companion Wilma Wilcox, Arbus spent hours poring over the images.

. . . .

Westbeth
77 Bethune Street at West Street

On July 28, 1971, Arbus committed suicide in her apartment at Westbeth, which had been converted into artists' housing two years earlier. She had been happy here for a period; she had friends in the building, and taught young photographers in an empty apartment. Westbeth was a vibrant, chaotic place; artists left their doors open and an atmosphere of bohemian decadence prevailed. Her own apartment, a ninth-floor duplex facing the Hudson, was decorated with negatives and proofs of her photographs, as well as odd and unsettling pictures by others. The complex, which still operates as a special residence for artists, once held the labs for Bell Telephone/Western Electric. Notable inventions that emerged from this building include the vacuum tube, radar, and "talkies," the first films with recorded sound.

Louis "Satchmo" Armstrong
JAZZ MUSICIAN 1901–1971

L ouis Armstrong was born in the Storeyville section of New Orleans, in the poor neighborhood known as "The Battlefield." As a boy, he supported his mother and siblings by delivering coal, working on a junk wagon, singing for pennies on street corners, and maintaining graves for tips. He bought his first cornet at the age of six and joined his first band at the Colored Waif's Home for Boys, where he had been sent for two years as punishment for prankishly shooting blanks into the air on New Year's Eve, 1912. After leaving the home, Satchmo—abridged from his nickname "Satchelmouth"—played with the eminent bandleader King Oliver in New Orleans and in Chicago. In his early twenties, Armstrong found work as a musician on the riverboats that chugged up and down the Mississippi. In 1929, he moved to New York, where he performed and recorded with his jazz peers, including Duke Ellington and Billie Holiday. He eventually toured the globe, playing an average of three hundred concerts a year. When not on the road, the greatest trumpeter in the world enjoyed a neighborly and modest life in Queens, surrounded by close friends and towers of correspondence from fans around the world.

. . . .

Louis Armstrong House
34-56 107th Street, between 34th and 37th Avenues
Corona, Queens
tel. (718) 478-8274, www.satchmo.net

In 1942, Armstrong married his fourth wife, Lucille Wilson, a dancer at the Cotton Club in Harlem. Armstrong had spent most of his life on the move between temporary abodes, but soon after their marriage, Lucille found and bought this house on 107th Street in Corona, Queens, while Armstrong was away on tour. In 1943, the Armstrongs moved in. They stayed in the house for the rest of their lives. Unassuming from the outside, the house's interiors were enriched over the decades with thousands of souvenirs and photographs from Armstrong's travels. The Armstrongs renovated many rooms of the house, adding a turquoise kitchen and an opulent master bath with mirrored walls and gold fix-

tures. When Armstrong's tour bus rolled into the neighborhood, local children ran to greet him, carrying his bags and trumpet to his house, where they ate ice cream and watched television with him in the den.

The restored home reopened to visitors as a museum in 2003. The Louis Armstrong House's forty-minute tour is designed to make visitors feel like guests in the home. No one has lived in the house since the death of Lucille Armstrong in 1983, and all furniture, memorabilia, clippings, and clothing are original to the house.

Louis Armstrong Archives

Queens College, The Rosenthal Library, Room 332
65-30 Kissena Boulevard, Flushing, Queens
tel. (718) 997-3670, www.satchmo.net

The Louis Armstrong Archives at Queens College maintains the richest collection of Louis Armstrong memorabilia. Exhibits from the collection are installed in the newly renovated Louis Armstrong House.

The Queens Jazz Trail Tour

Flushing Town Hall
137-35 Northern Boulevard, Flushing, Queens
tel. (718) 463-7700, www.flushingtownhall.org

A three-hour tour through the bright and crowded jazz history of Queens includes significant locations from the settled, last chapter of Armstrong's life. Stops include the Louis Armstrong House and Joe's Artistic Barber Shop, where Armstrong had his hair cut for many years.

Flushing Cemetery

163-06 46th Avenue, at 164th Street
Flushing, Queens

A stone engraved with "Satchmo" marks the grave of Louis Armstrong. He was laid to rest in Flushing Cemetery with Frank Sinatra, Ella Fitzgerald, Pearl Bailey, and Dizzy Gillespie—his Queens neighbor—acting as honorary pallbearers.

John Jacob Astor IV

HOTELIER 1864–1912

I n 1894, John Jacob Astor IV published *A Journey in Other Worlds*, a science-romance in which Astor-like gentlemen travel to Jupiter and Saturn, hunt strange game for science and sport, and meet with an oracle. Astor's characters predict that Manhattan will become the "perfection of civilization" by the year 2000: the "omnipotent fluid" of electricity will course through factories and homes, Anglo-Saxon gentlemen will triumph in the struggle for the cultural life of the city, and strolling New Yorkers will pluck ripe fruit from shade-giving trees lining wide avenues and "breathing-squares." Prescient about technology, Astor patented a new bicycle brake and a pneumatic road improver. Despite these forays into science fiction and engineering, Astor was inevitably most famous as the inheritor of the Astor fortune. At twenty-eight, he was worth fifty million dollars and became head of the American House of Astor (his rival cousin, William Waldorf Astor, had left for England). Astor was simultaneously a callous landlord of vast tenements in Lower Manhattan, singled out by muckraking journalist Jacob Riis as among the worst in the city, and a master hotelier whose Waldorf-Astoria became the unofficial national headquarters of exclusivity, propriety, and New York glamour. In 1911, he married eighteen-year-old Madeleine Force in his mother's famous ballroom. Society frowned on the match, and the newly married pair left for extended travel in Egypt and Europe. Upon their return on the *Titanic*, pregnant Force was saved in a lifeboat. Astor was last seen alive standing on the deck.

Private collection

Waldorf-Astoria Hotel
301 Park Avenue, between East 49th and East 50th Streets

The Empire State Building stands on the site of the original Waldorf-Astoria, which, in turn, stood upon the site of the first mansion of Astor's mother, Mrs. Caroline Astor—the arbiter of taste in New York City in the late nineteenth century. Mrs. Astor was effectively evicted by her nephew William Waldorf Astor, when he built a thirteen-story hotel named the Waldorf in 1893 on the Astor family lot at Fifth Avenue between 33rd and 34th Streets. Mrs. Astor resettled farther uptown. In retaliation, John Jacob Astor IV erected a taller, grander tower on the site of his mother's abandoned mansion. Full of contempt for each other, the cousins nonetheless cooperated for profit and merged their neighboring hotels. All connecting hallways and lobbies were designed so that they could be sealed off and the Waldorf and the Astoria could be run as separate hotels in the event of a renewed family feud.

Because of the celebrated balls thrown by Mrs. Astor, the dining room of the Waldorf-Astoria became the most important place to be seen by members of society. Henry James described the lobby of the Waldorf-Astoria as "a gorgeous golden blur, a paradise peopled with unmistakable American shapes."

The current Waldorf-Astoria was built in 1931.

St. Regis Hotel
2 East 55th Street at Fifth Avenue
tel. (212) 753-4500, www.stregis.com

The St. Regis is Astor's other great hotel, which opened in 1904. Behind the beaux-arts facade, Astor installed futuristic conveniences, and was among the first to provide private telephones in each room, personal thermostats that empowered guests with "climate control," and a centralized vacuum system. The King Cole Restaurant is designed around the Maxfield Parrish mural that once hung in the Knickerbocker Hotel Bar.

Site of Astor mansion
840 Fifth Avenue at East 65th Street

In 1927, the synagogue Temple Emanu-El was built on the former site of the mansion that architect Richard Morris Hunt had designed for Mrs. Caroline Astor. She and professional snob Ward McAllister drafted "the Four Hundred," a roster of New Yorkers they considered true members of society. Four hundred was the theoretical capacity of her ballroom, and the list was tightly guarded to prevent nouveau riches from creeping in. The papers covered Mrs. Astor's every public move: what she did was slavishly imitated, and what she did not do was instantly taboo among ladies. If a lady appeared hatless in public on the Sabbath, it was scandalous; if Mrs. Astor appeared hatless on the Sabbath, it launched a trend. John Jacob Astor IV married Madeleine Force in the ballroom at this address.

Bowling Green Offices Building
9-11 Broadway, between Beaver and Stone Streets

In April of 1912, the steps of this building, which housed the offices of the White Star Line, and the adjoining Bowling Green Park filled with distraught and curious New Yorkers trying to learn the fate of passengers on the *Titanic*. Among the best-known and wealthiest victims of the *Titanic* disaster were Peggy Guggenheim's father, Benjamin Guggenheim, and John Jacob Astor IV.

Astor's young, pregnant wife reported that to calm her after the ship's collision with an iceberg, her husband had accompanied her to the ship gymnasium, where they rode on the hobbyhorses while awaiting instruction from the crew. Astor's body was later recovered by a cable ship and identified by the "J.J.A." on the collar of his brown flannel shirt. His pockets contained a gold pencil, a pocketbook, a blue handkerchief, and currency in dollars, pounds, and francs.

Astor had provided for his wife and son in his will, though they were kept from the larger estate by agreements Astor had signed with his first wife (prohibiting his remarriage) and by prenuptial agreements he had asked Force to sign (prohibiting her remarriage). Madeleine Force went on to marry a wealthy banker from Maine and an Italian prizefighter before dying at forty-seven in her home on Palm Beach. Her son, whom she named John Jacob Astor, settled in Miami Beach and gained a reputation as a playboy.

Joseph Papp Public Theater
425 Lafayette Street, between 4th Street and Astor Place
tel. (212) 260-2400, www.publictheater.org

This building originally housed the library established by John Jacob Astor, the German immigrant who anchored the Astors in American life. Astor Library was the city's first free, non-circulating library. It housed a collection of one thousand volumes, the country's largest when the library opened in 1853. Washington Irving served as its first librarian. With the aid of a grant from the Tilden Foundation, Astor Library merged with its peer Lenox Library to form the New York Public Library in 1895. The building is now the Joseph Papp Public Theater.

W.H. Auden

POET 1907–1973

W H. Auden immigrated to the United States in 1939, after studies at Oxford, a disillusioning tour as a volunteer in the Spanish Civil War, and a period of sexual and social adventure in Berlin with friend and partner Chrisopher Isherwood. The English press lambasted Auden's decision to settle in New York just as England entered World War II. Auden did report to the American draft board, but was rejected because of his homosexuality. Auden the poet was a generous, guiding voice to young poets in the 1930s, but he could be brutally and condescendingly "instructive" in letters to friends, whose flaws he scrutinized without compunction. During his twenty years on the Lower East Side, sandy-haired Auden could be seen chain-smoking, shuffling along in signature black espadrilles and rumpled button-down shirts. He was a lifelong Benzedrine addict, who reasoned that his dependence on amphetamines sped up and streamlined his literary production. In 1972, Auden begged to return to Oxford and was granted residency in a small cottage on the grounds. It was an unhappy year; he was sluggish and ancient-looking due to a medical condition that caused his face to sag and crease. On the eve of his return to Oxford for a second year in residence, Auden died in his sleep.

. . . .

Former residence

1 Montague Terrace at Pierrepont Street
Brooklyn Heights, Brooklyn

Across the street from the Brooklyn Promenade is one of Auden's landmark former residences. A plaque beside the front door recalls his yearlong residency on the top floor from October 1939 to September 1940.

. . . .

Former residence

7 Middagh Street, between Willow Street and Columbia Heights
Brooklyn Heights, Brooklyn

Middagh Street is named for Lady Middagh, a wealthy benefactor of the neighborhood who spearheaded a movement to change the street names of Brooklyn Heights from those of wealthy benefactors to those of fruits: Pineapple, Cranberry, Orange. Lady Middagh's namesake street somehow weathered the fruitification of the neighborhood. Seven Middagh was a hub for the nomadic artists of the 1940s. Jane and Paul Bowles, Salvador Dalí, Carson McCullers, Richard Wright, and others all lived here at some point or passed through as guests. Auden instituted rules, collected the rents, and headed the dinner table—tasks reminiscent of his English schoolmaster days.

. . . .

Former residence

7 Cornelia Street, between Bleecker and West 4th Streets

Auden moved to this address in 1946, the year he became a citizen of the United

States. Visitors entered a small, dark room crammed with unshelved books, overflowing ashtrays, and an unmade army cot. He lived here until 1951, when he moved to 235 Seventh Avenue to live with his longtime partner, the poet and librettist Chester Kallman. The couple moved the following year to the Lower East Side.

W. H. Auden, ca. 1960s.

Former residence

77 St. Mark's Place, between First and Second Avenues

Auden was at odds with Beat culture, though he lived in the heart of it on the Lower East Side for twenty years. Auden and Kallman lived at 77 St. Mark's Place from 1953 to 1972, dividing their time between this apartment and a vacation house they owned in Austria. Auden brought home hundreds of artists, vagrants, misfits, and lovers. He cooked elaborate dinners in the tiny kitchen and entertained in the cramped, chaotic rooms. Close friends lamented that Auden and Kallman were continually robbed or exploited by their transient cast of houseguests.

St. Mark's in the Bowery Church

131 East 10th Street at Second Avenue
tel. (212) 674-0910, www.poetryproject.com

Later in life, Auden returned to the Christianity of his youth. While living at 77 St. Mark's Place, he became a steady parishioner of St. Mark's in the Bowery Church. The main church building was completed in 1799 on the site of Dutch governor Peter Stuyvesant's farm; he is buried under the foundation. In its first century, Episcopal St. Mark's served the most privileged New Yorkers and its churchyard contains some of the earliest marked graves in the city. In the last century, it became a bastion of progressive causes: immigrant advocates, labor unions, and the Black Panthers all found quarters here. Auden was among the poets (including Kahlil Gibran, Allen Ginsberg, and Edna St. Vincent Millay) who read here, and Andy Warhol screened his early films here. St. Mark's, still an active church, is now home to the Poetry Project.

James Baldwin, 1955.

Library of Congress Prints and Photographs Division

James Baldwin

WRITER 1924–1987

A s a child growing up in poverty in Harlem, Baldwin read voraciously and helped to raise his younger brothers and sisters. In his own words, he "took them over with one hand and held a book with the other." His stepfather pushed him to enter the ministry, and at fourteen, passionate and gifted, Baldwin became a preaching sensation in Harlem. Disillusioned by the hypocrisy of wealthy church leaders advising suffering congregants to accept their lot in life, he stepped down from the pulpit at seventeen. Baldwin's intellectual and literary gifts were recognized quickly by his teachers, including his high school advisor, the Harlem Renaissance poet Countee Cullen. Baldwin eventually left school to join the intellectuals, writers, and artists in Greenwich Village. In 1948, he moved to Paris where he finished his first novel, *Go Tell It On The Mountain*. This was only the first of many, prolonged periods abroad in Paris, London, Switzerland, and Istanbul. Beginning in 1957, Baldwin made numerous trips to the segregated South as a journalist and civil rights activist. Echoing the moral authority of the pulpit, Baldwin warned in novels, essays, and plays of the catastrophe awaiting all Americans if they failed to face racial and social injustice and the legacy of slavery.

Schomburg Center for Research in Black Culture

515 Malcolm X Boulevard, between West 135th and West 136th Streets
tel. (212) 491-2200, www.nypl.org

Encouraged by his teacher, Countee Cullen, Baldwin pursued his early reading and studying at the Schomburg Center when it was located nearby at 103 West 135th Street. He called it his sanctuary and spent much of his youth here. The modern research facility at 515 Malcolm X Boulevard was built in 1978.

. . . .

Former residence

81 Horatio Street, between Greenwich and Washington Streets

In December 1957, Baldwin signed a lease for an apartment here; he settled in during April of 1958, after his first trip to the South. The apartment would serve as his home and headquarters for many years. He worked on *Another Country* here.

. . . .

White Horse Tavern

567 Hudson, between West 11th and Perry Streets
tel. (212) 243-9260

Minetta Tavern

113 MacDougal Street, between Bleecker and West 3rd Streets
tel. (212) 475-3850

Baldwin began spending time in the Village around 1940, when he met Beauford Delaney, a fellow black artist who would become a mentor and lifelong friend. Delaney lived on the top floor of 181 Greene Street, and Baldwin often traveled downtown to spend time with him and with other artists and activists. Baldwin later socialized with the Beats in Greenwich Village, frequenting the now shuttered legends: the San Remo, Calypso, and Joe's Diner. He drank often at Minetta Tavern and White Horse Tavern, sometimes with Allen Ginsberg and Jack Kerouac. Despite its liberal reputation, the Village was not free of racism. At a popular Village bar, Baldwin and his close friend, a Turkish actor, were almost beaten to death by bar patrons after a white female friend casually rested her head on Baldwin's shoulder.

. . . .

El Faro

823 Greenwich Street at Horatio Street
tel. (212) 929-8210

Reportedly Baldwin's favorite neighborhood restaurant. After he mentioned El Faro in "If Beale Street Could Speak," Baldwin-seekers and celebrity-hounds started showing up.

. . . .

Actors Studio

432 West 44th Street, between Ninth and Tenth Avenues
tel. (212) 757-0870

Baldwin's adaptation of *Giovanni's Room*, his 1956 novel about a young man in Paris torn between his attachment to his fiancée and his attraction to another man, was produced here in 1958. The play was well received and deepened Baldwin's love of the theater and his involvement in it. He went on immediately to work with Elia Kazan on productions of Archibald MacLeish's *J.B.* and Tennessee Williams's *Sweet Bird of Youth*.

Tout Va Bien

311 West 51st Street, between Eighth and Ninth Avenues
tel. (212) 265-0190

During stormy rehearsals for *Blues for Mister Charlie* in 1964, Baldwin dined often at this fifty-year-old bistro. Encouraged by his early success in the theater, Baldwin wrote *Blues for Mister Charlie* to be produced at the Actors Studio with Lee Strasberg, with whom he quickly developed an openly hostile working relationship. It was his Broadway debut, but Baldwin was forced to fight forces both within the Studio and without to maintain the length, language, and harsh tone of the play. Though the theater filled up each night, low ticket prices—upon which Baldwin had insisted—dampened revenues and led the Actors Studio to close the play a month into its run.

The Cathedral Church of St. John the Divine

1047 Amsterdam Avenue at 112th Street
tel. (212) 316 7540, www.stjohndivine.org

In March of 1974, Baldwin received the "centennial medal in recognition of the artist as prophet" here. Thirteen years later, friends gathered here for Baldwin's funeral; he was eulogized by Maya Angelou, Amiri Baraka, and Toni Morrison before his coffin was carried through the streets of Harlem.

Lucille Ball

COMEDIENNE 1911–1989

Before Lucille Ball raced to keep pace with the conveyor belt at a candy factory or snuck into Ricky Ricardo's nightclub disguised as a lamp, she projected sleek seriousness as a platinum blonde runway model and a queen of B movies. Ball was born in Jamestown, New York. Her family moved up and down the line as her father, a telephone lineman, followed the expansion of the network from town to town. When she turned fifteen, Ball arrived in Manhattan to enroll in the John Murray Anderson School of the Theater. The head of the school encouraged Ball to drop out, which she did, dejectedly, within a couple of months. Ball returned to the city to work as a model for dress designers, until at seventeen she was forced by rheumatoid arthritis to leave again. She spent two years in a wheelchair, received experimental therapies, and eventually resumed her modeling career, often wearing full-length gowns to conceal leg braces. Filmmakers first noticed Ball when her image, as a Chesterfield Cigarette Girl, decorated the city. She soon appeared as a slave girl with a knee-length curtain of blonde hair in Samuel Goldwyn's *Roman Scandals* (1933). In Hollywood, Ball's friend Buster Keaton schooled her in the science of pulling faces and comic timing. She met and married Cuban bandleader Desi Arnaz in 1940, and she debuted as "Lucy" with hair dyed "Tango Red" in 1951. Demure and serenely composed in private life, Ball's onscreen antics made her the most watched and most lauded comedienne of her generation.

21 Club

21 West 52nd Street, between Fifth and Sixth Avenues
tel. (212) 582-7200, www.21club.com

The 21 Club has been an exclusive party place since 1929. During Prohibition, it was

Lucille Ball, 1948.

CBS Photo Archive

distinguished among speakeasies for its advanced evasions of police raids. A false two-ton brick wall concealed the deep wine cellar (now a private dining room), and bartenders triggered a system of weights and pulleys that apparently swept full bottles off the bar while sending empties down a chute into the New York City sewage system as "the Feds" stormed into the restaurant upstairs. The bar is now decked with toy airplanes, cars, and oil derricks to honor the business empires of current and former regulars. When Prohibition ended in 1933, 21 began its ascent as an above-board celebrity hangout. In the 1950s, Ball was a regular, as was Frank Sinatra. 21 is easy to spot: thirty-two painted jockeys line its red stone steps.

....

The Museum of Television and Radio

25 West 52nd Street, between Fifth and Sixth Avenues
tel. (212) 621-6600, www.mtr.org

The museum holds all episodes of *I Love Lucy* in its archives. Though the lobby and halls of this midtown museum display vintage movie posters, photographic portraits of television stars, and other memorabilia, most noteworthy is its library of 100,000 television and radio programs. The fourth floor houses a bank of computers on which visitors can locate particular shows before viewing them at private consoles. Special programs are aired in screening rooms and in-house theaters.

The germ of the character Lucy Ricardo began as a radio sitcom in which a goofy, hapless housewife maneuvered her way in and out of trouble. CBS offered to adapt the character to a television program, but Ball refused to proceed unless Desi Arnaz costarred. CBS then withdrew their offer. In 1950, Ball and Arnaz created Desilu Productions and took a vaudeville version of their act on the road. Once other studios put forth offers, CBS filmed the pilot episode of *I Love Lucy* featuring Arnaz as her husband. Fortuitously, they captured early episodes on 35mm film, so that they could be archived and preserved. *I Love Lucy* ran from October 15, 1951, the first show, to September 24, 1961; Ball filed for divorce the day after the final episode of the show was filmed in 1960. As a producer with great influence at CBS, Ball pushed the network to present pilots of *Star Trek, Mission Impossible*, and other eventual television classics.

Ricardo Family Home
623 East 68th Street

This was the New York address of the Ricardo family. The series was filmed in Hollywood on a soundstage, but the fictitious New York address would place them somewhere in the East River.

Site of Hattie Carnegie's Dress Shop
42 East 49th Street, between Park and Madison Avenues

The designer Hattie Carnegie acted as a surrogate parent to Ball, covering her medical expenses and employing her as a model throughout her struggles with rheumatoid arthritis. Ball's professional name, Diane Belmont, was inspired by the Belmont Racetrack on Long Island.

Tallulah Bankhead

ACTRESS 1903–1968

"Nobody can be exactly like me. Sometimes even I have trouble doing it."

T allulah Bankhead was the ethereally beautiful daughter of a prominent Southern family (her father and grandfather had served in Congress). After winning a national beauty search, she left Alabama at fifteen and moved to New York City. Evading and ignoring her chaperoning aunt, Bankhead plunged into the intellectually sophisticated crowd at the Algonquin Hotel, where she held her own among members of the Algonquin Round Table. She then moved to London, where she became a great dramatist and a beloved star of the English theater. In London, Bankhead was worshipped by her fans, mostly young women who imitated her manner, clothes, and hairstyle. Back in the United States, she succeeded onstage, struggled in Hollywood, and remained famous for being herself—talented, charming, and scandalous. Increasingly, her fame rested on the titillating inventory of her rumored bad behavior—affairs with hundreds of men and women, packs of Craven A cigarettes, and daily (Bankhead joked sixty) drinks of Old Grandad bourbon. Bankhead's quips are famous and legion. ("Cocaine, habit forming? Of course not. I ought to know, I've been using it for years.") At the end of her life, Bankhead reveled in playing the villain Black Widow on the Batman television series.

Algonquin Hotel
59 West 44th Street, between Fifth and Sixth Avenues
tel. (212) 840-6800, www.algonquinhotel.com

Bankhead lived here with her family chaperone, Aunt Louise. She landed small parts in the theater, dodged her aunt, and endeared herself to the hotel manager and staff. She became "the Baby of the Algonquin Roundtable." The Vicious Circle had planned to

dispatch the young beauty with a few cutting remarks, but Bankhead delivered her own leveling blows. When Bankhead turned eighteen, a despairing Aunt Louise left to volunteer for the Red Cross in Paris.

Theater District
From West 40th Street to West 53rd Street and from Sixth Avenue to Eighth Avenue

After her time in London, Bankhead returned to New York, where she enjoyed periods of success in the theater (most famously in 1939 in *The Little Foxes*). She performed at several theaters, including the Plymouth (236 West 45th Street), Ambassador (219 West 49th Street), Brooks Atkinson (256 West 47th Street), Martin Beck (302 West 45th Street), and Lyceum (149 West 45th Street). The Lyceum Theater, built in 1903, is a historic landmark and the oldest theater on Broadway.

Bronx Zoo

Fordham Road at the Bronx River Parkway
Bronx Park, The Bronx
tel. (718) 367-1010, www.bronxzoo.com

During a brief stint in Reno, where she was securing resident status in order to obtain a divorce, Bankhead purchased a lion cub from the circus and named it for her friend Winston Churchill. Bankhead added Winston to her troupe of animals at Windows, her house in Bedford Village, New York. As the lion cub matured, he menaced her frequent houseguests with increasing regularity, and Bankhead gave Winston Churchill to the Bronx Zoo.

Djuna Barnes

WRITER 1892–1982

D juna Barnes's parents, a failed artist and a minor violinist, were determined to mold a brilliant and unorthodox child. Their home was something of a social laboratory, in which Barnes was kept from school and allegedly presented to her father's friends as a sexual partner. Barnes arrived in New York City from Cornwall-on-Hudson, New York, to study drawing at the Pratt Institute and the Art Students League. Tall, angular, and strikingly beautiful, Barnes wore a long black cape, and was known for her dark and cutting wit. She had perfect disdain for public opinion and social convention of any kind. She worked as a reporter and illustrator, and became well known for her aloof, funny, and unconventional interviews with celebrities ("Nothing Amuses Coco Chanel After Midnight"). Barnes left for Paris in 1920, where she lived until 1931 with the love of her life, Thelma Wood (their tempestuous relationship inspired her novel *Nightwood*). While in Paris, she wrote poems, two novels, and a satiric account of the lesbian literary crowd with which she ran. T.S. Eliot edited and promoted *Nightwood*, which is dedicated, in part, to Peggy Guggenheim, securing its long tenure as a masterwork of modernism. After reading James Joyce's *Ulysses*, Barnes declared that no one else should attempt to write a novel. When she returned to New York during World War II, it was to live out the balance of her life in steady seclusion at 5 Patchin Place across the way from E.E. Cummings.

Greenwich Village

From Houston Street to West 14th Street and from Fifth Avenue to the Hudson River

In 1916, Barnes wrote "Greenwich Village As It Is," a journalistic defense of the good life among bohemians. In the mainstream press, bohemians were depicted as lost, glamorous, depraved, promiscuous, unhealthy, and unpredictable; curious visitors arrived in nervous groups to observe them only by the light of day. Barnes wrote, "The greater part of New York is soulless as a department store," and outsiders should not pity or fear the Greenwich Village bohemians. She described their "pleasant nightlife" at Café Lafayette, where she ate cold cuts and drank New Orleans fizzes before moving on to Bobbie Edwards's "Concolo Gatti Matti" (or Crazy Cat Club) at 64 West Eleventh Street.

Former residence

5 Patchin Place, off West 10th Street, between Greenwich and Sixth Avenues

In 1940, Barnes moved here, across the alley from E.E. Cummings. She lived as a recluse in a tiny apartment, weathering seasons of poverty, during which she often went for days without eating. She pined for Europe, wrote fiction at a furious clip, then destroyed her writing with equal fury. Grants from admirers, including Samuel Beckett and Peggy Guggenheim, covered her modest rent and the delivery of groceries. When other admirers, including an obsessed Carson McCullers, shouted to her window from the alley of Patchin Place, she yelled for them to move on and retreated back into her room.

Provincetown Playhouse
133 MacDougal Street at West 3rd Street
tel. (212) 998-5867

In 1920 and 1921, the Provincetown Players produced three of Barnes's one-act plays, when the theater was located at 139 MacDougal Street.

Coney Island

From Surf Avenue to the Boardwalk and from West 8th Street to West 16th Street
Coney Island, Brooklyn
www.coneyisland.com

Coney Island was still a major holiday destination when Barnes wrote a series of articles about its diversions for *The Brooklyn Daily Eagle.* Paying customers dodged predatory clowns, clambered to see a model *Titanic* that sunk hourly, and waited in line to be terrified on brightly lit thrill rides. Barnes described families from the city wandering the beach, eating fruit and "impossible chunks of bread," children drinking coffee from clamshells, and city people sprawling uncomfortably on the sand in rented and homemade bathing suits. In "If Noise Were Forbidden at Coney Island, a Lot of People Would Lose Their Jobs," Barnes chronicled the sad and seedy side of Coney Island. She described the flat look of hustlers in the afternoon sun and the despondent faces of the "freaks" on display. The policemen of Coney Island were "the most unconcerned uniformed individuals" Barnes had ever seen: "they never find anything wrong, for that would be absurd."

Statue of Ben Franklin

Intersection of Park Row, Nassau, and Spruce Streets

In the era before radio, television, and the Internet, political and religious activists reached the public by shouting their messages from soapboxes in public squares around New York. During the weekdays of 1913, small crowds gathered each noon under the statue of Ben Franklin across from City Hall. Barnes counted "Socialists, anti-Socialists, Prohibitionists, and revivalists" among the public speakers and sympathizers.

Bronx Zoo

Fordham Road at the Bronx River Parkway
Bronx Park, The Bronx
tel. (718) 367-1010, www.bronxzoo.com

In the autumn of 1914, Barnes visited the Bronx Zoo to interview Dinah, an African go-rilla brought to the Bronx by the New York Zoological Society. Though Dinah only lived until the following summer, she entered the record books at that time as the longest-surviving gorilla in captivity in New York. Barnes wrote about the embrace she received from Dinah: "It is at once impersonal and condescending, and yet rather agreeable. And when she laid her head upon my knees, I was not embarrassed but only pleased that she had found something in me, as a representative of the women she had come among, to make her trustful."

The Circle Line

Departs from Pier 83, West 42nd Street at Twelfth Avenue
tel. (212) 563-3200, www.circleline.com

In 1917, Barnes took a forty-mile boat tour that circumnavigated Manhattan Island. From the river, the Woolworth Building—then the tallest building in the world—was the prominent feature of the skyline. The boat floated under the Brooklyn Bridge, past ferries full of American troops heading to Europe, past the dark shapes of anchored warships of European allies, past the prisons on outlying islands. Though much has changed, today's Circle Line tour still creates the alien sense of the familiar that Barnes sought. She wrote: "To take a yacht trip around Manhattan Island is to find yourself in the awkward position of one who must become a stranger in his own house that he may describe it with necessary color."

P. T. Barnum

ENTERTAINER 1810–1891

I n P. T. Barnum's account of his past, a story he revised and reissued several times during his life, he maintained his belief that the "The People like to be humbugged." He never shrank from making a spectacle of objects and people that he deemed noteworthy or exotic. Shrewdly, he encouraged public skepticism about the authenticity of his exhibits, hoping that the temptation to judge for oneself would be impossible for ticket buyers to resist. He was right, and thousands of visitors from all over the country paid a few cents to investigate Barnum's claims. He made a fortune from mermaids, automatons, man-eating tigers, shrunken heads, miraculous miniatures, and people born with extreme physiques. His most famous live exhibits included General Tom Thumb, Jumbo, and the "Swedish Nightingale" Jenny Lind, billed as the beautiful possessor of the world's most extraordinary voice. Barnum later entered politics as a passionate advocate of temperance and abolition, and ultimately served as the mayor of Bridgeport, Connecticut. When he was a young boy, Barnum's parents and neighbors convinced him that he owned an island worth millions, an island that would make him wealthy and well loved for life. Years later, his family led him to his island—it was a worthless, mosquito-infested piece of swampland in Connecticut. Barnum vowed never to be humbugged again.

. . . .

Site of Barnum's American Museum
Broadway at Ann Street

Barnum spent the majority of his time in this neighborhood, overseeing his museum. In his autobiography, he describes some of the exhibits at the American Museum: "Industrious fleas, educated dogs, jugglers, automatons, ventriloquists, living statuary, tableaux, gypsies, albinos. Fat boys, giants, dwarfs, fire-dancers, caricatures of phrenology." A typical ad in the local paper for the American Museum invited guests to view: "The wax statuary, the Living Giraffes, the Living Boa Constrictor, the original Happy Family." When criticized for trickery, Barnum rebutted, "I should hope that a little 'clap-trap' occasionally, in the way of transparencies, flags, exaggerated pictures, and puffing advertisements, might find an offset in a wilderness of wonderful, instructive, and amusing realities."

His museum was burned with phosphorous by Confederate terrorists during the Civil War, in retaliation for Union victories. In a second fire in 1868, his menagerie of animals and specimens was destroyed—a fireman killed the lone escapee, a tiger, in the street.

. . . .

Grace Church
800-804 Broadway at East 10th Street
tel. (212) 254-2000, www.gracechurchnyc.org

On February 10, 1863, the dwarfs Lavinia Warren, "The Little Queen of Beauty," and Charles S. Stratton, "General Tom Thumb," were married at Grace Church. Mathew Brady produced cartes-de-visite photographs of the bride and groom, which the couple sold during world tours. Barnum had promoted the battle between Commodore Nutt and General Tom Thumb for Lavinia Warren's hand. He sold tickets to the wedding, in which an apparently reconciled Commodore Nutt appeared as Stratton's best man. Hundreds of thousands of people paid to see Lavinia Warren and her engagement ring in the weeks before the ceremony. Parts of Broadway shut down, as thousands more clogged the streets to catch a glimpse of the bride and groom and their glamorous guests. In the weeks after their wedding, Barnum arranged for the Strattons to appear in New York in a variety show that included songs, dance revues, and the chance to see the couple in their wedding clothes.

P.T. Barnum, undated.

Private collection

Pier A
Battery Place at New York Harbor

On April 8, 1882, America's most beloved elephant, Jumbo, arrived from England at this pier. City vendors sold "Jumbo" drinks and snacks—a marketing scheme still prized by merchants. Barnum never allowed Jumbo to be measured, but he was indisputably huge and prone to violence when penned up for too long. Handlers reportedly relied on Jumbo's dependence on whiskey to calm the animal's nerves during the transfer to the United States. Though Barnum had promised the long-waiting, rain-drenched crowds that Jumbo would walk up Broadway, his handlers decided the elephant should be kept in his crate. Horses and smaller elephants, brought downtown from Madison Square, pulled and pushed the crate up Broadway for hours, delivering Jumbo to his new home in the middle of the night. Jumbo was a tremendous success for Barnum. Four seasons after his arrival, the elephant was crushed by a freight train while crossing railroad tracks during a national tour.

American Museum of Natural History
Central Park West at West 79th Street
tel. (212) 769-5100, www.amnh.org

After Jumbo's death, Barnum donated his skeleton to the Museum of Natural History, which exhibited the bones for years. Barnum donated the stuffed hide to Tufts University. Many years later, the university's Barnum Museum of Natural History burned, destroying Jumbo's remains. Students gathered the ashes and, in this state, Jumbo lives on as the school mascot. Barnum was a dedicated student of taxonomy and biology, and usually donated or sold the deceased members of his menagerie to museums and universities for study.

Brooklyn Bridge
From Park Row (Manhattan) to Adams Street (Brooklyn)

Although Barnum campaigned to have Jumbo cross the Brooklyn Bridge first, the honor went to Emily Roebling, the wife of the debilitated engineer Washington Roebling.

Ethel Barrymore

ACTRESS 1879–1959

E thel Barrymore could not resist the pull of the family legacy, which some said was a curse. Her father, mother, grandmother, and two uncles were all prominent and celebrated theater actors. Though Ethel and her brothers, Lionel and John, had imagined careers off the stage, all three ultimately found fame as actors and later gained notoriety for public drunkenness and fierce family rivalries. In her early twenties, Barrymore began performing to critical acclaim and public adoration. Off the stage, her witty, attentive company was always in demand—at balls, on yachts, and by all her determined suitors, including Winston Churchill. She ultimately married an idle heir to the Colt family fortune, though the marriage did not last. While her brothers found success in Hollywood, Barrymore looked down on the new medium, and succumbed to its temptations only when financial crisis forced her. Often broke, she agreed unhappily to vaudeville tours to make ends meet. Though she made several astounding comebacks on Broadway, by the end of her life she was deeply disturbed by the diminishment of the American theater. During a vaudeville stint, Barrymore reportedly looked out at the audience and asked, "Who are they anyway?"

Algonquin Hotel
59 West 44th Street, between Fifth and Sixth Avenues
tel. (212) 840-6800, www.algonquinhotel.com

Barrymore and her family presided over the dining room from their table in the corner long before drama critic Alexander Woollcott settled his crowd here. At the Algonquin, the playwright Zoe Akins told Barrymore about a play she had written for her—*Declasse*. The play became a phenomenal success. Dorothy Parker wrote: "If, during my theater-going lifetime, there has been any other performance so perfect as the one Ethel Barrymore gives…I can only say that I had the hideous ill luck to miss it."

Barrymore looked down on the members of the Round Table as interlopers, and they quickly turned on her, publishing colder reviews of her work. Barrymore blamed the chilling of enthusiasm on professional jealousies. The "Baby of the Round Table," Tallulah Bankhead, however, remained a fan and noted with admiration Barrymore's "imperious manner, the scorn in her voice, the contempt in her eyes, the great reputation in which she was cloaked."

Ethel Barrymore, 1901.

Library of Congress Prints and Photographs Division

Plaza Hotel
768 Fifth Avenue at Central Park South
tel. (212) 759-3000, www.fairmont.com

Barrymore kept a regular table in the Palm Room, where reporters tracked her and made note of her avid public cigarette smoking. Newspapers fed public obsession with the actress by describing details of her loosely pinned hair, her low voice, and her opinions on literature. The press also followed her once-famous father's public tirades and hallucinations (later attributed to syphilis-induced dementia), and her brothers' emergence as theatrical stars and notorious drinkers.

Palace Theater
1564 Broadway, between West 46th and West 47th Streets

In 1899, Ethel's father, Maurice Barrymore, moved his family to a house on this site. In 1913, the Palace Theater was built here; it exists intact behind the billboards and neon that cover the building. Vaudevillians lived to "play the Palace," and performers from Sarah Bernhardt to the Marx Brothers have appeared on the Palace stage.

Ethel Barrymore Theater
243-251 West 47th Street, between Broadway and Eighth Avenue

Built in 1928, the Ethel Barrymore Theater is a landmark. Flamboyant, scroll-like wrought iron supports the marquee. In 1927, the Shuberts asked Barrymore to star in a new play they had commissioned, offering to build a theater in her honor if she accepted the part, which she did. The Ethel Barrymore Theater is still owned by the Shubert Organization.

I. Miller Building
167 West 46th Street at Broadway

Barrymore is depicted as Ophelia on the front of this building. Alexander Sterling Calder created sculptures of Barrymore, Mary Pickford, Rosa Ponselle, and Marilyn Miller, each immortalized in a title role, to fill the niches in the facade.

The Museum of the City of New York
1220 Fifth Avenue at East 103rd Street
tel. (212) 534-1672, www.mcny.org

The rotating installations of the ongoing exhibit "Broadway!" offer historic perspectives on aspects of Broadway theater.

Barrymore's
267 West 45th Street, between Broadway and Eighth Avenue
tel. (212) 391-8400

This old-fashioned pub was named in honor of John Barrymore, a prodigious boozer in the theater district. Caricatures and illustrations of John Barrymore hang on the wall, as do photographs of Lionel and Ethel Barrymore. Books and other Barrymore memorabilia are also on display.

Jesse Tarbox Beals

PHOTOGRAPHER 1870–1942

J esse Tarbox Beals was the first female photojournalist to receive credit for a photograph in an American newspaper. Beals started taking pictures at eighteen, with a rudimentary camera she had won in a contest; within a few weeks she traded it for a professional model. Beals's first subjects were neighbors and townspeople, who gathered on her front lawn dressed in dark suits and long skirts, clutching their most prized possessions for her to preserve for posterity. She married Alfred Tennyson Beals, a machinist, and convinced him that they could make a living as itinerant photographers; she shot the pictures, he developed them. They followed carnivals, big tent revivals, world's fairs, reunions, or any large gathering that would provide popular subject matter and guarantee sales. Beals got her break at the St. Louis World's Fair in 1904 when she photographed the "Giant Patagonians." She photographed four presidents, Mark Twain, society women, longshoremen, and children living in the slums of New York. Beals spent the last decades of her life contributing photographs of winter creeper, wild fern, and Sweet Williams to gardening columns in *The New York Times* and to books about the gardens of Greenwich Village.

Jessie Tarbox Beals at her Village Art Gallery, 6-1/2 Sheridan Square, ca. 1910.

The Museum of the City of New York

New-York Historical Society

2 West 77th Street at Central Park West
tel. (212) 873-3400, www.nyhistory.org

Beals has been featured in photography exhibits here and the society maintains a collection of her photographs. Among them are black-and-white shots of Greenwich Village: sun-dappled Patchin Place, slant-floored tearooms, dancing halls, rustic restaurants, and artists at work.

Site of Beals's studio

6-1/2 Sheridan Square, between West 4th Street and Washington Place

In 1923, Beals left her husband and moved to Greenwich Village, where she opened her own studio. Like other Villagers, she tried to make a little money off the curiosity of tourists who had overcome the widespread fear of the neighborhood and who were visiting in ever larger numbers. She reprinted her photographs of bohemians as postcards and wrote catchy couplets about life in the Village to accompany each image. In contemporary neighborhood guides, she was often named as the "official photographer for Greenwich Village." The site of her former studio is now filled by a 1970s apartment building.

The Gardens of Greenwich Village

Greenwich Village
From Houston Street to West 14th Street and from Fifth Avenue to the Hudson River

After years of "hustling," Beals returned to the relatively sedate pursuit of garden photography, in which she found renewed success. She started small, with the hidden gardens of New York City. Her commissions expanded to include the rolling estates outside the city, and her images began to appear in upscale magazines such as *Town & Country.*

To finance a move to California, Beals sold all but her most prized glass plate negatives to a picture manufacturer who stripped the plates of emulsion, and recycled them in picture frames. The Great Depression shrunk the market for photographs of wealthy, verdant estates, and Beals and her daughter wandered between Hollywood and Chicago, piecing together a meager income. Back in New York, her photographs of the comparatively small but lush gardens of the city brought her praise.

James Gordon Bennett, Jr.

NEWSPAPER EDITOR 1841–1918

J ames Gordon Bennett, Jr., underestimated heir to *The New York Herald,* perfected the art of creating exclusive news, instituted the cabled exchange of international political reportage, sent Stanley in search of Livingstone, brought the game of polo to America, and fought the last recorded duel in the United States. From the Civil War to World War I, he and his reporters anticipated the news with such acuity and impatience that they often landed in their own headlines. Bennett challenged the *Herald's* competitors to the first transatlantic yacht race and won, driving his paper to greater fame and circulation. At the *Herald,* Bennett saw conspiracy everywhere; he instituted the White Mice, an internal network that encouraged reporters and editors to spy on one another. Bennett relied on good reporters, including Mark Twain, Stephen Crane, and Walt Whitman, and he scooped his competitors by utilizing the transatlantic cable to report European affairs. In the race to report Custer's death at Little Big Horn, he hired hot air balloons, the ablest steamboat captains, and the fastest trains. When fresh news ebbed, Bennett, like most New York editors of the era, resorted to hoax, reporting on one occasion that ferocious zoo animals had been loosed on the streets of New York. According to the *Herald,* forty-nine New Yorkers had been killed and hundreds maimed.

. . . .

Woodlawn Cemetery

Entrances: East 233rd Street at Webster Avenue; Jerome Avenue north of Bainbridge Avenue
Woodlawn, The Bronx
tel. (718) 920-0500

In the second half of the nineteenth century, stories about heroic and missing explorers filled the newspaper columns. When news of their extraordinary discoveries could not be found, editors speculated over their long absences. Bennett sent Civil War hero George Washington Delong in search of a long-lost North Pole expedition (and the Pole itself). Delong steamed away from San Francisco in 1873, waving from the rail of a frail ship. When pack ice crushed their ship, Delong and his crew dragged their lifeboats to Bennett Island and took refuge. Many months later Delong and most of his men were found frozen to death. Rescuers reportedly pried Delong's journal from his hands. A few survivors were found adrift in a lifeboat and rescued, while others had been kept alive by families hunting and living along the Siberian coast. The survivors returned to tell their tale, and Delong's body was returned to New York and buried here. His grave is marked by a sculpture of Delong stepping out of a block of snow-white granite.

Site of old Steinway Hall

100 East 14th Street, between Union Square and Irving Place

"Doctor Livingstone, I presume?"—Henry M. Stanley

The missionary and explorer Dr. David Livingstone had been "missing" in Africa for three years when Bennett one-upped the standard editorial wagers over Livingstone's fate. He sent hard-boiled reporter Henry M. Stanley out to rescue Livingstone or to discover the details of his death, which had already been reported twice in other newspapers. In 1871, Stanley found white-haired Livingstone alive and well in Ujiji, a village on the shores of Lake Tanganyika. He traveled and studied with Livingstone for months, before returning to New York to lecture about his adventures.

In December of 1872, the newly minted celebrity, Henry M. Stanley, told the tale of the "discovery of Rev. Dr. Livingstone" to his first New York audience at Steinway Hall. *The New York Times* noted coolly that Stanley drew a few "marks of applause" as he rose to speak, dressed in a white flannel suit, summer helmet, and top boots. Stanley became a popular and controversial speaker on the US lecture circuit—the ultimate master of ceremonies, Mark Twain, introduced him in Boston. To many, it was unthinkable that an uneducated man of illegitimate birth had succeeded where professional explorers and gentlemen had failed. Stanley, a defensive and charmless man by all accounts, was caricatured mercilessly as a fake, and his reputation was ruined by the revelation that he had fought for both sides in the Civil War. Bennett did little to help him: it was intolerable to be in Stanley's shadow. Stanley returned to the Congo in 1874, attaching his name to great waterfalls and Bennett's to rivers and mountain peaks. Stanley made his most nefarious contribution to the colonization of Africa as a land-grabber, advisor, and aide to Belgian King Leopold II during Leopold's takeover of the Congo in the late 1870s.

Steinway Hall was one of Union Square's most venerable buildings until its demolition in 1925. The Steinway Company (New York's last piano maker) opened a new piano showroom and performance hall on West 57th Street later that year. The Landmarks Preservation Commission designated Steinway Hall a New York City landmark in 2001.

Herald Square

Sixth Avenue and Broadway, between West 34th and West 35th Streets

Herald Square is located at the hectic spot in front of R.H. Macy's department store where Sixth Avenue and Broadway cross. The petite park is dominated by an automated clock and bell. Now a monument to Bennett and his father, who founded *The New York Herald,* the clock and bell were formerly atop the Standford White-designed New York Herald Building from 1895 to 1921. Behind the bell looms a statue of Minerva, the ruthless defender of the city and the patron-protector of civilized life. Minerva, fierce with spear, shield, and armor of seething snakes, is flanked by powerfully built bell ringers, who swing sledgehammers against the bell each hour. Pigeons scatter.

Former residence of Caroline May

44 West 19th Street, between Fifth and Sixth Avenues

It was here, at the home of his fiancée, Miss Caroline May, where Bennett provided the enormous insult that drew him into the last recorded duel in American history. Bennett arrived wildly drunk and sabotaged his own engagement party by urinating into the fire crackling in the Mays' well-appointed fireplace. Guests fanned out across the city, and Bennett became a social pariah within hours. The next afternoon, May's enraged brother attacked Bennett, striking him with a horsewhip in the snow-blanketed streets, in full view of the Union Club. On January 7, 1877, the two men met again at Slaughter's Gap on the Maryland-Delaware border. Bennett and May paced apart and fired prudently wild shots, preserving the honor and health of all involved. Bennett was banished from New York society. Snubbed and sufficiently bored, he left for Paris, where he founded *The Herald Tribune* and devoted himself to his beloved dogs and owls.

Delmonico's

56 Beaver Street, betweeen William and Broad Streets
tel. (212) 509-1144, www.delmonicosny.com

Bennett often dined at Delmonico's. During a dinner with the actor Edwin Booth, the newspaperman leapt up from the table to chase down a passing fire truck. He was soon in the way of the firemen, who turned their powerful hoses on him. During another occasion at Delmonico's, Bennett was punched by what he described as a "little man." Infuriated by Bennett's loud, rude complaints over the slow delivery of a bottle

James Gordon Bennett, Jr., undated.

of champagne to his table, the man had decked him with a single blow. The "little man" turned out to be Bill Edwards, a well-known lightweight boxer. He later became one of Bennett's favorite drinking companions.

. . . .

New York Yacht Club

37 West 44th Street, between Fifth and Sixth Avenues
tel. (212) 382-1000, www.nyyc.org

Bennett was the youngest member ever elected to the New York Yacht Club and was elected Vice Commodore when he was only twenty-seven years old. He was the picture of young, flush social success, gliding up the Hudson on his polished, brass-tacked 120-foot yacht.

The site of the current clubhouse was donated by Commodore J. Pierpont Morgan. In 1900, Warren & Wetmore, the architects of Grand Central Terminal, designed the fanciful facade and serious interiors of the New York Yacht Club. The front of the building is a shallow stone wilderness of columns, colorful stained glass, and nautical flourishes including dolphins and waves. Each deep-set window frames a carved stone stern of a seventeenth-century ship that appears to be sailing through the facade and into the interior, churning the stone water. The interior of the building is closed to the public.

Sarah Bernhardt

ACTRESS 1844–1923

T he French tragedienne Sarah Bernhardt was hailed as the greatest actress of her generation, but her more lasting legacy may be her contribution to the invention of modern celebrity. She was an ingenious reinventor of her public self, manipulator of public sympathy and scandal, and was the secret promulgator of some of the most outrageous rumors about her private life. During her visits to New York, obsessed young men thrust their starched cuffs at her to be signed, women clipped feathers from her hat, and entire regiments gathered on 23rd Street to serenade her hotel balcony. Born to a Dutch courtesan, "The Bernhardt" inspired Victorien Sardou's play *La Tosca* and the character of Berma in Marcel Proust's *Swann's Way*. Ignored by her mother, Bernhardt bounced from convent to conservatoire to a coveted position at the Comédie-Française, only to be expelled for slapping one of its grande dames. She broke contracts, picked fights, painted, sculpted, flew hot air balloons, and, night after night, died tragically on stage as no one else could. In London she kept a cheetah, chameleons, a wolf, three dogs, and a parrot named Darwin. Her eccentricities only further suggested genius to a world of admirers. One million spectators lined the streets of Paris to watch the passage of her funeral cortege in 1923.

. . . .

Hudson River Pier

Specific site unknown

Bernhardt arrived in New York City from Paris for the first time on October 27, 1880. According to newspaper accounts, the Hudson had frozen over, and men walked ahead of her ship, breaking up the ice with pickaxes. Reporters and dignitaries thronged her ship, anchored in New York Harbor, and unruly crowds filled the quayside when she arrived at the pier. She was besieged by the New York press corps, which rushed to question Bernhardt and ignored a drably dressed and sad figure disembarking with her—Mary Todd Lincoln. Bernhardt claimed to have saved the famous widow's life during their passage. A sudden swell had almost pitched Mrs. Lincoln down the stairs, and Bernhardt had yanked her back to safety. Gifted at enlarging the dramatic possibilities of any event, Bernhardt mused in her autobiography that it must have dealt Mrs. Lincoln a second psychological wound to have been saved by an actor, when an actor, after all, had assassinated her husband.

Sarah Bernhardt, ca. 1896.

Library of Congress, Prints and Photographs Division

Site of Booth Theater
West 23rd Street at Sixth Avenue

During her 1880 visit, Bernhardt debuted here in *Adrienne Lecouvreur*—nicknamed the "Play of Five Dresses" for its fast rotation of extravagant costumes. New York did not impress the great French actress during her first days there. Crooked customs agents held forty trunks of her stage costumes hostage. Bernhardt's first impression of New York was of a pushy, frantic, uncultured city obsessed with making money. In line with the anti-immigrant and anti-Jewish rhetoric that had taken hold of the city, much press coverage caricatured her Jewishness and foreignness. Walt Whitman, however, recognized and praised Bernhardt's own "American" traits—her bossiness, impudence, and deft self-promotion.

During the same trip, Bernhardt drove out to Menlo Park, New Jersey, to visit "the Wizard," Thomas Edison. As she and her companions bumped along the icy, dark road in their carriage and drew near to Edison's house, the thick woods and clustered icicles suddenly blazed with hundreds of bright, white lights. Bernhardt was delighted and declared Edison a genius.

Delmonico's

56 Beaver Street, betweeen William and Broad Streets
tel. (212) 509-1144, www.delmonicosny.com

James Gordon Bennett, Jr. hosted a banquet in honor of Bernhardt here during her 1880 visit. Bernhardt was shunned by society women who considered her a de facto courtesan and by American preachers who warned their congregations not to see her performances. It did not necessarily help her racy reputation that Bennett's Delmonico's banquet was for men only; no other women had been invited.

Brooklyn Bridge

From Park Row (Manhattan) to Adams Street (Brooklyn)

The Brooklyn Bridge was still under construction during Bernhardt's 1880 visit to New York. Her visit had been a trial, adoration of the crowds notwithstanding. The rabid New York reporters had shaken her with their special brand of nasty caricature. She felt oppressed by the American custom of "le handshake" and called American food "a horror." She was ultimately won over by the Brooklyn Bridge, which she visited by special permit. Bernhardt found the bridge beautiful, and the noise of construction ingenious. She compared the chaos of building to the "chaos of the universe." Standing upon the Brooklyn Bridge, she claimed to be "reconciled with this great people."

Caswell-Massey

518 Lexington Avenue at East 48th Street
tel. (212) 755-2254, www.caswellmassey.com

Established in 1752, Caswell-Massey is still the purveyor of original formula No. Six Cologne, the favorite of George Washington. In 1887, Caswell-Massey shipped thirty jars of cucumber night cream to Sarah Bernhardt, who had requested that the jars be sent express, so she could take them on an upcoming European tour.

Chelsea Hotel

222 West 23rd Street, between Seventh and Eighth Avenues
tel. (212) 243-3700, www.hotelchelsea.com

The Chelsea became a hotel in 1905, and Bernhardt was one of its earliest celebrated guests. It was whispered around the city that Bernhardt slept in a coffin, which she carried with her on tour. Though it remains unclear whether she traveled with a coffin, Bernhardt did keep one in her Paris bedroom. She liked to lie there, snug in the satin-lined confinement while memorizing the lines of the tragic heroines she played. Upon her death, she was laid to rest in the same coffin.

The Players

16 Gramercy Park South, between Park Avenue South and Irving Place
tel. (212) 475-6116, www.theplayersnyc.org

In the intervening century between the founding of The Players in 1888 and its decision to include women as members in 1989, the club acknowledged the work of legendary people of the theater, including notable women, during traditional Pipe Nights, named for the festive smoking of churchwarden pipes. Bernhardt was the first woman to be honored on Pipe Night in 1911.

Palace Theater
1564 Broadway, between West 46th and West 47th Streets

In 1913, Bernhardt played at the Palace Theatre and received, by her own account, a "tidal wave" of applause. She took the praise sitting down, as a chronic knee injury made it unbearable to stand after a full performance. In 1915, still tortured by pain, abscesses, and interminable bed rest, Bernhardt begged her physician to amputate her leg above the knee. He obliged. After her recovery from surgery, she felt a kinship with the many young men who had lost limbs in battle. She was carried out to the Front in an ornate chair so that she could entertain the troops.

. . . .

Brooklyn Academy of Music
30 Lafayette Avenue, between Ashland Place and St. Felix Street
Fort Greene, Brooklyn
tel. (718) 636-4100, www.bam.org

Bernhardt performed here during her last American tour in 1917. She was accorded the respect of a living legend, but her dated acting style failed to move new audiences.

. . . .

Prospect Park
From Prospect Park West to Flatbush Avenue and from Prospect Park Southwest to Ocean Avenue
and Parkside Avenue
Prospect Park, Brooklyn

During her last visit, in 1917, Bernhardt's declaration of solidarity with Americans was rendered particularly emotional by the American decision to enter World War I. Bernhardt addressed crowds from the Prospect Park bandstand on Independence Day—50,000 joined her in shouting, "*Vive l'Amerique, Vive la France!*"

Elizabeth Bishop
POET 1911–1979

Elizabeth Bishop's poetic genius and struggles in life were belied by what fellow poet James Merrill called her "instinctive, modest, lifelong impersonations of an ordinary woman." Her poems translate the innocent and abundant features of the natural world—icebergs, fish, insects, leaves—into sly reminders of human tragedies. Bishop moved to New York in 1934, following her graduation from Vassar. Her first book of poetry was published when she was thirty-five. She seemed, to her many admirers, incapable of self-promotion, but she was championed by her most celebrated contemporaries, including Robert Lowell and Marianne Moore. She had spent a transient childhood among different family members in Massachusetts and Nova Scotia. Bishop settled down only once in life—with Lota de Macedo Soares in Brazil, where she moved in 1951 and stayed, often happily, for years, adding Brazil's light, culture, flora, fauna, sights, and sounds to her catalogue of images: "big symbolic birds," "scaling-ladder vines, oblique and neat." Though Bishop was troubled by her low poetic output—the product of perfectionism complicated by bouts of drinking and depression—she was honored with almost every poetry prize in the country, including the Pulitzer Prize, the National Book Award, two Guggenheim Fellowships, and the Books Abroad/Neustadt Prize for Literature. After the apparent suicide of Soares in New York, Bishop spent her final years in the United States.

New York Public Library

Fifth Avenue at West 42nd Street
tel. (212) 930-0830, www.nypl.org

Bishop met Marianne Moore for the first time on a bench outside the public Reading Room at the New York Public Library in March 1934. The meeting had been arranged by the librarian at Vassar, Bishop's alma mater. Bishop greatly admired Moore, and by the time they met, she had spent years searching literary journals and poetry anthologies for Moore's work. Moore became Bishop's mentor; it was an enormously important friendship in both of their lives. Bishop sent Moore her early poems to edit, and Moore was instrumental in getting Bishop's first book of poetry published. They continued to send each other poetry throughout their lives and maintained an intense correspondence; four of Bishop's posthumously published poems were found in letters to Moore.

Elizabeth Bishop, 1956.

AP/Wide World Photos

The Metropolitan Museum of Art

1000 Fifth Avenue at East 82nd Street
tel. (212) 535-7710, www.metmuseum.org

Bishop and Moore (and Mrs Moore, who accompanied them almost everywhere) visited the Met often. They took pleasure in noting and exchanging idiosyncratic details. In a letter from January 1935, Bishop wrote to Moore about an odd museum label: "Some of their inscriptions baffle me—a perfectly sensible crystal fish, for example, something like a perch, labeled 'Porpoise.' And a young man on a Greek vase who is obviously cutting the ends of his hair with his sword, called 'Boy Washing Hair (?)'". Bishop's alertness to the unintended or unexpected inspired several of her poems, including "The Man-Moth"(a misprint of "mammoth" that she read in a New York City newspaper), a creature who represented perfectly the peculiar loneliness of the city.

Chelsea Hotel
222 West 23rd Street, between Seventh and Eighth Avenues
tel. (212) 243-3700, www.hotelchelsea.com

Bishop lived here briefly in the mid-1930s after a stint at the Hotel Brevoort. The transience of her life in New York was familiar to Bishop, who had not settled in one place for long since being orphaned as a young child by the death of her father and the institutionalization of her mother.

Former residence
16 Charles Street, between Greenwich Avenue and Waverley Place

Bishop lived here in 1934. Bishop struggled whenever she was in the city. The classic aggravations of city life—noise, brusqueness, and isolation—affected her deeply. Her departure from the city for Brazil, a move encouraged by many of her close friends, launched the happiest and most productive chapter in her life.

Former residence
61 Perry Street, between West 4th and Bleecker Streets

Bishop was living here in 1967, when her partner Soares visited from Brazil. It was here that Soares took an overdose of tranquilizers and collapsed in Bishop's arms. Soares died days later at St. Vincent's Hospital.

Elizabeth Blackwell
PHYSICIAN 1821–1910

I n 1849, Elizabeth Blackwell became the first woman in the United States to be licensed as a physician. At that time, Victorian social convention held that it would be "unbecoming in a woman to receive instruction from males in the nature and laws of her organism." Blackwell nonetheless applied to two dozen medical schools and was summarily rejected by all but one. The administration of the Geneva Medical School in New York placed her application before the student body for a vote, with the caveat that a single "no" vote would result in her rejection. Motivated by an opportunity to embarrass the faculty (and apparently believing the application was a hoax submitted by a rival school), the students voted unanimously in 1847 to admit Elizabeth Blackwell. Students initially harassed her, pausing to note her "admirable phrenology" as they dropped folded notes onto her head from the balcony in the lecture hall. Women in town snubbed her or stopped to stare at her in the streets. By the end of her term, however, she was admired by her fellow students and graduated at the top of her class. Determined to practice, she returned to New York City in 1851. During her first residency, male interns walked out of wards en masse (with the patients' medical charts) when she entered the room. In New York, Blackwell opened the first hospital and free clinic to be staffed by female physicians and founded a successful medical college. In 1869, Blackwell returned to her native England to practice.

Elizabeth Blackwell, undated.

Library of Congress Prints and Photographs Division

Cooper Union
7 East 7th Street at Cooper Square
tel. (212) 353-4100, www.cooper.edu

Thousands of women filled Cooper Union in the spring of 1861 to create the Women's Central Association of Relief for the Sick and Wounded of the Army. The organization was established to aid field doctors, who were overwhelmed by the number of ailing and injured soldiers brought in from the Civil War battlefields. Working with Florence Nightingale, Blackwell devised an accelerated training program for nurses willing to volunteer in the war effort. Several wealthy and socially prominent women joined and helped to organize the effort. At churches and private homes, women of all classes helped by sewing miles of bandages for Union troops.

Site of The New York Infirmary for Women and Children
East 7th Street at Tompkins Square

Blackwell returned to New York City in 1851 after further studies in Europe. Shut out of existing hospitals and clinics on the basis of her sex, she resolved to open her own clinic and sought quarters for a medical practice. She was barred from leasing rooms on all but squalid blocks, but finally secured a house on Bleecker Street. After delays and suspicions, patients, particularly poor women and their children, crowded the small clinic. Two years later, she opened a dispensary on East 7th Street close to Tompkins Square and was joined by her sister, Dr. Emily Blackwell, and by Dr. Marie Zachrzewska, the former chief midwife of Prussia's largest hospital. The practice continued to specialize in the needs of poor women, who traveled from all over the city to visit the infirmary. Blackwell's New York Infirmary for Women and Children continues to operate as a respected medical institution, though since 1979 it has been part of what is now known as NYU Downtown Hospital and is located at 170 William Street, between Beekman and Ann Streets.

....

Site of the Woman's Medical College of the New York Infirmary
126 Second Avenue, between East 7th Street and St. Mark's Place

Blackwell initially rejected the idea of establishing a women's medical college, of which there were only a handful in the country, believing that integrated instruction at long-standing medical schools provided the best education. Since, however, established medical schools continued to turn women away, Blackwell established The Woman's Medical College of the New York Infirmary in 1868, which held students to more stringent graduation requirements than most of the established all-male medical schools in the city. In training courses and in popular lectures around the city, Blackwell advocated improved hygiene, higher educational standards, physical education for boys and girls, and preventative health care. The college was closed when Cornell University began to admit women to its medical school.

Nellie Bly
JOURNALIST 1867–1922

A s an investigative journalist, Nellie Bly willingly put herself in the most dangerous of circumstances. She threw herself anonymously into the bleak social systems of New York City in order to expose their corruption and cruelty. In the process, she exposed sham spiritualists, the trade in newborns, the hard life of domestics, the dangers of factory work, the mistreatment of prisoners, and the torture of the mentally ill. She feigned insanity to gain access to the notorious asylum on Blackwell's Island; she engineered her own arrest for larceny to investigate the mistreatment of female prisoners by male guards; she circumnavigated the globe in a race against Jules Verne's fictitious Phileas Fogg and won by completing her global loop in seventy-two days, notwithstanding a stop to visit the skeptical author in Europe. As an entrepreneur, she owned and operated factories and patented the first steel barrel. While in Austria to promote her barrel business, she visited the four-day-old Eastern Front of World War I. During the war years in Austria, her attitudes were shaped by German propaganda. In unpopular letters and articles, she vented her intensely anti-English, anti-French views, and warned ominously of the "creeping" Bolshevism against which the Germans were struggling. Back in the United States after the war, Bly found work as an "empathy columnist" answering the letters of those suffering quietly in marriages and in unhappy families. She watched her emulators from a cool distance: the new crop of "stunt girls," desperate to break into journalism, who volunteered to be shot while wearing

Nellie Bly, 1896.

The Museum of the City of New York

the first bulletproof vests and stood on streetcar tracks to demonstrate the potential dangers of unmaintained brakes.

Site of The New York World Building
Beneath access ramp to Brooklyn Bridge

Bly concluded her circumnavigation of the globe at the offices of *The New York World*, then located at 31 Park Row across from City Hall. At the time, The New York World Building was the tallest building in the world: twenty stories of arched windows capped by a golden dome. Years earlier, Bly had arrived at Park Row determined to work as a New York reporter. She had a considerable reputation in the provinces, but no New York editor would meet with her. She volunteered for a hot air balloon stunt, but it was deemed too dangerous for a lady and her offer was declined. She finally cracked the Park Row world by posing as a well-connected but discouraged job applicant. Falsified letters of introduction assured her access to managing editors of the city's papers; she asked them if women had a chance in journalism—all replied with an unequivocal no. She published the embarrassing piece in a regional paper, and Joseph Pulitzer's *The World* hired her immediately. For her first assignment, he commissioned her to impersonate a mentally ill woman, in order to get a story from inside the notorious Women's Lunatic Asylum on Blackwell's Island.

The New York World Building was at 31 Park Row until Frankfort Street was enlarged and Park Row changed course in 1955. The New York World Building was torn down; the original site is now beneath the access ramp to the Brooklyn Bridge. This stretch, then known as Newspaper Row, was once home to *The New York Herald*, *Times*, *Tribune*, *Sun*, and *World*. In Bly's day, it was the most important and most difficult to breach cluster of institutions in the country for an aspiring journalist.

Roosevelt Island

In the East River from East 47th to East 96th Streets

On May 7, 1893, Bly's exposé of the insane asylum at Blackwell's Island (the former name of Roosevelt Island) appeared under her byline in *The World*. In her scheme to appear insane to the authorities and thereby to be admitted to the asylum, Bly had dressed in out-of-fashion clothes, let her hair become disheveled, and perfected a far-away look with which she wandered the streets. Having set the stage, she checked into Irene Stenard's Temporary Home for Women at 84 Second Avenue.

Pouncing on the romantic mystery (possibly fueled by Pulitzer himself), other newspapers asked their readers to help identify the young, beautiful, apparently affluent amnesiac by publishing her photo under headlines such as: "Who is this Insane Girl?" (*The Sun*) and "Mysterious Waif with the Wild Hunted Look in Her Eyes" (*The New York Times*). Though the warden at the Lunatic Asylum insisted, after the fact, that he had been suspicious all along, three doctors at Bellevue diagnosed Bly as "undoubtedly insane." She was ferried across the East River to Blackwell's Island where she spent ten days before Pulitzer sprung her from the nightmarish place.

The Octagon Tower, formerly the central structure of the Lunatic Asylum, is extant and protected as a historic site on Roosevelt Island. The Asylum, designed in 1839, was New York's first. Charles Dickens toured the hospital in 1841 during his visit to New York; he noted with familiar sadness the "long, listless, madhouse air."

New York Union Square Theatre

100 East 17th Street, between Park Avenue and Irving Place
tel. (212) 505-0700

Bly delivered a series of lectures here about her record-breaking trip around the globe. As happened with many star reporters of the era, Bly's editors, once overshadowed, stopped promoting her. Bly left *The World*, feeling she was underpaid and underappreciated. She was forced to return to the staff after a failed stint as a novelist.

Site of The Tombs

100 Centre Street, between Worth and Leonard Streets

This site, now occupied by the Criminal Courts Building, once held the city's massive, nineteenth-century prison complex. The complex had been styled after an Egyptian mausoleum and was known popularly as "the Tombs." Though the building that inspired the nickname is long gone, the city's central detention center is still called "the Tombs." Bly interviewed anarchist Emma Goldman here in 1893, after Goldman was imprisoned for allegedly inciting the poor to take bread "by force." Hers was the first interview with the notorious Goldman in the mainstream press. In her article published in *The World*, Bly addressed her readers: "You see her in your mind a great raw-boned creature, with short hair and bloomers, a red flag in one hand, a burning torch in the other; both feet constantly off of the ground and 'murder!' continually upon her lips." Bly encountered instead a petite woman of twenty-five with "very expressive blue-gray eyes" and a gentle manner. Bly informed her readers that Goldman was "very pretty and girlish" and spoke Russian, German, French, and English; it was a sympathetic portrait, in which Goldman was quoted at length.

Jefferson Market Library
425 Sixth Avenue at West 10th Street
tel. (212) 243-4334

This building was Jefferson Courthouse when Bly appeared before a judge here after arranging her own arrest for larceny, so that she could report on the abuse of female prisoners by the male guards and lawyers.

Former residence
15 West 37th Street, between Fifth and Sixth Avenues

At the height of her celebrity, Bly married a bachelor industrialist forty-four years her senior. They lived here with her husband's brother. The three battled over money, particularly the money necessary to renovate the once-grand house that the elderly brothers had let fall into gothic disrepair. The trio was often the subject of newspaper gossip, and her jealous husband had Bly tailed around New York. After many publicly rocky and dramatic years, Bly settled in as his caretaker, and he ultimately left his business empire to her.

Washington Square Arch
Washington Square North at Fifth Avenue

Bly donated one hundred collectible photographs of herself to aid in funding the building of the Arch.

Woodlawn Cemetery
Entrances: East 233rd Street at Webster Avenue; Jerome Avenue north of Bainbridge Avenue
Woodlawn, The Bronx
tel. (718) 920-0500

Bly is buried here, in a field of modest grave markers. Hers reads: "Dedicated June 22, 1978 to Nellie Bly by the New York Press Club in Honor of a Famous News Reporter."

Humphrey Bogart

ACTOR 1899–1957

A fter an elite prep school expelled him, Humphrey Bogart shipped out as an enlisted serviceman on the *Leviathan* during World War I. Back in New York after the war, Bogart worked as a chess hustler, challenging all at Coney Island and Times Square. Encouraged by friends, he pursued acting, appearing onstage for the first time as a Japanese waiter. In his first celebrated role, he played a hunched, hard-hearted murderer in *The Petrified Forest*; his authentic portrayal frightened theater audiences and brought him critical acclaim. He was never expected to succeed as a leading man—his signature lisp, wry delivery, and the villainous bent of his earliest roles all qualified him, in Hollywood, for the terminal role of the criminal. Bogart broke the mold and went on to star in such films as *The Maltese Falcon, Casablanca,*

and *The African Queen*, for which he won the Academy Award for Best Actor and became the leading man of his generation. Bogart met nineteen-year-old Lauren Bacall on the set of *To Have and Have Not*—the two fell in love, existing relationships with others notwithstanding, and married in 1946. They starred in film classics including *The Big Sleep*, *Key Largo*, and *Dark Passage*, had two children, and stayed together until Bogart's death in 1957.

Former residence
245 West 103rd Street, between Broadway and West End Avenue

This was Bogart's childhood home. His father, a prominent doctor, kept his offices in the parlor, and Bogart's mother, a well-known illustrator, worked under a skylight on the fourth floor. Her drawing of infant Bogart appeared in a national ad campaign for Mellin's Baby Food.

Broadhurst Theater

235 West 44th Street, between Seventh and Eighth Avenues

Bogart made his debut here in 1935 in the Robert E. Sherwood play, *Petrified Forest*, produced by Leslie Howard. In gratitude to Howard, Bogart named one of his children Leslie. Bogart went on to star in the film adaptation of *Petrified Forest*.

....

Gramercy Park Hotel

2 Lexington Avenue at East 21st Street
tel. (800) 221-4083, www.gramercyparkhotel.com

Bogart married his first wife, fellow actor Helen Menken, on the roof of the Gramercy Park Hotel in 1926. She filed for divorce a few years later on the grounds that Bogart cared only for his acting.

....

BOGART AT LARGE

Though Prohibition had done little if anything to curb drinking in New York, its repeal was still a cause of major celebration around the city. On the night that the Eighteenth Amendment sailed into history, Bogart and his friends dressed in tails and drank at the Ritz-Carlton (formerly at Madison Avenue and East 54th Street). They headed on to the Waldorf-Astoria, where liquor supplies had not quite caught up with demand. The friends abandoned the high-end, legal boozing and returned to their old favorites, speakeasies like Tony's (formerly on 49th Street where Rockefeller Center now stands), Hotsy Totsy, and others. Bogart was a frequent patron of 21—a former speakeasy—during its aboveboard days.

....

Former residence

434 East 52nd Street, between First Avenue and FDR Drive

Bogart lived at this address with his second wife, Mary Philips, during the Great Depression. At this time, chess tournaments in storefronts were a popular diversion and moneymaking scheme, and Bogart, an expert chess player, took on all comers in storefronts matches around Times Square, several blocks west.

....

Elaine's

703 Second Avenue, between 88th and 89th Streets
tel. (212) 534-8103

Bacall came to Elaine's often during her performances on Broadway. Elaine protected Bacall from irrepressible male admirers, all of whom seemed to come up with the same brilliant approach: to imitate Bogart's whistle in *To Have and Have Not* when attempting to make her acquaintance.

Mathew Brady

PHOTOGRAPHER 1823–1896

W hen Mathew Brady's photographs of Civil War dead—encrusted in mud and strewn on the bloody battlefields of Antietam—appeared at his gallery in Lower Manhattan, New Yorkers witnessed for the first time the true horrors of the war. Brady often transformed public perception of political events and figures through photographic portraiture. If not for Brady, current generations would be without (in many cases, the only) photographic images of princes, Union and Confederate soldiers, ailing and youthful presidents, poets, and assassins. Brady was the only son of a farming family in upstate New York; he moved to New York City at the age of sixteen and learned to make daguerreotypes from the leading American master of the process, Samuel F.B. Morse. Determined to photograph all the great men and women of his world, Brady compiled his "Gallery of Illustrious Americans" by enticing the famous into his studios in New York and Washington, D.C., their other natural habitat. When the Civil War broke out, soldiers and their loved ones overwhelmed photography studios with demands for cardboard likenesses of one another to carry into battle or to keep close to the hearth. Against the advice of everyone he consulted, Brady threw himself and his personal fortune into photographing the Civil War. He was recognizable in the field in his long, pale dustcoat, low straw hat, and thick blue-tinted glasses; his fleet of "What-Is-It" wagons (darkrooms on wheels) rumbled through the theaters of war. His greatest photographic legacy ruined him financially and brought him little acclaim in his day. Bankrupt, Brady sold his collection of war images to the War Department at a steep loss. Most of the plates were lost or broken; Brady died penniless and forgotten by his contemporaries.

· ·

Cooper Union

7 East 7th Street at Cooper Square
tel. (212) 353-4100, www.cooper.edu

Mathew Brady, 1861.

"Brady and the Cooper Institute made me President."—Abraham Lincoln

On February 27, 1860, Abraham Lincoln stood before a crowd assembled at Cooper Union; he was among the contenders for the presidential nomination of the Republican Party. Observers noted his height, his apparent melancholy, and the shabbiness of his clothes. After his electrifying speech, however, he became a political celebrity, whose image—as captured by Mathew Brady—appeared in all of the newspapers and magazines the next day. Brady had photographed Lincoln young, clean-shaven, confident, and relaxed in his third studio at 643 Bleecker Street near Broadway the morning of the speech. Brady's studio marketed cartes-de-visite (small cardboard photographic likenesses) of Lincoln, which became best sellers.

. . . .

Site of Daguerrian Miniature Gallery
205-207 Broadway at Fulton Street

In 1844, Brady opened his first studio at the frenetic Broadway/Fulton intersection, across from P.T. Barnum's American Museum. Brady developed his technique and wrecked his eyesight making tens of thousands of daguerreotypes here. He built greenhouse-like rooms on the roof and punched through the ceiling with skylights to drench his subjects in natural light. Within a few years competing studios appeared everywhere. Photographers tried to outdo each other, in part, by selling pictures of the odd or the unbelievable: octogenarian triplets were popular. In the beginning of the 1850s, Brady traveled to Europe with his friend James Gordon Bennett, Jr. Brady won a medal for his photography at the Crystal Palace Exhibition in London and traveled for several more months, seeing Europe and encountering innovations in photographic technique. By the time Brady returned to New York in 1853, the daguerreotype was giving way to new technology: the wet plate process. The commercial giants of photography competed with ever-larger prints: "imperials" (life-size portraits) were popular among the wealthy. Brady took competition to the extreme with a promotional display of three monumental photographic portraits, each twenty-five feet tall, which hung on the exterior of his Broadway building. At the opposite end of the spectrum were affordable cartes-de-visite, which replaced the calling card and were traded during the Civil War by soldiers and their loved ones. Brady received international acclaim and grew wealthy from his studios, which were increasingly operated by carefully selected and trained assistants.

. . . .

Site of Brady on Broadway
359 Broadway, between Franklin and Leonard Streets

In 1853, upon his return from Europe, Brady opened his second studio above a popular saloon called Thompson's. Each of Brady's studios was grander, better equipped, and more popular than the last. Socialites and celebrities endured the discomforts (an immobilizing head clamp, for one) of the long exposure time required to transfer their images onto glass plates. At Brady on Broadway, Brady built up his "Gallery of Illustrious Americans."

. . . .

Site of National Portrait Gallery
785 Broadway at East 10th Street

Brady outfitted his flagship, the pinnacle of American photography studios, with the finest technology and most lush environs. In long, grand rooms chandelier crystals, display cases, daguerreotypes, and etched glass doors shone softly in the gaslight. Portraits of every size gazed solemnly from the wall, while clients posed on the rose-red carpets or in an engineered suffusion of sunlight.

Margaret Wise Brown

WRITER 1910–1952

Margaret Wise Brown wrote hundreds of books, *Goodnight Moon* and *Runaway Bunny* among them, and almost single-handedly produced a new kind of literature for children. Brown became involved in childhood education and development at Lucy Sprague Mitchell's Bank Street School, where she was envied by peers for her ability to disappear effortlessly into the world of children. The decor of her homes reflected her eccentric nature: she lined her Manhattan house with fur (she had written a book, *The Little Fur Family*, about tiny furry people living in a fur house), and she refused to have a refrigerator at her summer house in Maine, choosing instead to tie milk, butter, and beer to labeled ropes in the ice-cold river. For all of her success and optimism in work and life, Brown fell into fraught, obsessive friendships with domineering, wealthy women, and she was deeply troubled that her literary talents did not register in the world of adult critics. Hopeful of forging a literary friendship, Brown convinced her publisher to solicit a children's book from Gertrude Stein, *World is Round*, in which Stein wrote her best-remembered phrase: "a rose is a rose is a rose." In the gradual dimming of light and noise in the pages of *Goodnight Moon* and the abiding love of the mother in *Runaway Bunny*, Brown continues to enchant new generations of children.

Margaret Wise Brown, 1939.

Cobble Court
Northeast corner of Greenwich Avenue and Charles Street

Brown's house, Cobble Court, appears in her book *Mister Dog*. This nineteenth-century farm cottage was moved from the courtyard of an apartment building on York Avenue between East 71st and East 72nd Streets to its present location in 1967. Still a private home, the cottage is an eccentric collection of angles and additions that stands behind an ivy-covered wall. Brown used this space as a writing studio when she no longer kept offices at 69 Bank Street. The house had scant amenities: just waxed brick floors and an open hearth always crackling with fire in the winter. When her longtime collaborator and illustrator Clement Hurd—returned from World War II—arrived in New York, he and his wife stayed at Cobble Court. Brown had upholstered the walls and furniture with fur and filled the house with flowers. Cobble Court is also where her friends gathered on what would have been Brown's forty-third birthday, May 12, 1953, for a memorial service.

. . . .

Site of Bank Street School
69 Bank Street between Bleecker and West 4th Streets

Since the 1940s, the Bank Street School has been the generator and laboratory for progressive ideas about education and language development. Run by social reformer and educational philosopher Lucy Sprague Mitchell, Bank Street teachers believed that in order to teach children, adults must grasp how children see and experience reality. At Bank Street, Brown found her most significant mentor in Mitchell, who insisted that it was "rhythm, sound quality and patterns of sound" that drove children to acquire language, not a desire to communicate. Mitchell guided Brown in her early efforts to write for children; together they rejected most traditional fairy tales because they were contaminated by "the stimulus of adult fancies." The Bank Street School is now located on West 112th Street between Broadway and Riverside Drive.

. . . .

Former residence
21 West 10th Street, between Fifth and Sixth Avenues

Here, friends encountered Brown's menagerie: goats, a flying squirrel, and numerous cats. After receiving the publisher's advance for *When the Wind Blew*, Brown bought the entire contents of a horse-drawn flower cart, filled the rooms and halls of her apartment with flowers, and invited all of her friends in to celebrate.

Lenny Bruce

COMEDIAN 1925–1966

L enny Bruce paved the way for contemporary, edgy stand-up comedy and fought on multiple fronts for the freedom of speech guaranteed under the First Amendment. When Bruce was rushed to the hospital after a serious fall in 1964, his reputation for invective was so notorious that doctors reportedly taped his mouth shut to protect the nuns working there. Bruce's parents (a moralizing podiatrist and a restless actress) met at a leap year dance on Long Island. The marriage collapsed and Bruce was trafficked between family members and a happy, firmly settled farming couple whom Bruce begged to adopt him. Bruce married Honey Harlow (her stage name) and moved with her to New York, where they lived with Bruce's mother, then enjoying success as a "crazy-legs-dancer." Mother, son, and Honey spent summers on the Catskills circuit performing in vaudeville-like variety shows. Back in New York, Bruce acted as emcee between acts at strip clubs: there he developed his ad-lib satirical style, leafing through newspaper articles on stage and plumbing the great reservoir of 1950s taboo. In New York, Bruce and Harlow sank into the mainlining drug culture that finally claimed Bruce's life years later. He became a liberal cause célèbre among fellow artists after he was arrested repeatedly on obscenity charges and drug possession. Hounded by the authorities and the courts, Bruce fired his lawyer, studied legal briefs frantically, and took over his own defense. He spent his last years at the mercy of the political legal system he had satirized so fearlessly.

Lenny Bruce, 1961.

LENNY BRUCE

Library of Congress Prints and Photographs Division

Site of Café au Go Go

152 Bleecker Street, between LaGuardia Place and Thompson Street

This building once housed Café au Go Go. By the time Bruce performed here in 1964, he had already been arrested in Chicago, San Francisco, and Los Angeles for using obscene language and indecent material in his performances. He continued to spout "obscenities" here, satirizing, among other political matters, the assassination of John F. Kennedy. Tape recorder-wielding police officers and CIA agents soon joined the audience and took copious notes of Bruce's performances. Bruce was arrested on obscenity charges in New York on April 3, 1964. Actors, artists, and Beat celebrities signed petitions and generated publicity in defense of his First Amendment right to free speech. Despite their efforts and more than two thousand errors discovered in the police transcripts of Bruce's act, he was found guilty and sentenced to four months in the workhouse on Rikers Island. Thirty-nine years later, on December 23, 2003, Bruce was posthumously pardoned by Governor George E. Pataki.

The Marlton
3-5 West 8th Street, between Fifth and Sixth Avenues

Now a dormitory for students at the Parsons School of Design, this was once the Marlton Hotel, home to Bruce during his obscenity trial in 1964.

Former Residence
11 St. Mark's Place, between Second and Third Avenues

Bruce lived here in the 1960s.

Former offices of theater talent scouts
1650 Broadway at West 51st Street

This was once a hive of Catskills-circuit talent booking agents. Comics and other performers, including Bruce, hoping to launch a turn on the lucrative and prestigious Catskills circuit lingered outside this building, and at diners in the Times Square area, including Lindy's (now at 825 Seventh Avenue at West 53rd Street and 401 Seventh Avenue at 32nd Street). Bruce's first act as a comedian—"The Bavarian Mimic"—was a long way from the barbed satire for which he became famous.

Truman Capote
WRITER 1924–1984

 eft by his teenage beauty queen mother to be reared by doting aunts and cousins in the South, Truman Capote had a lonely childhood that left him largely to his own imagination. He moved to New York City at the age of seventeen. In his first novel, *Other Voices, Other Rooms*, he wrote about a love affair between men. Delicate, boyish Capote appeared on the cover reclining, buttoned into a sharp, small vest and gazing provocatively at the reading public. His putative masterpiece, *In Cold Blood*, is a chronicle of the murder of a Kansas farm family, the Clutter family. With it, Capote invented a literary form: the nonfiction novel. The literary celebrity Capote waved off criticism of his social life—indulging and being indulged by members of high society—by claiming all experience as research for his writing. In the wake of his monumental success as a writer and master social planner, Capote finished his literary career with *Answered Prayers*, a novelistic account of the important people whose friendships he had cultivated. Those who recognized their unflattering portraits in excerpts published in *Esquire* magazine in 1975 snubbed Capote, proving that, even shaken, the old guard could deliver the expert social cut.

Former residence
70 Willow Street, between Pineapple and Orange Streets
Brooklyn Heights, Brooklyn

In the 1950s, Capote lived in Brooklyn—"by choice," as he asserted in a *Holiday* magazine piece, "A House on the Heights." Capote wrote *Breakfast at Tiffany's* and *In Cold*

Blood here, after the owner of the house, theatrical designer Oliver Smith, gave into Capote's sustained petitions for residency. Before becoming a tenant, Capote visited the yellow-brick mansion in 1957, recording with envy an inventory of twenty-eight rooms, twenty-eight "marble-mantled fireplaces" and walls "thick as buffalo"; he admired the rear porch, which reminded him of Louisiana, where guests drank wine under a canopy of leaves and wisteria. The garden blossomed with pear trees, tulip trees, and forsythia. In the basement apartment, Capote lived among filigreed and extravagant relics from a past of travel and eccentric acquisition—a pair of butterfly-shaped mirrors hovered over the room. Though Capote lived in the basement, he took emotional possession of the entire house, obsessing over its "beautiful staircase floating upward in white, swan-simple curves to a skylight of sunny amber-gold glass." Capote walked along the waterfront regularly during the bustling day and during the shuttered warehouse hush of late night.

Site of Gage & Tollner

372-374 Fulton Street at Jay Street
Brooklyn Heights, Brooklyn

Truman Capote, ca. 1940s.

© Bettmann/CORBIS

Founded in 1879 and occupying its current location by 1892, Gage & Tollner was a landmark Brooklyn institution. After 125 years in business, Gage & Tollner closed on Valentine's Day in 2004. A new restaurant is likely to open in this space. Since both the interior and exterior are designated historic landmarks, its cut glass chandeliers, solid mahogany furniture, mirror-lined walls, and flickering gas lights will remain. In Capote's day, diners assembled around marble-topped tables and praised the fresh fish, chowder, and seasonal soft-shell crabs. Capote recalled "Chowders the doughtiest down-Easter must approve. Lobsters that would appease Nero."

Tiffany & Co.

727 Fifth Avenue at East 57th Street
tel. (212) 755-8000, www.tiffany.com

"What I've found does the most good is just to get into a taxi and go to Tiffany's. It calms me down right away, the quietness and the proud look of it; nothing very bad could happen to you there."—Holly Golightly in *Breakfast at Tiffany's*

Capote wrote *Breakfast at Tiffany's* while he was living in Brooklyn Heights, though the story follows the narrator around the Upper East Side (Capote's first address in New York), as he marshals Holly Golightly through the ups and downs of city life. The book was adapted as a film starring Audrey Hepburn. Tiffany's moved to Fifth Avenue and 57th Street from an extant building at 409 Fifth Avenue in 1940.

Plaza Hotel

768 Fifth Avenue at Central Park South
tel. (212) 759-3000, www.fairmont.com

In the Grand Ballroom here, Capote celebrated his social and literary success by throwing a party in honor of *Washington Post* publisher Katherine Graham on November 28, 1966. The "Black and White Ball" caused a thrilling upheaval in the social worlds of New York. Capote created a masterpiece of a party, fine-tuning a list of 500 guests, (quipping that in the process he had made 15,000 enemies), that included Frank Sinatra, Marianne Moore, Norman Mailer, Andy Warhol, and Tennessee Williams. Like Mrs. Astor before him, Capote chose the elite, but he drew from diverse reservoirs: neither society nor the art world could relax in the certainty of an invitation. All of the guests were required to appear in black and white and to wear elaborate masks. An unprecedented crush of journalists, cameras, and fans crowded the red carpet laid outside the Plaza Hotel. Once inside, guests eyed each other, danced, and drank. More than one guest compared the glittering, masked, and silk-hooded procession past the throngs at the door to the numbered days before the French Revolution.

The Museum of the City of New York

1220 Fifth Avenue at 103rd Street
tel. (212) 534-1672, www.mcny.org

The museum owns a collection of invitations, masks, fans, and other memorabilia from "The Black and White Ball."

Library of Congress Prints and Photographs Division

Enrico Caruso

OPERA SINGER 1873–1921

E nrico Caruso, considered by many to have possessed the greatest voice of the twentieth century, was the eighteenth of twenty-one siblings, and the first to survive infancy at a time when cholera epidemics swept frequently across southern Italy. Celebrated in his youth for his performance of popular Neapolitan songs, Caruso was called up for military service at the outset of his operatic career. At the insistence of commanding officers enthralled by Caruso's voice, he was released from the army to pursue his career, while his younger brother dutifully filled his slot in the army. Caruso debuted at the Metropolitan Opera House in New York in 1903 and was soon hailed as the most gifted tenor in the world. Caruso's voice was also among the first to enter American homes on gramophones; his recordings virtually launched the recording industry and made opera accessible to a broader public. In recognition of his public support of the police, Caruso was made honorary police chief by the New York City Police Department. The public loved him fanatically, though saboteurs, angry over fees rumored to top $10,000 a performance, ignited a bomb under the stage during a performance in Cuba. Caruso escaped uninjured, and he remained a jovial and generous presence around New York until his death in 1921.

Enrico Caruso Museum of America

1942 East 19th Street, between Avenue S and Avenue T
Gravesend, Brooklyn
tel. (718) 368-3993, www.enricocarusomuseum.com

Up the narrow stairs of an adapted Brooklyn home is the Enrico Caruso Museum, a remarkable constellation of rare recordings, photographs, letters, and personal effects of Enrico Caruso, including his death mask. The collection has been cultivated over many decades by second-generation Caruso devotee Aldo Mancusi. Highlights of the museum include original wooden chairs and a gold-leaf angel from the roof of the Old Metropolitan Opera House, Caruso's opera costumes, his orchid-and-black dress shoes, his last pack of Egyptian Prettiest Cigarettes, and the last cigarette itself, which is stamped with "The Sheik Restaurant." Also noteworthy is Mr. Mancusi's collection of antique music boxes, symphoniums, victrolas, and paper organs, which play popular instrumentals dating from the 1870s on. It is the chance to hear Caruso as his contemporary New Yorkers, relaxing at home, would have: Caruso's Neopolitan love song "Ungrateful Heart" reaches listeners by way of a steel phonograph needle and a golden amplifying horn. Caruso was a gifted caricaturist, and his self-portraits and sketches of fellow celebrities and friends are on display. Caruso once entertained a skeptical public standing in line to see modernist works at the Armory Show by making fast caricatures of Duchamp's *Nude Descending a Staircase, No. 2* and throwing them out into the crowd.

Site of Old Metropolitan Opera House
Broadway, between West 39th and West 40th Streets

Caruso performed at the Old Metropolitan Opera House 861 times. The Old Met provided a haven for the newly rich families of the late 1880s who, millions aside, struggled to breech the institutions of the old money set, including the Academy of Music on Union Square. The nouveau riche applied their millions to the construction of the Metropolitan Opera House and to the establishment of their own opera company, which opened with *Faust* in the fall of 1883. On November 23, 1903, Caruso made his American debut there. In 1909, Dr. Lee De Forest improved experimental radio and transmission devices; he broadcast Caruso singing *Pagliacci* at the Old Metropolitan Opera House and then picked up the broadcast in his home, to the amazement of his guests. Caruso's coevolution with radio and recording technology helped to broaden exposure to opera beyond the exclusive and expensive arena of the opera house. Relics from the demolished Old Metropolitan Opera House—including original gold-and-red chairs and sections of the ornate interiors—can be seen at the Enrico Caruso Museum.

Brooklyn Academy of Music
30 Lafayette Avenue, between Ashland Place and St. Felix Street
Fort Greene, Brooklyn
tel. (718) 636-4100, www.bam.org

Caruso performed here on November 14, 1908 in a Metropolitan Opera production of *Faust* that marked the opening of BAM on Lafayette Avenue (their Civil War-era home at 176-194 Montague Street in Brooklyn Heights burned down in 1903). It was on the same BAM stage in 1921 that Caruso appeared in *L'Elisir d'Amore* during the Metropolitan Opera's last season at BAM. During the performance, a blood vessel in Caruso's throat burst, forcing him from the stage, but only after he had struggled on, coughing blood into several handkerchiefs. He gave his final performance two weeks later at the Old Metropolitan Opera House.

Former Knickerbocker Hotel
1466 Broadway at West 42nd Street (now 6 Times Square)

Caruso lived in a fourteen-room suite in this building from 1908 until 1920. He dined most nights in the hotel restaurant and frequented the hotel bar, which was dominated by a Maxfield Parrish mural. (The mural was saved and can still be seen in its new home, the St. Regis Hotel bar.) On Armistice Day, November 9, 1918, Caruso sang from the balcony of his hotel suite to entertain the crowds celebrating the end of World War I in Times Square. He sang the national anthems of the United States, France, and Italy.

Former Vanderbilt Hotel
4 Park Avenue, between East 33rd and East 34th Streets

In 1920, Caruso moved here from the Knickerbocker Hotel. This former grand hotel was also converted into office space. The vaulted crypt, originally the hotel bar, is now a landmark. Caruso, who spent most of his life in fine hotels, would only sleep on stacked mattresses in order to spare his voice the humid, low air that drifted closer to the floor.

Marble Collegiate Church
272 Fifth Avenue at West 29th Street

Caruso and Dorothy Benjamin were married here on August 20, 1918. Benjamin's father, an affluent patent lawyer, disowned his daughter for marrying the opera star who was twenty years her senior.

Chun Kong Chow

ENTREPRENEUR 1892–1984

C ivil rights advocate and community leader Chun Kong Chow was a major force in the founding of twentieth-century Chinatown. Chun's family had left their fishing village in the Guangdong province of China, settling first in Australia and then in San Francisco. In 1927, Chun followed the path opened by earlier Chinese immigrants fleeing discrimination in the West, and traveled cross-country to New York. The following year, he opened the New York branch of the family imported goods emporium, Sun Goon Shing. The shop became a hub of news, social life, and political organization that lasted for forty years. As a merchant, Chun was a Section Six exception to the 1882 Exclusion Act, which banned all Chinese immigrants—save merchants, scholars, and students—from entering the United States, though even Section Six immigrants could not apply for US citizenship, making the Chinese the first nationality barred by law from becoming US citizens. The Exclusion Act was prolonged through sequel legislation: in 1922, the Cable Act revoked the citizenship of any woman who married an "alien," and quotas favoring immigrants from European nations effectively continued exclusion until 1943. Chun devoted his retirement years to activism: he fought for the removal of immigration quotas, for the right of Chinese immigrants to attend New York public universities, and for the posting of street and subway signs in Chinatown in both English and Chinese.

Chinatown
From Canal Street to Worth Street and from Mulberry Street to the Bowery

Beginning in the 1870s, many Chinese immigrants fled the West Coast, where anti-Chinese rhetoric had escalated into riots and violent attacks against the Chinese

community. Many traveled to New York City and established a new community in an area now roughly bounded by Canal, Worth, and Mulberry Streets, and the Bowery. Canal, now a traffic-battered asphalt and cobblestone street laid over the path of an actual canal that once drained an inland spring, remains the main artery of Chinatown. On it, visitors can find shops specializing in light bulbs, plastics, delicacies, clothes, lamps— almost anything. Early Chinatown was a "bachelor society," as immigrant men could neither apply for citizenship nor bring their families over. Retail centers like Sun Goon Shing provided a social center and meeting place for the community.

Museum of Chinese in the Americas

70 Mulberry Street, between Canal and Bayard Streets
(212) 619-4785, www.moca-nyc.org

The Museum of Chinese in the Americas (MoCA) is the nation's first permanent, fully staffed museum devoted to the cultural heritage of the Chinese in the western hemisphere. Located on the second floor of a hundred-year-old school building in the center of Chinatown, MoCA offers a core exhibit ("Where is Home? Chinese in the Americas") with artefacts and photographs documenting prominent lives in Chinatown—including that of Chun Kong Chow. Rotating exhibits cover everything from political struggle to the performing arts, and walking tours of the neighborhood are available in the summer.

Site of Sun Goon Shing
55 Mott Street, between Canal and Bayard Streets

The original Chinatown was framed by Mott, Pell, Doyers, and Bayard Streets. Chun led the expansion into surrounding neighborhoods with Sun Goon Shing, the first store to open on the traditionally Italian side of Bayard Street. Sun Goon Shing was a social, cultural, and culinary hub of Chinatown from 1929 to 1968. Chun stocked imported water chestnuts, soy sauce, dried fish, silk scarves, candied ginger, porcelain dinnerware, and other housewares, and oversaw the preparation of roasted ducks, pigs, and chickens. Beginning in the 1930s, Chun catered events at the Copacabana and other nightclubs around New York, though he never neglected his own community and kept the store open until midnight to serve late-night workers. He designed a customized and efficient kitchen and pioneered the use of new technologies and progressive management, including air conditioning and health benefits for employees. The site is now a cluster of smaller shops called "Chinatown Gift Center."

Mott Street General Store
32 Mott Street, between Mosco and Pell Streets

Just a few doors down from the former site of Sun Goon Shing is Mott Street General Store, offering many of the traditional items Chun would have sold from his general merchandise store. Mott Street General Store is the oldest operating business in Chinatown and has been open since 1891.

Site of Chinese Seamen's Club
24 Pell Street at Doyers Street

Chun helped to establish this institution during World War II as a gathering place for Chinese seamen on shore leave, which had been forbidden until he and others campaigned for the right of liberty for Chinese sailors.

De Witt Clinton

GOVERNOR 1769–1828

D e Witt Clinton graduated from Columbia University at seventeen and became secretary to Governor Clinton, his uncle, at twenty-one. With characteristic nimbleness, he leapt from post to post and was elected mayor of New York City at thirty-four. Clinton envisioned a futuristic New York, one in which goods from the state and the nation would stream into Manhattan and Brooklyn along a system of canals. As governor, he supported the construction of the Erie Canal, an ambitious scheme to connect the Great Lakes to New York City that would require workers to dig a 360-mile ditch from Buffalo to New York Harbor. Clinton campaigned for decades, surmounting federal resistance to funding and ignoring mockery of "Clinton's Ditch" in the press. In 1817, the canal was given official sanction in Albany; it was cut and built largely with Welsh and Irish immigrant labor and finished two years ahead of schedule. The canal was a phenomenal success: it triggered a canal-building craze throughout the region and it dramatically altered the economy of the city and the state. The value of European imports fell, and farmers in Brooklyn switched crops to fill idiosyncratic niches in the tastes of city folk (e.g., asparagus, peas). Though New York had not yet developed above Houston Street, Clinton predicted that by the end of the century, "the whole island of Manhattan, covered with inhabitants and replenished with a dense population, will constitute one vast city." Clinton and others worked to eradicate eccentric lots, oddly shaped parks, plazas, and snaking roads in the settled part of the city. According to his plan, except for the southernmost knot of streets in the oldest area of the city, all streets would be patterned in a grid running from north to south and east to west. Surveyors who hacked and trekked into the hostile, rocky, overgrown, dark forest of Upper Manhattan risked attack by animals and by armed people defending their doomed encampments from the city dwellers creeping northward.

Battery Park
Southern tip of Manhattan

An estimated two-thirds of all New Yorkers left their homes to watch Clinton complete his maiden voyage down the Erie Canal and into New York Harbor. The guns of the Battery fired in celebration as Clinton and his party floated into view on their flat-bottomed canal craft; candle-illuminated transparencies of the Erie Canal decked City Hall; and social and labor organizations marched in regiment through the streets of Lower Manhattan. Spectators enjoyed festooned steamships, triumphal music, and the "marriage of the waters" ceremony in which Clinton emptied casks of Erie water into the Harbor.

New-York Historical Society
2 West 77th Street at Central Park West
tel. (212) 873-3400, www.nyhistory.org

On display here is the barrel—petite, deep brown, and decorated in watery blue letters—used by Clinton to transport Lake Erie water down the Erie Canal into New York Harbor.

Castle Clinton National Monument
Southern end of Battery Park
tel. (212) 344-7220, www.nps.gov/cacl

At the outset of the War of 1812, Battery Park was protected from potential naval attack by a modest necklace of island fortifications in New York Harbor. One of the fortifications, the Southwest Battery, had been built on rocks off the southern tip of Manhattan in 1811; it was joined to Manhattan by a 300-foot causeway, though the little island has since been subsumed by Manhattan's landfill expansion. The fort's guns were manned but never fired. Five years after the War of 1812, the Southwest Battery was rechristened Castle Clinton in honor of De Witt Clinton. Within another five years, soldiers left the fort and New York City took control of the site, renaming it Castle Garden and building a restaurant and opera house on the site. Thirty years later, Castle Garden reverted to government use as a processing center for almost eight million immigrants.

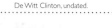

In 1896, the institution morphed into the popular New York City Aquarium, which shut down in 1941. Today, Castle Clinton is free and open to visitors who wish to explore on their own or join guided tours led by rangers in period costume. In its most prosaic capacity to date, Castle Clinton also serves as the ticket office of the ferry service to the Statue of Liberty and other New York Harbor destinations.

South Street Seaport Museum
12 Fulton Street at Front Street
tel. (212) 748-8600, www.southstseaport.org

The South Street Seaport Museum plans to open a museum with a permanent exhibition, "World Port New York," in 2005. The exhibition will be housed in the upper floors of Schermerhorn Row, a block of renovated nineteenth-century warehouses. The exhibition will trace the history of New York as a world port—from the earliest colonial days through the Erie Canal boom to the present.

Anthony Comstock
MORAL CRUSADER 1844–1915

A s head of the New York Society for the Suppression of Vice, Anthony Comstock crusaded against pornography, contraception, obscenity, and all else that he felt contaminated mainstream American society. He endeared himself to the powerful upper class by stoking their fear of the growing immigrant population and the new social activism of the working classes. He was made a special agent of the US Post Office, empowering him to monitor mail and to stop the publication and distribution of any materials he deemed obscene. Robust, broad-shouldered, with legs like tree trunks, Comstock paced the streets of New York in black-and-white policeman's shoes, armed with a Winchester rifle and a revolver. He kept an eye out for gamblers and trou-blemakers; he shut down Eugene O'Neill's *All God's Chillun Got Wings* because of an interracial kiss; he battled the insidious influence of James Joyce's *Ulysses*; he banned Ovid's *Art of Love* for its racy title; and he raided the Art Students League of New York, enraged by a life drawing of nudes that had appeared in a class catalogue. George Bernard Shaw, whose play *Mrs. Warren's Profession*, was shut down by Comstock, asked incredulously how New York could allow "comstockery" to rule their lives. Comstock's stamp of disapproval took on such perverse cachet that lesser artists asked him to ban their works in order to boost sales. At the end of his life, he was an easy target for car-toonists and critics, as he continued to lash out, increasingly comic and puny, in what was ultimately a losing battle.

Anthony Comstock, undated.

Private collection

Site of Comstock's office
150 Nassau Street, between Spruce and Beekman Streets

From his earliest crusading days, Comstock kept offices here. He perused publications and catalogues for evidence of illegal enticements. He entrapped prostitutes and strip-pers by enduring entire performances before having the women arrested. He railed against the short-haired women and long-haired men of Greenwich Village. From this office, he organized his famous campaign against Victoria Woodhull; the court battle led to the stringent Comstock Laws of 1873, which effectively blocked birth control and the vote for women for many more decades.

Site of The Tombs
100 Centre Street, between Worth and Leonard Streets

Comstock visited one of his heroes, Harry K. Thaw, here during the Stanford White murder trial in 1906. Comstock claimed to have posted spies throughout White's architectural masterpiece, the first Madison Square Garden (since demolished), and to have heard more than enough about follies, parties, and intrigues there to be convinced that the place was a quagmire of depravity, into which Thaw had gone bravely to assassinate a ruiner of young women (see page 214).

Site of Madame Restell's shop
East 52nd Street at Fifth Avenue

At a house on the northeast corner of this intersection, Ann Lohman, known notoriously as the abortionist "Madame Restell," peddled contraceptive powders to wealthy clients. Popular images often depicted her as a gothic, evil figure (sometimes with bat wings) that swooped down to destroy the innocent. Comstock entered her house in 1878 and posed as a young man who had gotten his girlfriend pregnant. She sold him illegal, pregnancy-terminating powder and was jailed in the Tombs. Awaiting the verdict and terrified of returning to the Tombs, she chose to end her life here. She was found in the bathtub with her throat cut on the morning of April 1. Comstock boasted that Lohman was the fifteenth person he had driven to suicide.

The Art Students League
215 West 57th Street, between Seventh Avenue and Broadway
tel. (212) 247-4510, www.theartstudentsleague.org

On August 2, 1906, Comstock raided this building and ordered a baffled nineteen-year-old bookeeper to turn over all copies of the school's catalogue, "The American Art Student." The booklet, which offered an overview of the coursework available to en-rolling students, included examples of drawings of nudes from their life drawing classes. Comstock hauled the student off to the West Side Court and ordered the destruction of 2,500 copies of the booklet. Angry students hung Comstock in effigy from the third-story window of this building.

Joseph Cornell

ARTIST 1903–1972

J oseph Cornell collected the raw materials for his collages and boxes long before he imagined their construction. A true obsessive, he wandered the city, buying trinkets and harvesting the city's cast-offs. He filed everything away in the house he shared with his mother and brother in Queens, and supported himself by selling woolen goods and designing textiles. He was shy, melancholy, and usually alone; he loved iced tea and cake; he revered Henry David Thoreau and Harry Houdini. By chance, in the 1930s he watched art dealer Julian Levy unpacking surrealist art at his gallery in New York and recognized in the work a way of putting together the enormous vocabulary of objects he had accumulated while walking the city. When he started to create his collages and, later, his boxes—framed three-dimensional assemblages of images, paint, text, and objects—Cornell had amassed thousands of items: Japanese prints, miniature caskets, astral maps, train schedules, clay pipes, wooden birds, and much else. Each small

Joseph Cornell, ca. 1940.

box emphasizes the elusive significance of common objects by placing them on a shallow stage behind a ragged proscenium (Cornell and his family spent much of their time at ballets, plays, and symphonies). Cornell often said that his art stemmed from his love of New York City. He lived out his days crafting little utopias in his mother's house in Queens, preserving his forays into imagined foreign territories.

CORNELL AT LARGE

Like Walt Whitman, who ranged all over New York noticing synchronisms and incongruities, Cornell devoted much of his time to exploring New York, watching fellow city dwellers talking, fighting, and idling. While tuned in to all the human agitation and ambition in the city, he collected both odd and everyday objects. In particular, he loved going to the Metropolitan Museum of Art (which exhibited his collages in 1970), the Brooklyn Museum of Art, the Pierpont Morgan Library, the American Museum of Natural History, and its Hayden Planetarium, the second-hand bookshops along Fourth Avenue, and Washington Square Park. He bought knick-knacks, costume jewelry, stamps, and other items for his art from Woolworth's when it was still a five-and-dime store.

C.O. Bigelow Chemists

414 Sixth Avenue at West 9th Street
tel. (212) 533-2700, www.bigelowchemists.com

Bigelow's, the oldest pharmacy in the nation, was founded in 1838 and moved to its present location in 1902. Its motto, stenciled on the front window reads, "If you can't find it anywhere else, try Bigelow's." In this old-fashioned neighborhood apothecary, variety still reigns, as it did when Cornell combed the shelves for objects for his artwork.

The Old Print Shop

150 Lexington Avenue, between 29th and 30th Streets
tel. (212) 683-3950, www.theoldprintshop.com

Founded in 1898 and settled at the current address in 1925, the Old Print Shop—packed with antiquarian maps, Currier & Ives images, and eighteenth- and nineteenth-century prints of everything from horse racing to ice boating—was another favorite Cornell destination.

Solomon R. Guggenheim Museum

1071 Fifth Avenue at East 89th Street
tel. (212) 423-3500, www.guggenheim.org

Even during the 1960s, Cornell remained virtually unknown outside of art circles, but the Guggenheim retrospective in 1967 brought him wider fame and recognition. Highlights of the collection include *Fortune Telling Parrot* (circa 1937–1938); *Space Object Box* (mid-1950s–early 1960s); *Setting for a Fairy Tale* (1942); and *Grand (Grand Hotel de l'Observatoire)* (1954).

E.E. Cummings

POET 1894–1962

A fter graduating from Harvard, E.E. Cummings moved to New York on New Year's Day 1917. He worked for *Collier's Weekly* briefly—a stint of gainful employment Cummings declared would be his last—before volunteering for the ambulance corps in France, where he was imprisoned for three months on the suspicion of espionage. His account of his imprisonment, *The Enormous Room*, was his first published book. When he returned to New York in 1918, he gave himself over completely to painting, poetry, and drinking with like-minded friends. Cummings battled the typographical old guard, and broke the fetters of standard punctuation to put his poems more concretely upon the page. His first book of poetry, *Tulips and Chimneys*, appeared in 1923: many critics dismissed with annoyance the anarchical syntax of his otherwise sincere poems, but others praised the ambition of the experiment. For Cummings, a few honest people composed the elite of individuals who felt and noticed their worlds, who carried a special alertness to life and fellow beings. The rest were the harmfully oblivious, ("a salesman is an it that stinks Excuse/Me"), and Cummings remained opposed, as the self-demoted lower-case "i" in his poetry, to the dehumanizing powers of advertising, technology, political complacency, and fashion.

Former Collier's Weekly Building

416-430 West 13th Street, between Washington Street and Ninth Avenue

The popular magazine has disappeared, but the building where Cummings first worked in New York (responding to the superabundance of mail sent in by readers) still stands. Cummings worked at *Collier's* for three months in 1917, sifting through letters loaded with exotic syntactical, grammatical, and typographical errors, which he loved to study and collect.

Site of Cummings's studio
50-1/2 Barrow Street at West 4th Street

Cummings often walked to the offices of *The Dial*, just a few blocks away from his studio on Barrow Street. His poetry appeared in the journal in the 1920s and brought him celebrity among the avant-garde.

. . . .

McSorley's Old Ale House
15 East 7th Street, between Cooper Square and Second Avenue
tel. (212) 473-9148

Open and serving ale since 1854, McSorley's is reputed to be the oldest saloon in New York City. It was founded by "Old John" McSorley and has been handed down or sold only to those who resist the call to "make improvements" and who have made even smallest changes grudgingly. Long a watering hole for immigrants, laborers, Cooper Union students, pensioners, writers, and regulars, the pub is dim, haunted-feeling, and encrusted with memorabilia: gas lamps, vintage menus, autographs, hanging boots, political posters, and many storied objects to discover. Cummings drank ale here often and wrote a poem titled: [i was sitting in mcsorley's]

"i was sitting in mcsorley's. outside it was New York and beauti-
fully snowing.
Inside snug and evil."

. . . .

Minetta Tavern
113 MacDougal Street, between Bleecker and West 3rd Streets
tel. (212) 475-3850

Once a speakeasy called The Black Rabbit, Minetta Tavern was a favorite gathering place for the literati, including Cummings, Ezra Pound, and Ernest Hemingway. Photographs and caricatures of legendary regulars crowd the walls.

. . . .

Former residence of Elaine Thayer
3 Washington Square North, between University Place and Fifth Avenue

Cummings attended the popular teas hosted here by Elaine Thayer, the urbane and accomplished wife of Cummings's friend Scofield Thayer, editor of *The Dial*. Cummings and Elaine Thayer formed a close friendship that gave way to a six-year affair that resulted, ultimately, in Thayer's pregnancy in 1919. With Scofield's support, Elaine left him to marry Cummings, who formally adopted their child, Nancy. The Cummings lived here as a family but not for long—Elaine left E.E., frustrated by his inability to tend to the practical things in life. In 1946, while painting her portrait, Cummings revealed to his "adopted" daughter, Nancy, that he was, in fact, her biological father.

. . . .

Former residence
4 Patchin Place, off West 10th Street, between Greenwich and Sixth Avenues

Two rows of sleepy houses, built in 1848 as living quarters for Basque restaurant workers, face each other across a serene and tree-shaded courtyard. Cummings moved to 4 Patchin Place in 1923 and stayed until his death in 1962. (His third wife, the fashion model Marion Morehouse, joined him here in 1932.) Cummings reportedly liked to shout across the courtyard to the hermit Djuna Barnes, in 5 Patchin Place: "You still

Photograph by Edward Weston. Collection of Center for Creative Photography. © 1981 Center for Creative Photography, Arizona Board of Regents

alive in there?" Now a landmark, the mews were slated for destruction and redevelopment in the late 1950s; Cummings petitioned Mayor Wagner to preserve the row of historic houses. In 1958, Cummings wrote to a friend: "I appeared not long since, at City Hall (NY) & was copiously snapshotted with-&-without Mayor Wagner…this being the price we paid, M&I, for not being thrown out of our 35year residence at 4 Patchin; after a lawsuit lasting about a year."

Sammy Davis, Jr.

ENTERTAINER 1925–1990

F rom the age of four, when he was known in vaudeville as "Silent Sam, the Dancing Midget," reputedly to evade child labor laws, Sammy Davis, Jr. was a natural on stage. Over a sixty-year career of singing, dancing, and acting, Davis starred on Broadway, appeared in dozens of films and television shows, including his own, and wrote two best-selling autobiographies. A member of the Rat Pack, a loosely bound band of entertainers, public drinkers, and comedic performers whose members included Frank Sinatra and Dean Martin, he embodied the group's irreverent, at times reckless, attitude towards life. His marriage to Swedish actress May Britt, his conversion to Judaism, and his friendships with Presidents Nixon and Kennedy stirred controversy. Early in his career, Davis performed in Las Vegas and New York hotel nightclubs where he was barred, on the basis of race, from staying as a guest. On his death, all the marquees of the Vegas Strip were dimmed in honor of his passing.

Site of Copacabana
10 East 60th Street, between Fifth and Madison Avenues

Davis signed his first record deal (with Decca Records) after a performance here in 1954. In a 1959 review of another Copacabana appearance, Robert W. Dana wrote: "Out of a small body, with a waistline a high-fashion model might aspire to, comes such richness of tone, such high voltage movement and such facile wit as to astound even the most inveterate cafegoer."

The "Copa," formerly a speakeasy called the Villa Vallee, was the hub of the nightclub life of the 1940s and 1950s. Glamorous crowds dined on fine cuisine, a rarity for the nightclub scene, and saw repeat performances by the up-and-coming and the celebrated, including Davis, Frank Sinatra, Harry Belafonte, Tony Bennett, Nat King Cole, and Desi Arnaz.

Sammy Davis, Jr., 1953.

© Bettmann/CORBIS

21 Club
21 West 52nd Street, between Fifth and Sixth Avenues
tel. (212) 582-7200, www.21club.com

According to 21 lore, Davis once arrived for dinner wearing a turtleneck sweater and jacket, but no tie, as required by the house dress code. Supplied with a tie by management, Davis tied it around his head.

Radio City Music Hall
1260 Sixth Avenue at West 50th Street
tel. (212) 307-7171, www.radiocity.com

Davis performed many of his greatest hits, including "The Candy Man" at Radio City Music Hall. Throughout the 1960s, he performed here with the Rat Pack.

Majestic Theatre
245 West 44th Street, between Broadway and Eighth Avenue

In 1964, Davis launched a fabulous Broadway run in *Golden Boy*: he gave 568 performances here between 1964 and 1966. The interior of the theater is a landmark space; it first opened to the public in 1927.

....

Museum of Television and Radio

25 West 52nd Street, between Fifth and Sixth Avenues
tel. (212) 621-6800, www.mtr.org

Davis's many television appearances, including his short-lived *The Sammy Davis, Jr. Show*, can be seen here.

....

Former residence

2632 Eighth Avenue at West 140th Street

As a child, Davis lived here with his grandmother in an apartment in the front of the building.

Dorothy Day

ACTIVIST 1897–1980

I n her twenties, Dorothy Day was a determined, passionate, but rudderless Greenwich Villager swept up in the radicalism of the neighborhood. She wrote provocative articles calling for social change, drank and caroused until late every night, and had a child out of wedlock. Despite the rowdiness of her youth, Day became a staunch Catholic activist, for which she is best known today. Though she was initially suspicious of organized religion and disenchanted with the social inaction of many seemingly pious people, she converted to Catholicism in 1928. She lived by and promoted a deeply religious daily life, one that was uncompromising in its renunciation of worldly goods. She was arrested many times while protesting social injustice. She and Peter Maurin, a French scholar, itinerant worker, and peace activist, launched *The Catholic Worker* in 1933 and in the same year opened the first "house of hospitality" for homeless and hungry New Yorkers. Day remained a committed pacifist through both world wars. She was arrested and imprisoned in New York City in the 1950s for refusing the order to find shelter during nuclear attack practice drills. Brooklyn-born Day is considered a saint by many, and the case for her canonization has been opened at the Vatican.

....

Site of *The Masses* offices

91 Greenwich Avenue, between Bank and West 12th Streets

This was the site of an innocuous-looking brick building deemed by the federal government to be the cradle of a treasonous conspiracy. *The Masses*, founded in 1911, advocated fair wages, safe working conditions, universal suffrage, and public education about birth control. Day joined friends Floyd Dell and Max Eastman in writing for and occasionally editing the publication. *The Masses* was shut down in 1917 by the federal government for its editorial opposition to involvement in World War I, which the editors argued was being championed by industrialists hungry for war profit. The August 1917 issue was banned by the US Post Office under the Espionage Act and its mailing permit revoked; the magazine was defunct by December. Dell and Eastman were charged with conspiracy against the government for "interfering with enlistment." After two hung juries and with the war winding down, the case was dropped.

Jefferson Market Library

425 Sixth Avenue at West 10th Street
tel. (212) 243-4334

Day is numbered among the famous women, including Ethel Rosenberg, Valerie Solanas, and Mae West, who were inmates here when it was the Women's House of Detention. The prison was severed from its adjoining courthouse and the space converted into the present-day garden. The former courthouse is now a branch of the New York Public Library.

Webster Hall

125 East 11th Street, between Third and Fourth Avenues
tel. (212) 353-1600, www.webster-hall.com

Webster Hall, now a nightclub and performance space, was built in 1886 and described as the "Jewel of the Village" by Eugene O'Neill. It was a hub of bohemian happenings where radical artists celebrated the political and artistic coups of Emma Goldman, Marcel Duchamp, and others, with rambunctious and eccentric balls, such as "The Blind Man's Ball" and "The Futurist Ball." The radical banquets, which Day often attended, morphed into hedonistic free-for-alls during the repressive Prohibition era.

St. Joseph's Church

371 Sixth Avenue, between Waverly and Washington Places

Day sometimes stopped in here for late-night reflection or morning Mass after long, wild nights out in the Village. The cornerstone of St. Joseph's was laid on June 10, 1833, qualifying it as the oldest Catholic edifice in Manhattan.

Former residence of Leon Trotsky

77 St. Mark's Place, between First and Second Avenues

While in New York, Leon Trotsky lived and worked in the basement of this building, editing his Russian-language newspaper, *Novy Mir*. Here, as a reporter for *The American Call* in 1917, Day interviewed him shortly before he left to join the Russian Revolution. Decades later, when W.H. Auden occupied this same building, Day became a frequent visitor to this address. Auden called Day "part of the atmosphere of [his] home."

The Catholic Worker

36 East 1st Street, between First and Second Avenues
tel. (212) 777-9617, www.catholicworker.org

Day and Peter Maurin founded the Catholic Worker movement in 1933, and the movement has since expanded its mission to include communities throughout the world, all committed to "nonviolence, voluntary poverty, prayer, and hospitality for the homeless, exiled, hungry, and forsaken." *The Catholic Worker* newspaper, as established by Day and Maurin in the 1930s, stands against racism, injustice, and violence of any kind, including war. Day edited *The Catholic Worker* from 1933 until her death in 1980. It still sells for a penny.

Maryhouse

55 East 3rd Street at Second Avenue
tel. (212) 777-9617, www.catholicworker.org

One of many houses of hospitality established by Day and *The Catholic Worker* throughout the city, Maryhouse provides food, shelter, comfort, and communion to homeless New Yorkers. It does not solicit donations. Day died at Maryhouse on November 29, 1980.

Dorothy Day, 1934.

Spanish Camp
Raritan Bay, Staten Island

In 1924, Dorothy Day bought, with money earned from her autobiographical novel, *The Eleventh Virgin*, a cottage at Spanish Camp—a collection of beach cottages built in the 1920s by the *Sociedad Natura Hispana*, a group of eco-minded Communists who had fled Spain. The cottages were arranged to facilitate communal life: residents shared mowed commons, parking areas, and paths between the cottages and the beach. Day spent much of her time here from the 1920s until her death in 1980. She credited the natural beauty of Staten Island and the serenity of her days in the cottage with inspiring her religious feeling. In 1999, descendants of the original owners sold the seventeen acres to a developer and Day's three small cottages were razed in 2001. Though both the Dorothy Day Historic Site and Spanish Camp Historic Site have been scheduled for discussion by the Landmarks Preservation Commission, million-dollar houses have been designated for the beachfront. Dorothy Day is buried near Tottenville, Staten Island, in Resurrection Cemetery.

John Dos Passos
WRITER 1896–1970

A s a political novelist, John Dos Passos was among the first to capture and characterize the class struggles shaping American society in the 1920s. Following the success of books such as *U.S.A.* and *Manhattan Transfer*, Dos Passos was tagged as a modern master ascendant with comparatively apolitical writers like Ernest Hemingway and F. Scott Fitzgerald. The restless Dos Passos lived abroad for years, rooting his intellect and his writing in leftist European politics. He settled back in New York during the calm of his first marriage and added the homegrown radicalism of his Greenwich Village peers to his social and literary work. Dos Passos, like many of his leftist contemporaries, became disenchanted with Communist ideology after the rise of Stalin. In the 1930s, he drifted away from leftist friends and by the 1960s he viewed most of the political upheaval in the United States with suspicion, speaking scornfully of the youth swept up in antiwar protests during the Vietnam War.

Former residence

3 Washington Square North, between University Place and Fifth Avenue

In 1922, Dos Passos rented a cramped, dimly lit room behind this house, where he worked out the vast complex of *Manhattan Transfer*'s plots and subplots. Before E.E. Cummings's marriage to Elaine (then Thayer), Dos Passos had been a regular guest at the fireplace teas given by the Elaine and Scofield Thayer, also at 3 Washington Square North.

Former residence

11 Bank Street, between Waverly Place and Greenwich Avenue

Dos Passos lived here between 1924 and 1925, while working on *Manhattan Transfer*, his ambitious account of the social, technological, and political turmoil of New York in the 1920s.

Former residence

Washington Mews
From Fifth Avenue to University Place, between Washington Square North and East 8th Street

John Dos Passos, ca. 1940s.

© Bettmann/CORBIS

Dos Passos lived along this private cobblestone alley, lined on its north side by converted stables where the wealthy Washington Square crowd kept their carriages and on the south side by 1939 stucco houses. Other notable former residents include Edward Hopper and Sherwood Anderson.

....

John's
302 East 12th Street, between First and Second Avenues
tel. (212) 475-9531

Dos Passos lunched at this venerable café with Carlo Tresca, the Italian anarchist and editor of the radical newspaper *Il Martello* (The Hammer), on January 11, 1943—the day of Tresca's murder. Tresca had a multitude of enemies—Mussolini, local fascists, organized crime, and the federal government numbered among them. Dos Passos remembered that Tresca ate heartily as they talked for hours about the fall of Mussolini and the scourge of Stalin. Walking home from the offices of *Il Martello,* Tresca was gunned down on the northwest corner of Fifth Avenue and 15th Street by a contract killer, and was later pronounced dead at St. Vincent's Hospital.

....

Site of Café Royale
Southeast corner of 12th Street at Second Avenue

Café Royale closed in the 1950s after thirty years as the "Yiddish Sardi's." It was popular among agents, actors, and writers in the Yiddish theater, and the lively atmosphere was a great draw for Dos Passos and E.E. Cummings, who became regulars.

....

Former residence
110 Columbia Heights, between Orange and Pineapple Streets
Brooklyn Heights, Brooklyn

Dos Passos lived here in 1929. It is the same building from which Brooklyn Bridge engineer Washington Roebling, crippled by the bends, watched the progress of his great work.

Marcel Duchamp
ARTIST 1887–1968

M arcel Duchamp introduced American audiences to Dadaist and other avant-garde art as a painter, curator, and designer of books, catalogues, and art installations. The public first set eyes on Duchamp's *Nude Descending a Staircase, No. 2* at the Armory Show in 1913—the painting immediately became a handy symbol of the Armory Show and modernism as a movement. The painting brought Duchamp national attention and proved an easy target of caricature, derision, and genuine anxiety in the newspapers. Theodore Roosevelt compared the modernists to a "bunch of lunatics." In the eyes of traditionalists, Duchamp further debased the art world by exhibiting unaltered, mass-produced objects such as bicycle tires and urinals, which he dubbed "readymades." He enlisted his friend Man Ray in many of his institution-bucking schemes—Man Ray sold photographic portraits of Duchamp to bankroll Duchamp's trip to Monte Carlo, where he tested a system for beating the roulette wheel; in 1921, Man Ray photographed Duchamp looking sultry as Rose Selavy (a "ready-maid"), his female alter ego. Selavy wrote lascivious verse and was named, by Duchamp, as the

copyright holder for much of his work, which further aggravated art dealers. Duchamp became an American citizen in 1955 but is buried in Rouen, France beneath a tomb-stone of his design that reads: *"D'ailleurs c'est toujours les autres qui meurent"* ("But it's always other people who die").

Washington Square Arch

Washington Square North at Fifth Avenue

Duchamp joined the small, rebellious band of artists, including John Sloan and Gertrude Drick, who stormed the roof of the arch under cover of night and declared the "Free and Independent Republic of Greenwich Village" in 1917. They decked the arch with Chinese lanterns and balloons and read their declaration of independence, composed of the repeated phrase "whereas." They fired cap guns into the dark air, toasted their victory by candlelight, and descended after their revolutionary night picnic.

Site of 69th Regiment Armory

68 Lexington Avenue, between East 25th and East 26th Streets

On February 17, 1913, the International Exhibition of Modern Art, remembered as The Armory Show, opened to the public here. More than a thousand pieces by the European and American avant-garde were on display. Duchamp's cubist study of form and movement, *Nude Descending a Staircase, No. 2*, was the object of the most intense criticism and praise. The piece made him an instant celebrity. The painting had earlier been rejected by the *Salon des Independents* shows in Barcelona and Paris.

Webster Hall

125 East 11th Street, between Third and Fourth Avenues
tel. (212) 353-1600, www.webster-hall.com

Duchamp was a guest of honor at the "Blind Man's Ball" in the early summer of 1917.

That year, Duchamp had cofounded the Society of Independent Artists and become its director. Yet this ultra avant-garde institution quickly rejected Duchamp's *Fountain* (an unaltered urinal) on the grounds that it was not art, and Duchamp just as quickly resigned in protest. At the "Blind Man's Ball," guests in eccentric attire filled Webster Hall in support of Duchamp and his *Fountain*. With Man Ray and the artist/art collector Katherine Dreier, Duchamp formed the more radical Société Anonyme, Inc. in 1920.

Villard Houses, now the New York Palace Hotel

451-455 Madison Avenue, between East 50th and East 51st Streets
tel. (212) 888-7000, www.newyorkpalace.com

Duchamp and André Breton exhibited the "First Papers of Surrealism" here between October 14 and November 7, 1942. The group show, an effort to raise funds for the French Relief, included work by Man Ray and Duchamp, who designed the catalogue cover: a photograph of five embedded bullets, which Duchamp had shot into the stone foundation of a friend's upstate country house. Duchamp installed the artwork and then wound the gallery in sixteen miles of string that required viewers to navigate the visual web in order to obtain an unobstructed view of the work.

Former studio

210 West 14th Street, between Seventh and Eighth Avenues

Duchamp's studio was on the fourth floor of this building in 1943. He reportedly communicated with his friends by telegram, as he was too poor to install a telephone. By 1943, Duchamp publicly claimed that he had retired from making art, but he was quietly constructing *Given: 1 The Waterfall, 2 The Illuminating Gas* in this studio. The exterior of the piece is an ordinary, weathered wood-plank door with dual peepholes. When viewers step onto the welcome mat and peer in through the peepholes, engines and lights activate the interior: a faceless woman lies on a nest of twigs, a glowing lamp in her hand; a lit waterfall seems to crash into the distant landscape. Duchamp wrote a detailed "Manual of Instructions" for breaking down and rebuilding the piece. The piece was not exhibited publicly until after Duchamp's death.

Marshall Chess Club

23 West 10th Street, between Fifth and Sixth Avenues
tel. (212) 477-3716, www.marshallchessclub.org

A brilliant strategist and master chess player, Duchamp was elected to the French Olympic Chess Team in 1928. In 1932, he was appointed French delegate to the International Chess Federation. He published a work of chess strategy (with Vitaly Halberstadt), "Opposition and Sister Squares are Reconciled." Duchamp lived a block away from this chess institution, which was founded in 1915 by US chess champion Frank Marshall. Duchamp was one of its most successful players, winning a perfect sweep of the New York State Chess Association Tournament of 1949.

Woolworth Building

233 Broadway, between Barclay Street and Park Place

Duchamp's readymades elevated to the status of art the everyday objects (bicycle tires, bottle racks) mass produced and taken for granted by most people. In the third and final installment of Duchamp's notes, *The White Box*, published in the 1960s, is a photograph of the Woolworth Building with a note in his hand scribbled along its height. The inscription reads "for Woolworth Bldg as readymade."

Solomon R. Guggenheim Museum

1071 Fifth Avenue at East 89th Street
tel. (212) 423-3500, www.guggenheim.org

In 1957, Duchamp and his brothers, Jacques Villon and Raymond Duchamp-Villon, were exhibited together in "Three Brothers." The show had been Duchamp's idea; he selected many of the images and he designed the catalogue. Duchamp's works in the permanent collection include: *Apropos of Little Sister* (October 1911); *Nude (Study), Sad Young Man on a Train* (1911–12); and *Study for Chess Players* (late 1911).

Museum of Modern Art (MoMA)

11 West 53rd Street, between Fifth and Sixth Avenues
tel. (212) 708-9400, www.moma.org

One of Duchamp's readymades, *Bicycle Wheel*, an overturned wheel mounted on a stool, is part of MoMA's collection. Duchamp made it in 1951 to replace two earlier versions, the first from 1913, which he had lost. A 1968 exhibition entitled "Dada, Surrealism, and their Heritage," featured twelve pieces by Duchamp. Other highlights of the collection include *Why Not Sneeze Rose Sélavy?* (1964; replica of 1921 original).

Thomas Alva Edison

INVENTOR 1847–1931

E dison is credited with more than 1,093 inventions, and he still holds the record for most patents held by an individual. Though conservative in his private life, Edison was a fearless and flamboyant experimenter who used nuts from the rain forest for phonograph needles and Japanese bamboo for the filament of his incandescent light. Edison was a fantastic and talented promoter of his innovations, and he attracted New Yorkers to his feverish ideas about the high-tech future of the city. He lit the Brooklyn Bridge, Coney Island, and the homes of captains of industry with his incandescent lights; he marketed the first talking doll; he created the first recordings on phonograph, the first electric chair, and some of the first motion pictures. Limited by little formal education, Edison filled his laboratories with brilliant engineers, mathematicians, and designers. On the evening of his burial, power plants across the country shut down generators and dimmed lights, but only for an instant, before racing ahead into the future Edison had envisioned.

Site of J.P. Morgan & Co. building

23 Wall Street at Broad Street

On September 4, 1882, in the J.P. Morgan & Co. building formerly at this site, Edison ceremonially flipped the light switch. Shops and offices along Fulton and Nassau Streets came to life as the electricity spread down the lines for the first time from Pearl Power Plant at what was then 255-257 Pearl Street. *The New York Times* reporters noted approvingly that Edison's electric lights gave off a "soft, mellow" glow.

Throughout his career, Edison endeared himself to the wealthy and influential in New York, seeking capital and access to the centers of power. This intersection, the nexus of financial power in the nation, was also a target for anarchist terrorists in 1920. A suicide bomber, Mario Buda, detonated a wagonload full of dynamite near the current building to protest the arrest of Sacco and Vanzetti. Thirty-nine were killed and four hundred injured in the blast; the lower part of the building still bears the scars of the explosion.

Pierpont Morgan Library
33 East 36th Street, between Madison and Park Avenues
Closed for expansion and renovation until early 2006.
tel. (212) 615-0610, www.morganlibrary.org

In the nineteenth century, New York went from dark, moonlit, and gaslit to brightly lit by electricity. In 1882, J.P. Morgan's mansion on Madison Avenue was the first private home to be completely fitted with incandescent lights. Despite a plague of small fires and complaints from neighbors over the noise of the generator in his garden, Morgan stuck to the new light, and the rest of the exclusive block was soon similarly ablaze. Morgan's home is now the Pierpont Morgan Library, designed by McKim, Mead & White in 1906.

Site of first traffic light in Manhattan
Fifth Avenue at 42nd Street

In 1919, New York City set up the first traffic light in a tower at Fifth Avenue and 42nd Street. It was a rudimentary signal modeled after railroad switching signals.

Nikola Tesla Corner
West 40th Street at Sixth Avenue

Thomas Alva Edison, ca. 1920.

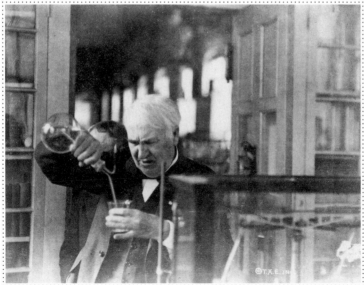

This corner and street sign honors Nikola Tesla, Edison's brilliant one-time employee and later rival who invented alternating current, the mode of electric transmission still in use. When Tesla found a financial backer in George Westinghouse, alternating current suddenly posed a market menace to Edison and his patented direct current technology. Edison had built his generators, which he named "dynamos" and "jumbos," for use with direct current, and his fierce, impractical refusal to switch to alternating current, the safer and more efficient method, soon led him into dark territory. Edison had been staunchly opposed to the death penalty, until he realized it could be used to his competitive advantage. He pushed and politicked for the electric chair—he argued that electricity, specifically Tesla's alternating current, offered a reliable means for executing condemned men. Edison hoped to provide an unforgettable commercial association between alternating current and death; in trying to coin a name for the new form of execution, Edison suggested "to Westinghouse" a criminal. In the end, he and his backers settled on "electrocution."

....

Site of Luna Park

From Surf Avenue to the Boardwalk and from West 8th Street to West 16th Street
Coney Island, Brooklyn
www.coneyisland.com

Edison, who had been allowing the execution of luckless dogs and other small animals in his Menlo Park, New Jersey, laboratories in order to test the effects of electricity on these creatures, found an excellent opportunity to test the real power of electricity when Topsy, an aging elephant at Coney Island, attacked two drunk stable hands after they fed her a lit cigarette. She had crushed the head of one of the men under her foot and was condemned to death. When New York City handed down a decision that deemed hanging inhumane for the elephant, Edison stepped forward cheerfully with a solution: Topsy could be electrocuted. Topsy was put to death on January 4, 1903 at Coney Island. Edison also used the occasion of the execution to make a silent film. The film can be viewed at the Brooklyn Museum of Art [200 Eastern Parkway, Brooklyn, tel. (718) 638-5000, www.brooklynmuseum.org], and a Topsy memorial is planned in the Coney Island Museum [open but undergoing renovations; 1208 Surf Avenue at West 12th Street, tel. (718) 372-5159, www.coneyisland.com/museum.shtml].

Duke Ellington

MUSICIAN AND COMPOSER 1899–1974

Duke Ellington, considered by many to be America's greatest composer, was charismatic and confident of his talents from early childhood. In 1923, he moved to New York as the pianist in Elmer Snowden's Washingtonians. When Snowden left after a dispute over money, the remaining band members elected Ellington to lead them. Within seven years, the Duke Ellington Orchestra included a dozen musicians whose compositions were heard on national radio and in Hollywood films. Ellington's regular broadcasts "From the Cotton Club" made him the most pursued recording artist in the country. Ellington played for all crowds and atmospheres from the nightclub to the cathedral. He introduced "swing" into the general lexicon. He played for queens and presidents, and performed with fellow jazz royalty including Ella Fitzgerald, Louis

Armstrong, and Miles Davis. He received the US Presidential Medal of Freedom and the Legion of Honor from the French government, both representing the highest possible decoration for a citizen.

Duke Ellington, 1962.

Library of Congress Prints and Photographs Division

Duke Ellington Memorial

East 110th Street at Fifth Avenue

Across the street from the northeast corner of Central Park is Frawley Circle, an elevated performance area ringed by steps and trees. At a height of twenty-five feet, a larger-than-life Ellington stands among the trees and looks straight down Tito Puente Way. His statue shares the platform with a grand piano, all held aloft by ten-foot columns. It is the first monument in New York City dedicated to an African-American, and the first Ellington memorial in the United States. It was unveiled in July of 1997.

Duke Ellington Boulevard

106th Street from Riverside Drive to Central Park West

West 106th Street has been renamed Duke Ellington Boulevard in honor of the composer's nearby home, River Mansion, at 337 Riverside Drive.

Showman's

375 West 125th Street, between Morningside and Manhattan Avenues
tel. (212) 864-8941

Showman's opened in 1942 and became the "living room" of Apollo entertainers like Duke Ellington and Sarah Vaughan, who hung out and performed here after their shows at the Apollo. The present location (since 1998) is a long, narrow room that runs the length of the bar and ends in an elevated stage. There are photographs of jazz greats over the bar and a Hammond B-3 organ on stage. A congenial and historic atmosphere prevails.

Sugar Hill Historic District
From Edgecombe Avenue to Convent Avenue and from West 145th to West 149th Streets

Ellington sang "You must take the A train, to go to Sugar Hill way up in Harlem." Emblematic of African-American achievement and affluence, life on Sugar Hill was sweet and refined. Between the 1920s and the 1950s, Sugar Hill was home to Duke Ellington, Langston Hughes, Ralph Ellison, W.E.B. DuBois, Aaron Douglas, Thurgood Marshall, and Walter White.

Former residence
935 St. Nicholas Avenue at West 157th Street

Ellington lived on the fourth floor of this building from 1939 until 1961.

Cotton Club
656 West 125th Street, between Riverside Drive and Broadway
tel. (212) 663-7980

The Cotton Club was opened in 1920 by a former heavyweight boxing champion as the Club Deluxe at 644 Lenox Avenue, between West 142nd and West 143rd Streets. The second owner, Owney Madden, rumored to be linked to organized crime, changed the name to the Cotton Club, where whites-only audiences watched black performers in a jungle- and plantation-theme setting. Many New York nightclubs catering to white audiences romanticized the antebellum South with names like the Plantation Club and Club Kentucky. In 1927, Duke Ellington's Orchestra became the resident band, the most celebrated in the club's history. Madden moved the club in 1935 to Midtown after race riots in Harlem kept fearful white audiences away. The current Cotton Club, now back in Harlem, has no connection to the original, but promotes and preserves the musical and black cultural legacy of the Cotton Club's heyday.

Hotel Pennsylvania
401 Seventh Avenue at 33rd Street
tel. (212) 736-5000

The Café Rouge Ballroom in the Hotel Pennsylvania was an integrated performance space during the big-band era. Ellington performed here with his orchestra. Best known from Glen Miller's song "Pennsylvania 6-5000," the hotel has had the same phone number since 1919.

Carnegie Hall
156 West 57th Street at Seventh Avenue
tel. (212) 903-9765, www.carnegiehall.org

Ellington launched his annual concerts at Carnegie Hall in January 1943 with "Black, Brown, and Beige," which he intended as a "tonal parallel to the history of the American Negro." The experimental and ambitious forty-five-minute composition was panned by critics who argued that Ellington had pushed jazz beyond its natural scope. Though Ellington performed sections from the piece throughout his career, he never again presented the epic in its entirety.

Woodlawn Cemetery

Entrances: East 233rd Street at Webster Avenue; Jerome Avenue north of Bainbridge Avenue
Woodlawn, The Bronx
tel. (718) 920-0500

Ellington is buried here, across the lane from Miles Davis. He lies beneath a sheltering hood of linden tree branches, and between two large crosses etched with "The Lord is My Shepherd." Woodlawn Cemetery is a beautiful place for a walk—its (former) remoteness from the city, its winding lanes, and carefully landscaped vistas are all products of the rural cemetery movement of the mid-nineteenth century.

F. Scott Fitzgerald

WRITER 1896–1940

"It was three years before we saw New York again. As the ship glided up the river, the city burst thunderously upon us in the early dusk. A band started to play on deck, but the majesty of the city made the march trivial and tinkling. From that moment I knew that New York, however often I might leave it, was home."

I n works that ranged from literary masterpieces to fluff pieces for popular magazines, F. Scott Fitzgerald memorialized the excess and rebellion of the Lost Generation. He chronicled its alcoholic exuberance and its deep isolation; he popularized "flappers," the "Jazz Age," and the allure of the "modern girl." Obsessed with winning the hand of Zelda Sayre, Fitzgerald finished his first novel, *This Side of Paradise*, in New York and thus secured Zelda's consent. Their troubled life together provided the source material for much of his writing. Their money-burning marriage, his alcoholism, and the devastation of Zelda's mental illness drove Fitzgerald and his fortunes into the abyss just as the country plummeted into the Great Depression. Fitzgerald's finest work, *The Great Gatsby*, pulled back the veil of youthful, rich, urban confidence, revealing desolation postponed only briefly by the excitement of a party. Throughout his life, Fitzgerald identified fatalistically with Edgar Allan Poe and monitored the portentous track that his life was on: great talent and literary longing thwarted by poverty, drink, and runaway bad luck.

. . . .

Former residence

200 Claremont Avenue at Tiemann Place

Following a lackluster showing in the US Army, in 1918 Fitzgerald headed to New York to see his friend from Princeton, the literary critic Edmund Wilson. He surveyed Wilson's cultivated Greenwich Village life, and decided he must have it too. He ended up writing slogans for an advertising agency while living far uptown on Claremont Avenue, just south of 125th Street. He finished a draft of *This Side of Paradise* at this address and is said to have pasted 122 rejection slips from publishers on the walls of his apartment. Believing his first attempt at the New York life had been a disaster, he drank himself into one last big city stupor and left town.

Fitzgerald's putative alter ego in *This Side of Paradise* is Amory Blaine, who launches a three-week drinking binge after losing love and quitting his job in advertising. After deciding to leave New York for good, he takes the bus to West 127th Street (two blocks north of Claremont Avenue) and crosses into Riverside Park. He "followed a winding,

descending sidewalk and came out facing the river," where he notices the "barely distinguishable flat odor of the Hudson."

When Fitzgerald returned to New York in September 1919, *This Side of Paradise* had been accepted for publication and was released the following year. The novel's popularity shaped the age it described and brought Fitzgerald money and fame. The hedonism of his characters underwrote Fitzgerald's own, and he poured most of his money into clothes and cars for himself and Zelda.

St. Patrick's Cathedral

Fifth Avenue at 51st Street
tel. (212) 753-2261

Fitzgerald married Zelda Sayre here. By his own account, he had reached the pinnacle of happiness—he was rich, young, published, famous, and now marrying elusive, brilliant Zelda. Few friends and no parents attended the wedding. In contrast to Zelda's ultimately glamorous reputation, Scott's New York friends were dismayed when she arrived in town sporting the dreaded "look of the provinces." They re-dressed her fashionably in time for the ceremony.

. . . .

FITZGERALD AT LARGE

Pre-Prohibition hipsters met at the Biltmore Bar under the clock. ("Meet me at the clock" was a favorite phrase of Fitzgerald's crowd.) The hotel has been destroyed but the clock remains, absorbed into the lobby of an office building at 43 East 43rd Street.

In *This Side of Paradise,* heart-broken Amory Blaine reels from hotel bar to hotel bar, fueled by highballs and Bronx Cocktails. At the Knickerbocker Bar, Blaine is "beamed upon by Maxfield Parrish's jovial, colorful 'Old King Cole.'" (The painting is now in the historic St. Regis Hotel at 2 East 55th Street.) After a slight lull in the drinking, Blaine moves on to the Biltmore Hotel (formerly at Madison and 43rd Street): "At noon he ran into a crowd in the Biltmore Bar, and the riot began again."

Fitzgerald sometimes capped off a marathon night of club hopping with breakfast at Child's Restaurant, a popular chain. Fitzgerald did not always retire to Child's with the dawn—he once herded a few remaining revelers on to a final stop to see bodies at the morgue.

. . . .

Plaza Hotel

768 Fifth Avenue at Central Park South
tel. (212) 759-3000, www.fairmont.com

The Fitzgeralds stayed here off and on, as they boomeranged through hotels, many of which forced them to leave after disreputable episodes. After one such eviction, Fitzgerald reputedly evaded capture by spinning through the revolving doors for several minutes while helpless hotel employees and guests watched. The Fitzgeralds were well known in New York for being wild, and they were proud of their degenerate fame. They loved disturbing the peace, diving into public fountains (including the Pulitzer Fountain that fronts the Plaza), having long, loud arguments that trailed all over the city (as one chased the other). Zelda is said to have dared Scott to start fistfights with bouncers, dares that Scott accepted in his strenuous, ongoing effort to cast off social constraints. Rebellion came more naturally to Zelda who, on one occasion, hired a taxi so that she could ride around New York on the hood.

Library of Congress Prints and Photographs Division

Kahlil Gibran

POET 1883–1931

K ahlil Gibran revolutionized American and Arabic literature as a poet, teacher, and member of Arribitah (the Pen Bond), a 1920s group of Arab-American intellectuals and writers living in New York. With his mother and siblings, he left his village in the mountains of Lebanon and immigrated to the United States in 1895. By 1912, he had settled in New York and gained a reputation as a gifted artist who wrote compellingly of the need for reconciliation among all faiths and nations. As a poet-prophet, Gibran warned of the turmoil that would engulf the world if opposing forces were not reconciled. He became a passionate advocate of forming a Christian-Muslim alliance to defeat Ottoman oppression in Lebanon. From his studio in the West Village, Gibran preached sensible living, mastery over one's life, and the merging of opposite charges—male and female, East and West. Long after his death, his poetry in works such as The Prophet remained a deep influence on the popular spiritualism of the 1960s and 1980s. Gibran was also an accomplished painter who talked at length about spirituality and psychology with Carl Jung and W.B. Yeats as they sat for their portraits.

Site of Studio Building
51-55 West 10th Street at Sixth Avenue

Gibran kept his studio here between 1911 and 1931. Built in 1858, it was the country's first engineered studio space for artists, designed around the provision of light and exhibition space. Visitors to Gibran's studios recalled the tapestries, hanging lamps, carpets, religious icons, candles, church table, and incense smoke. In 1920, Gibran moved to a bigger studio in the building, where Arrabitah met in 1920 and drew up its bylaws and designed its seal. With Arrabitah, Gibran was a steady voice against oppression from without and censorship from within the Arab world. By 1924, Gibran was a Greenwich

Village celebrity with a highly cultivated, at times theatrically mysterious, public life. The building was razed in 1956.

. . . .

Atlantic Avenue
From the Promenade to Flatbush Avenue
Brooklyn

Gibran and other members of the Pen Bond met in cafes and restaurants along Atlantic Avenue, already known as "Little Arabia" and "Little Syria" by the time of Gibran's immigration in 1895. The track for Atlantic Avenue, known as the "Main Street of Arab America," was laid in the 1700s as a private road. By 1855, the private farm road had been subsumed by the incorporated Village of Brooklyn and renamed Atlantic Street. Elevated to Atlantic Avenue in the 1870s, it was, for decades, a fashionable shopping district. By the turn of the last century, the arrival of thousands of immigrants from the Middle East, predominantly Christians emigrating from the Ottoman Empire, supported the opening of numerous restaurants and specialty food shops. Immigration was cut off in the 1920s, as stringent new immigration laws appeared, but it resurged in the 1960s, as a second wave of immigrants, predominantly Muslim, began arriving in the United States. Many settled along Atlantic Avenue in Brooklyn, adding a proliferation of mosques to the neighborhood.

Althea Gibson

ATHLETE 1927–2003

O n her twenty-third birthday, Althea Gibson made history as the first African-American to compete in the national tennis championship, the future US Open. Gibson had grown up in Harlem, playing paddle tennis in parks and community centers, where youth activist and former bandleader Buddy Walker recognized her talent and placed her under the tutelage of a tennis coach at the Cosmopolitan Tennis Club. Throughout her career, Gibson was mentored by African-American community leaders, including Sugar Ray Robinson; Dr. Hubert Eaton, who took her into his family in North Carolina (Gibson had been living at a Catholic girls' school and in low-income housing); and Walter "Whirlwind" Johnson, who inducted her into the summer tennis circuit. In her second bid for the national championship in 1957, Gibson won Wimbledon and the US Tennis Championships. She won both titles again in 1958. The City of New York hosted a ticker-tape parade in her honor, but the absence of professional endorsements forced Gibson to retire from the game in order to make a living. She taught tennis, wrote her autobiography, took small parts in films, and played exhibition matches on the Harlem Globetrotters tour in 1959. In the 1960s, she became the first African-American woman to play on the Ladies Professional Golf Tour.

. . . .

United States Tennis Association (USTA) National Tennis Center
Flushing Meadows-Corona Park
Flushing, Queens
www.usta.com

In 1950, Gibson became the first African-American player to compete in the championships here—the future home of the US Open. When the USTA National Tennis Center

Althea Gibson, 1950.

© Bettmann/CORBIS

is not hosting the US Open, its courts are open (for a fee) to members of the public who want to ace friends in the footsteps of tennis legends.

Mount Morris Park (now Marcus Garvey Memorial Park)
From Mount Morris Park West to Madison Avenue and from 120th to 124th Streets

Gibson practiced and played tennis around Harlem, at the Harlem River Tennis Courts; at Mount Morris Park; and off the brick walls at Public School #136. As a teenager, she won tournaments organized by the Police Athletic League in New York, before moving to North Carolina to attend high school.

The Harlem Tennis Center
369th Regiment Armory
2366 Fifth Avenue, between West 142nd and West 143rd Streets
tel. (212) 283-4028, www.htc.8m.com

For fifty years, the Harlem Tennis Center has been an important sporting facility in Harlem. Eight courts fill the former drill shed floor of the armory. In the late 1950s, Gibson practiced on the indoor courts during the winter months, and she returned to Harlem as a tennis champion and taught children in the community tennis league here.

Allen Ginsberg

POET 1926–1997

A llen Ginsberg entered Columbia University in 1943 with dreams of becoming a labor lawyer. At Columbia, Ginsberg formed fateful friendships with William S. Burroughs, Neal Cassady, and Jack Kerouac, the future vanguard of the Beat poetry movement. Ginsberg was suspended from Columbia for insults (written in the accumulated dust of his dorm room) directed at the housekeeper and the president of the university. He spent the following year at sea as a Merchant Marine before returning to Columbia to finish his studies. After graduation, Ginsberg migrated to San Francisco, where he was an energetic creator of a new kind of poetry—insistent and unorthodox, fueled by apparent spontaneity, contemporary reference, and independent authority. In 1956, Ginsberg published "Howl" ("I saw the best minds of my generation destroyed by madness"); the poem was banned and landed Ginsberg in court on obscenity charges the following year. Ginsberg and "Howl" emerged victorious. As an antiwar and civil rights activist during the 1960s and as a student and teacher of Buddhism, Ginsberg traveled extensively. His poetic meditation on his American travels, *Fall of America*, won him the National Book Award in 1973.

Allen Ginsberg, ca. 1953.

© Allen Ginsberg/CORBIS

The West End

2911 Broadway, between West 113th and West 114th Streets
tel. (212) 662-8830

Ginsberg, William S. Burroughs, Joan Vollman, Jack Kerouac, and other members of the future Beat generation often drank here in the 1940s when Ginsberg was a student at Columbia. The West End is a Columbia watering hole in constant use by waves of new students, so the atmosphere is current rather than nostalgic, though the well-worn wooden bar and grafitti-etched booths attest to its long use.

Miller Theater at Columbia University

2960 Broadway at West 116th Street
tel. (212) 854-7799, www.millertheater .com

Before its overhaul in 1988, this space was called McMillan Theater, where Ginsberg read parts of "Kaddish" for the first time in 1959. "Kaddish," considered by many to be Ginsberg's masterpiece, is a lament for his mother's death and life, which was plagued by severe mental illness. Ginsberg remained his mother's closest ally during years of delusion, paranoia, extended hospitalizations, and violent outbursts. In 1948, Ginsberg and his brother consented to the suggestion of doctors that Naomi Ginsberg undergo a frontal lobotomy, severing her brain's access to emotional experience.

Café Figaro

184 Bleecker Street at MacDougal Street
tel. (212) 677 1100

Café Figaro provided a regular meeting place for Ginsberg and his fellow Beat poets. After a few intervening years as a less illustrious eating establishment, Café Figaro has reopened as a café and bar under its old moniker.

St. Mark's Bookshop

31 Third Avenue at East 9th Street
tel. (212) 260-7853, www.stmarksbookshop.com

Ginsberg spent many hours among the stacks of this independent bookshop, founded in 1977. After ten years at 13 St. Mark's Place, the bookshop moved to its current, more spacious location, a former German shooting club.

St. Mark's in the Bowery Church

131 East 10th Street at Second Avenue
tel. (212) 674-0910, www.poetryproject.com

Ginsberg was active in the Poetry Project from its beginning in 1966. The Poetry Project continues to offer readings, writing workshops, and special events that promote poetry and poets. A dogwood tree, planted in 1999 in memory of Ginsberg, grows in the churchyard.

Former residence

206 East 7th Street, between Avenues B and C

Ginsberg lived here with Gregory Corso and William S. Burroughs in 1952 and 1953, when Burroughs began work on *Naked Lunch*, which Ginsberg edited. The photograph on page 81 was taken on the rooftop of this apartment building.

Former residence

170 East 2nd Street, between Avenues A and B

Ginsberg lived here with his partner, the artist Peter Orlovsky, from 1958 to 1961. Here, Ginsberg completed much of "Kaddish."

Jackie Gleason

ENTERTAINER 1916–1987

T he gregarious and rotund Jackie Gleason perfected the character of bedeviled Brooklynite, Ralph Kramden of *The Honeymooners*, who reflected his own troubled upbringing in Brooklyn. In the years leading up to his television celebrity, Gleason hustled for any entertainment industry work he could find: he was an itinerant emcee for carnivals, a boxer, a disc jockey, a professional daredevil, and a star diver in the water follies. His acting success was just as varied: he won a Tony Award for *Take Me Along* in 1959, and was nominated for an Academy Award for his performance in *The Hustler* in 1963. He composed music, including the theme for *The Honeymooners*. He had an acerbic onstage style, and he could silence hecklers with a word. Having pioneered a new kind of serial television, Gleason retired *The Honeymooners* after thirty-nine episodes, refusing to cheapen or stretch thin material so dear to his heart. *The Jackie Gleason Show*, on the other hand, was a busy extravaganza of high-kicking chorus girls, kaleidoscope shots, and Glea Girls who lit his cigarettes and accompanied him around stage. Borrowing his own closing line of each evening's show, Gleason had engraved the steps to his grave: "And Away We Go."

The Park Central

870 Seventh Avenue, between West 54th and West 55th Streets
tel. (212) 247-8000, www.parkcentralny.com

Gleason called this Midtown hotel home during the taping of *The Honeymooners* in 1955 and 1956. He filmed scenes for some of the episodes inside the hotel.

Jackie Gleason, undated.

Museum of Television and Radio

25 West 52nd Street, between Fifth and Sixth Avenues
tel. (212) 621-6800, www.mtr.org

All thirty-nine episodes of *The Honeymooners* can be viewed here.
....

Statue of Jackie Gleason

Port Authority Bus Terminal
West 40th Street at Eighth Avenue

In honor of television's most heroic bus driver, a larger-than-life statue of Jackie Gleason as Ralph Kramden has been placed at the entrance to the Port Authority Bus Terminal.
....

Former residence

358 Chauncey Street, between Howard and Saratoga Avenues
Bushwick, Brooklyn

In *The Honeymooners*, Ralph Kramden lives at 358 Chauncey Street in the Bensonhurst section of Brooklyn. Gleason designed the painted-cardboard set to resemble his family's home at this address in the neighborhood of Bushwick in Brooklyn.
....

Brooklyn Botanic Garden

Entrances: Washington Avenue at Eastern Parkway; Empire Boulevard at Washington Avenue
Institute Park, Brooklyn
tel. (718) 623-7200, www.bbg.org

The Celebrity Path in Brooklyn Botanic Garden, edged by rhododendrons and daffodils, is laid with stones commemorating Brooklynites, including Gleason, who went on to artistic, literary, and athletic achievement.
....

Ye Waverly Inn

16 Bank Street, between Waverly Place and West 4th Street
tel. (212) 929-4377

Tucked into the basement of an 1845 farmhouse, Ye Waverly Inn is a cozy bar with a working fireplace. Gleason is rumored to have been a frequent occupant of the bar stools here.

Emma Goldman

POLITICAL ACTIVIST 1869–1940

E mma Goldman was among the thousands of Jewish immigrants who entered the US from Eastern Europe in the 1880s. Sixteen-year-old Goldman wept at the ship's rail when she first set eyes on the Statue of Liberty, but she was soon horrified to find working conditions worse in New York than in the Russia she had left behind. She would spend the rest of her life fighting for radical causes. Throughout her years of activism in New York, American authorities tried desperately to drive her out of the country, especially after her partner Alexander Berkman attempted to assassinate Henry Clay Frick. The New York press depicted her as a monstrous den mother to young, bearded, "swarthy, half-clad and grimy Anarchists," but many of the fundamentals of her radicalism are now accepted tenets of federal law. She advocated an eight-hour workday, education for women about contraception, as well as access to birth control. She supported efforts to organize labor unions, and demanded equal protection under the law. In 1905, she opened a successful massage parlor, where she acted as counselor and comforter to women from all walks of life. She was arrested twice for breaking the Comstock Law, which prohibited printed discussion of birth control. Goldman's anti-draft speeches, rallies, and protests at the outset of World War I provided the federal government with the pretext it had long sought, and Goldman was imprisoned until a twenty-four-year-old J. Edgar Hoover arranged for her exile. As she wandered Europe and Canada she remained active in radical causes, but longed to return to her home in New York. Franklin D. Roosevelt permitted Goldman to visit the United States for ninety days on strict terms, but she was not allowed to remain. Only death brought Goldman brought back to the US. She is buried beside the Haymarket Martyrs in Chicago, as was her wish.

Former Offices of *Mother Earth*
210 East 13th Street, between Second and Third Avenues

The plot now occupied by 208 East 13th Street (the addresses were shifted when the block was redeveloped) is the site where Goldman lived while writing, editing, and publishing the influential radical journal *Mother Earth* (1903–1913). The journal was the first to publish the work of Strindberg and Ibsen in America. During the anarchist-uprooting Palmer Raids, the offices of *Mother Earth* were ransacked and left a wreck of overturned office chairs and rifled-through papers. The building was gutted by fire in the 1970s, though a plaque marks the exterior.

Elmer Holmes Bobst Library
70 Washington Square South, between West Broadway and Washington Square East
tel. (212) 998-2500, www.library.nyu.edu

The Tamiment Library and Robert F. Wagner Archives are on the tenth floor of this

Emma Goldman, 1934.

Library of Congress Prints and Photographs Division

NYU library (Elmer Holmes Bobst Library) and are open to the public. You can see old copies of Goldman's journal *Mother Earth*, and peruse a rich collection of radical literature from the period.

··

Christopher Street / Sheridan Square subway station
Christopher Street at Seventh Avenue South

Goldman in glasses and glazed in red, white, and black tile, dominates one mural of the Rebel mosaic series that decorate the Uptown 1/9 platform of the station.

··

Former residence of Emma Goldman
36 Grove Street, between Bedford and Bleecker Streets

Goldman lived here before her deportation in 1919 to the Soviet Union via Ellis Island.

··

Former residence
20 East 125th Street, between Fifth and Madison Avenues

On June 17, 1917, *The New York Times* reported that police had raided the "Berkman-Goldman headquarters" at this address. In the raid, the police arrested workers, malcontented "never-smilers," and recent immigrants, and collected incriminating materials including a "card index believed to contain names of ninety percent of the anarchists of consequence in this country."

Henry Honeychurch Gorringe
NAVAL OFFICER AND EXPLORER 1841–1885

T he son of an English cleric stationed in the West Indies, Gorringe traveled to the United States to enlist as a common sailor for the Union at the outset of the American Civil War. Officers noted his gallantry in battle and he rose quickly through the ranks until he commanded his own sloop in the South Atlantic fleet. In postwar years, Gorringe enjoyed an excellent reputation for charting submerged volcanoes and dangerous coastline for the US Navy. He achieved national celebrity as the mastermind behind the transplant of "Cleopatra's Needle" from Alexandria, Egypt, to Central Park. The obelisk was a gift from Ismail Pasha, the Khedive of Egypt, who hoped to bolster relations between the United States and Egypt after the opening of the Suez Canal. Initial ideas for the transport of the obelisk included sending it upright across the seas; hanging it from the bow of a steamer; boxing it up in a giant buoyant coffin and towing it through the swells of the Atlantic. Gorringe studied French, English, and Russian solutions to the problem of relocating massive monuments and designed a crane, which lifted, tipped, and lowered the obelisk around its center of gravity.

··

The Obelisk (Cleopatra's Needle)
Inside Central Park, behind the Metropolitan Museum of Art

The Obelisk, also called Cleopatra's Needle, towers over its small octagonal park behind the Metropolitan Museum of Art. Black bronze crabs (replicas of those installed by the Romans) are wedged beneath each corner of the obelisk's base. Many of the hieroglyphics have eroded in the polluted air of New York, but a few remain distinct.

Translations of the hieroglyphics can be found on plaques at each side of the obelisk. On a quiet day, this nicely secluded part of the park has a desolate atmosphere that almost makes the obelisk seem like a ruin indigenous to the park.

Henry Honeychurch Gorringe, undated.

Print Collection, Miriam and Ira D. Wallach Division of Art, Prints and Photographs, The New York Public Library, Astor, Lenox and Tilden Foundations

Originally one of a pair erected at the Temple of the Sun at Heliopolis around 1450 BCE, the obelisk is engraved with hieroglyphic panegyric of the reign of Tuthmosis III. Ramses II re-inscribed the obelisks. In 22 BCE, the occupying Romans moved the pair of obelisks to Alexandria, where they formed an encouraging marker to sailors approaching the Mediterranean port. The other obelisk, a gift to the British on the occasion of Lord Nelson's defeat of the French, stands on the banks of the Thames.

Upon his arrival in Alexandria, Gorringe wrote to the New York papers that he had encountered crowds of angry Egyptians protesting the removal of the obelisk, but he took it all in stride. Such apparent nonchalance in the face of "angry natives" was a standard feature of exploration and adventure reportage at the time. Gorringe worked quickly with a crew of one hundred Egyptians to excavate the base of the obelisk. The furious mob reportedly fell into anxious silence as the obelisk was lifted from its base, creaked against the ropes, snapped the supporting timber, and swung over the spectators. The monumental obelisk eventually settled safely onto its trellis and began its glacially slow trip to New York. Gorringe braced the interior of an iron steamer with a nest of wood and steel beams and lowered the obelisk into the hold through a hole in the prow. Months later, the obelisk steamed into New York and was hauled by sixteen pairs of harnessed horses on a trellis loaded with canon balls that acted as giant ball bearings. Over many months, through late summer, autumn, and winter, the obelisk inched across the city and through Central Park. In January of 1881, the obelisk was swung back into its vertical position atop its original pedestal. William H. Vanderbilt underwrote the costly extraction of the obelisk from its 2,000-year-old pocket of earth and its slow and unorthodox conveyance to Central Park.

The Metropolitan Museum of Art
1000 Fifth Avenue at East 82nd Street
tel. (212) 535-7710, www.metmuseum.org

Past the collection of scrolls, mummies, sphinxes, and miniature amulets of gods, crocodiles, and ships in the Department of Egyptian Art stands the Temple of Dendur. Six statues of the lion-headed Sakhmet, the god responsible for war, violent storms, and pestilence, flank the entrance to the light-flooded gallery. Two glass cases contain the original bronze crabs installed on the obelisk by the Roman prefect Barbarus and the architect Pontius during the eighteenth year of the reign of Augustus. The label reads: "Gift of Henry Gorringe."

Site of Old Metropolitan Opera House
Broadway, between West 39th and West 40th Streets

Gorringe's calm retrieval of the obelisk and his gentlemanly management of his celebrity made him a sought-out guest at exclusive parties. He attended the Bachelor's Ball of 1884 at the old Metropolitan Opera House. The former merchant marine was now keeping the best company: Astors and Vanderbilts were also in attendance. The lobby and dining room were transformed, according to *The New York Times,* into a "huge hothouse" by a profusion of evergreen branches and geraniums. Guests admired a replica of a castle on the opera house stage and passed through halls decked with colorful Chinese lanterns swaying under a canopy of fresh flowers. The society column noted with admiration the many varieties of blooms on display, adding that the affair was pleasantly lacking in "wall-flowers," who were an inevitable drag for young bachelors at lesser balls.

The Brooklyn Navy Yard
From Flushing Avenue to the East River, and Navy Street / Hudson Avenue to Kent Avenue
Fort Greene, Brooklyn

Gorringe was stationed here in the 1880s. During this time he traveled widely, and his opinions on matters of engineering and shipbuilding were followed closely. He delivered an optimistic report on the progress of the Panama Canal, as workers were struggling to cut through the deep hills of the isthmus. The abandoned buildings of the Navy Yard are now occupied by businesses and municipal facilities, including a prison. A fifteen-acre complex of television and film studios is under construction. The Navy Yard is surrounded by high brick walls, coils of barbed wired, and the rusted broadsides of guarded entrances that resemble decrepit ships. It is off-limits to the general public.

After Gorringe's resignation from the Navy, friends encouraged him to capitalize on his good reputation and naval experience by launching an American shipbuilding company.

Spurred on by patriotic ambition and the dashing figure of Gorringe, investors heaped money into the American Shipbuilding Company in Philadelphia. Mismanagement bankrupted the company.

. . . .

Grace Church

800-804 Broadway at East 10th Street
tel. (212) 254-2000, www.gracechurchnyc.org

The funeral of Commander Gorringe was held here. He had died soon after leaping from an express train onto a platform, injuring his back. White roses, lilies, and myrtle draped his casket, mounted with a plaque bearing his name and the word "rest" in Arabic. His head lay upon a small pillow with his name transliterated into Arabic script. Gorringe's body was stored in the vault of Grace Church for many months, while the family arranged for an ideal burial site: a grassy knoll overlooking the Hudson River at Rockland Cemetery. His friends and colleagues commissioned the miniature of the obelisk that marks his grave.

Martha Graham

DANCER AND CHOREOGRAPHER 1894–1991

O ver the course of seventy years, modernist visionary Martha Graham created 181 ballets and trained hundreds of young dancers at her school in New York. Before Graham, dance was praised for its fluidity and for the beauty of its movement—something she rejected outright. She wanted emotion—in all its angularity, directness, and force—to be evident in the dancer's movements. She believed that dance should be a form of disclosure; it should be "fraught with inner meaning, excitement and surge." Graham was born in Pittsburgh, then the nation's center of coal production. She recalled that the soot-filled air made the city seem "spun entirely out of evening and dark thread." Graham's father later moved the family to healthy, spacious California, where Graham first saw pioneering dancer Ruth St. Denis perform in 1911. Graham enrolled in St. Denis's prestigious dance school, Denishawn (the school's other founder was Ted Shawn), and spent the next eight years as a student, company dancer, and teacher. Graham returned to New York to join the mildly scandalous Greenwich Village Follies from 1923 to 1924, where she had some liberty to choreograph her own work. With a loan of $1000 from Gotham Book Mart owner Frances Steloff, Graham staged her debut and launched her solo career. In 1926, Graham founded her own dance company, and became pivotal in defining the modern dance movement. In 1976, she received the US Presidential Medal of Freedom. To her great unhappiness, Graham had to stop dancing professionally in her mid-70s. She continued to choreograph and re-interpreted Stravinsky's "The Rite of Spring" at the age of ninety.

. . . .

Site of Greenwich Village Follies

Seventh Avenue South, between Christopher and West 4th Streets

This 1931 building occupies the former site of Greenwich Village Theatre, home to the smash review, the Greenwich Village Follies. Graham was a dancer and choreographer in the Follies in the early 1920s. Though it was considered the thinking person's variety show, ultimately the popular format prevented Graham from experimenting to the extent that she had hoped.

Central Park Zoo

830 Fifth Avenue at East 64th Street
tel. (212) 439-6500, www.nyzoosandaquarium.com

As a young, poor dancer in New York, Graham spent hours here watching the animals—the lions in particular—in the hope of emulating their movements.

··

Carnegie Hall

156 West 57th Street at Seventh Avenue
tel. (212) 903-9765, www.carnegiehall.org

Graham's first dance studio was located here. Number 819 on the sixth floor was, ac-

Martha Graham, ca. early 20th century.

cording to visitors, an incredibly small space. She lunched often with choreographer Louis Horst at the nearby Horn & Hardart's Automat (977 Eighth Avenue between West 57th and West 58th Streets). Automats, now extinct, were a favorite of budget diners all over the city. Inside the automat, gleaming glass doors framed single servings of everything from macaroni and cheese and baked beans to chicken casserole and apple pie. For a few nickels, the machines dispensed the selected item and diners ate at cafeteria tables.

The Martha Graham School of Contemporary Dance

316 East 63rd Street, between First and Second Avenues
tel. (212) 838-5886, www.marthagrahamdance.org

Graham opened her school in 1926, in her tiny studio in Carnegie Hall. Located its present address since 1952, the Martha Graham School is the longest-operating dance school in the country. In her autobiography, Graham describes quiet afternoons alone in the dance studio before taking the company on tour. She rehearsed surrounded by crates of Isamu Noguchi's stage sets and sculptures, which would accompany the troupe.

Isamu Noguchi Museum

9-01 33rd Road, between Vernon Boulevard and 10th Street
Long Island City, Queens
tel. (718) 204-7088, www.noguchi.org

In the museum's permanent collection is a 1976 model (10" × 24" × 24") of a proposed Martha Graham Dance Theater. The open, honeycombed dome reflects the geodesic domes of utopian architect R. Buckminster Fuller. Noguchi and Fuller met in 1929; it was the beginning of fifty years of friendship and collaboration.

New York Public Library for the Performing Arts at Lincoln Center

40 Lincoln Center Plaza (west of Broadway and Columbus Avenues, between West 62nd and West 65th Streets)
tel. (212) 870-1630, www.nypl.org

The Jerome Robbins Dance Division, housed in the Library for the Performing Arts, is the largest and most diverse dance archive in the world. The library has a collection of articles, films, and artefacts from Martha Graham's career. On the ground floor of the library is the Donald and Mary Oenslager Gallery, a glassed-in gallery that features exhibits on the performing arts, ranging from shadow puppetry to Balanchine.

Peggy Guggenheim

ART PATRON 1898–1979

P eggy Guggenheim was always alluring in an edgy way—from a bohemian flair for layered, shapeless clothes in the 1920s to flamboyant sunglasses in the 1960s. Her father, millionaire playboy Benjamin Guggenheim, died on the *Titanic*, a loss from which she never fully recovered. More interested in the world beyond the wealthy and conventional crowd into which she had been born, she volunteered at her cousin's radical bookstore, where she met Alfred Stieglitz. At his gallery, 291, he handed her an abstract painting by Georgia O'Keeffe—a baffled Guggenheim turned the painting clockwise and counter-clockwise, which amused and delighted Stieglitz. She committed the rest of her life to avant-garde art. She moved to France in 1921, the heyday of American expatriates in Paris. She was photographed by Man Ray, hung out with the luminaries resident in the city (James Joyce, Samuel Beckett, Marcel Duchamp, Constantin Brancusi, Fernand Léger, André Breton, Marc Chagall, Alexander Calder, Ernest Hemingway, Djuna Barnes, Piet Mondrian, Pablo Picasso, Salvador Dalí, and future husband Max Ernst), and began to collect modern art. When the Nazis invaded France, Guggenheim searched for a safe haven for her collection. The Louvre deemed the work too new and rejected it, so Guggenheim hid her artworks under bales of hay at a friend's farm. Her collection is now installed in her former home on the Grand Canal in Venice. It is open to the public and run by the Guggenheim Museum.

Solomon R. Guggenheim Museum
1071 Fifth Avenue at East 89th Street
tel. (212) 423-3500, www.guggenheim.org

In 1939, the Museum of Non-Objective Painting opened under the auspices of the Solomon R. Guggenheim Foundation with a mission to promote new art forms of art.

Peggy Guggenheim, 1942.

In 1959, the museum took occupation of its current home, the building designed by Frank Lloyd Wright. Peggy Guggenheim disapproved of the Wright building for her uncle's museum. She complained that the signature interior ramp "coils like an evil serpent."

In the mid-1970s, Guggenheim deeded her house in Venice and her entire private collection to the foundation established in her uncle's name. The Guggenheim has run the Peggy Guggenheim Collection in Venice since 1979.

....

Central Park
From Central Park South (59th Street) to Central Park North (110th Street) and from Fifth Avenue to Central Park West (Eighth Avenue)

The Guggenheims lived near Central Park at East 72nd Street, where Peggy was home-schooled until the age of fifteen. It was a lonely house, full of tutors, nurses, and her father's mistresses. She spent time riding sidesaddle through Central Park. Once, while passing beneath one of the park's stone footbridges, Guggenheim was knocked from her horse and dragged several feet. She lost a tooth and broke her jaw.

....

Former residence, Hale House
440 East 51st Street at the East River

Upon their escape from Europe during World War II, Guggenheim and husband Max Ernst moved into a renovated, two-story brownstone overlooking the East River. The house had been named Hale House in honor of patriotic martyr Nathan Hale, rumored to have been hung on the property. Guggenheim loved the "chapel-like" living room and ancient-looking fireplace, which she thought looked like it was from "some baronial hall in Hungary." The house became a refuge for artists and others fleeing the war. Guggenheim and Ernst made regular visits to MoMA, established in 1929 and open at its current location since 1939; the Guggeheim Museum; The Museum of Natural History; and the Museum of the American Indian, which was reportedly Ernst's favorite.

In addition to being a collector, Guggenheim was a monumentally important benefactor who supported most of the important artists of the period. A partial list includes Berenice Abbot, Djuna Barnes (who wrote most of *Nightwood* as Guggenheim's house-guest in Europe), Constantin Brancusi, Alexander Calder, Alberto Giacometti, Frida Kahlo, Henri Matisse, Joan Miró, Piet Mondrian, Henry Moore, Pablo Picasso, and Jackson Pollock.

....

Site of "Art of This Century" Exhibition
30 West 57th Street, between Fifth and Sixth Avenues

On October 20, 1942, Peggy Guggenheim launched "Art of This Century" at this address. The opening of her gallery was a phenomenal success and declared a "must see" by art critics, despite its unorthodox exhibition style and radical modernist bent. At the opening, which she organized as a benefit for the American Red Cross, Guggenheim wore one Yves Tanguy earring and one Alexander Calder earring to demonstrate her "impartiality between surrealist and abstract art." In the gallery, paintings were not framed but suspended before concave wooden shields or blocked out along serpentine galleries. Novel gadgets abounded: a mechanical arm swung Paul Klee paintings before the viewer in ten-second intervals, unless the viewer held a piece in place by pressing a button.

Woody Guthrie

MUSICIAN 1912–1967

F olk hero Woody Guthrie moved to New York in 1940. As a new arrival alone in a Times Square hotel room, he wrote "This Land is Your Land," which he intended as a protest and parody of Irving Berlin's "God Bless America." Guthrie settled in Greenwich Village, where he and fellow future folk legends Pete Seeger, Lee Hays, and Millard Lampell formed the prototypical folk group The Almanac Singers. G᠂ ˙hrie was an important participant in leftist and art scenes in New York: in his jeans, work boots, black cap, and pea coat, he was a conspicuous character in the formal, buttoned-down 1940s, but he prefigured the counterculture uniform of the following decades. In New York, money was perennially scarce, but Guthrie found steady success recording American folk songs for the Library of Congress. The recordings led to a record contract and a radio program, "Pipe Smoking Time," which was short-lived because

Guthrie found the format constricting and the censorship oppressive. Before and during American involvement in World War II, Guthrie wrote anti-Nazi and anti-Fascist songs. He shipped out three times with the Merchant Marines and survived dual torpedo attacks. In the mid-1940s, Guthrie played often at the Martha Graham School (his second wife Marjorie Mazia danced with the company), where he was the unofficial mascot of the troupe. Guthrie settled into family life on Coney Island, but it was not long before he started rambling again, this time to the West Coast. The cause of Guthrie's increasingly erratic behavior was discovered in 1952, when he was diagnosed with Huntington's Chorea, a degenerative neurological disorder that had killed his mother. He continued roaming in and out of wards and was last hospitalized in Greystone Park in New Jersey, where friends and admirers visited him on the weekends. His visitors included folk musicians such as Bob Dylan and Joan Baez, who ensured that Guthrie's songs were popularized during his lifetime.

Almanac House

130 West 10th Street, between Greenwich Avenue and Waverly Place

"This is the house where the Almanacs use to stay
This is the place where the records used to play."

Guthrie lived here in 1940, soon after arriving in the city, with a community of artists and musicians who played together in impromptu sessions and in political and personal fund-raising hootenannies. Guthrie, Lee Hays, Millard Lampell, Pete Seeger, and other folk musicians lived here communally and named their band The Almanac Singers, after the house. The group moved on to other apartments and houses that they likewise dubbed "Almanac Houses."

McSorley's Old Ale House

15 East 7th Street, between Cooper Square and Second Avenue
tel. (212) 473-9148

Guthrie was photographed at McSorley's for the publicity photos of his album "Bound for Glory."

Former residence

74 Charles Street, between Bleecker and West 4th Streets

Guthrie lived here in 1943, waiting for Mazia to leave her marriage and join him. While he waited, he entertained and played music with friends, including blues guitarist Leadbelly.

92nd Street Y

Theresa L. Kaufman Auditorium
1395 Lexington Avenue at 92nd Street
tel. (212) 415-5500, www.92ndsty.org

On May 3, 1942, Guthrie played "Two Dust Bowl Ballads" accompanied by Martha Graham dancers.

Coney Island

From Surf Avenue to the Boardwalk and from West 8th Street to West 16th Street
Coney Island, Brooklyn
www.coneyisland.com

Guthrie loved Coney Island and wrote several songs about it. In the 1948 tune "Coney Island & Me" he sang: "Coney Island and me ain't two different things."

. . . .

Nathan's Famous

1310 Surf Avenue at Stillwell Avenue
tel. (718) 946-2202

Opened in 1916 as a nickel hotdog stand, Nathan's is a bustling synecdoche of Coney Island nostalgia and good times in American popular culture. Guthrie loved Nathan's and took his children and visiting friends to hotdog breakfasts here before walks along the beaches and jetties.

. . . .

Site of former residence

3520 Mermaid Avenue between West 35th and West 36th Streets

This was the address of the Guthrie family's Coney Island home in the mid-1940s. Guthrie wrote his collection of children's songs, "Songs to Grow On," at this address.

. . . .

Washington Square Park

From Washington Square North (Waverly Place) to Washington Square South (West 4th Street) and from University Place to MacDougal Street

In the 1960s, Guthrie was preeminent among the guitarists and songwriters who performed folk and protest music in the park. Struggling against Huntington's Chorea and alcohol, Guthrie—bearded, disoriented, lying on the ground—was also a spectacle to the youth whose cultivated look (jeans, work boots, white work shirts, pea coat) he had sported when he arrived in New York twenty years earlier.

Alexander Hamilton

STATESMAN 1757–1804

T he illegitimate son of a Scottish merchant, Alexander Hamilton enrolled at King's College (now Columbia University) in 1773. The American Revolution ended Hamilton's formal schooling, and he became George Washington's aide-de-camp during the war. In post-Revolutionary New York, Hamilton rose to eminence as "the little lion of Federalism"—although he had to prove himself again and again to the cautious, embedded aristocrats of the nascent nation. The author of *The Federalist*, Hamilton envisioned a strong national government as a bulwark against the potential chaos of a fractured and free-for-all conglomeration of separate interests and provinces. As the first Secretary of the Treasury, he created the Bank of the United States and pushed the federal government to assume all state debt in the aftermath of the Revolutionary War. His vision for the country was cut short after he joined Thomas Jefferson and others in campaigning against candidate Aaron Burr. Hamilton declared him unfit for public office and Burr, whose reputation was already battered, challenged Hamilton to a duel. In the summer of 1804, they faced each other at ten paces on the New Jersey bank of the Hudson across from present-day Midtown. Burr fired the first shot successfully, and Hamilton fell. Burr fled New York, and Hamilton's body was carried through the streets, trailing a crowd of mourners, to Trinity Church, where he is buried.

Hamilton Grange National Memorial

287 Convent Avenue, between West 141st and West 142nd Streets
tel. (212) 283-5154, www.nps.gov/hagr

Commissioned by Hamilton and designed by John McComb, Jr., the Federal style house originally stood on thirty-two acres of rural sprawl in upper Manhattan. Hamilton occupied the house in 1802 and dubbed his estate "The Grange" in honor of an ancestral Scottish home.

New-York Historical Society

2 West 77th Street at Central Park West
tel. (212) 873-3400, www.nyhistory.org

On display here is a tall mahogany clock with a great white face, presented by Hamilton to the Bank of New York to celebrate its opening at 48 Wall Street. The clock chimed employees through banker's hours (10 a.m. to 3 p.m.) from 1797 to 1858, when it was donated to the Historical Society.

In the Luce Center upstairs is the pale, weathered stone that long marked the bluff across the Hudson where Hamilton fell. In the mezzanine, a mourning handkerchief commemorates Hamilton's death: angels and weeping women linger under cemetery trees and around his tomb, and the black script reads, "Five years have not passed since your tears flowed for the Father of your country and you are once again called to shed them over her eldest son."

Among the daily objects from life in New York from that era (patriotic butter molds, a cobbler's bench, pewter candlesticks, diamond-encrusted shoe buckles, eel traps, etc.) is an over life-size heroic bust of Alexander Hamilton with furrowed brow and set mouth. He shares the glass display case with a cast of Aaron Burr's head.

Alexander Hamilton, undated.

Former residence

58 Wall Street at Hanover Street

Hamilton lived at this address while working on *The Federalist*.

. . . .

Cemetery at Trinity Church

74 Trinity Place, between Rector and Thames Streets
tel. (212) 602-0800, www.trinitywallstreet.org

The body of Hamilton is interred here beneath a pyramid-shaped monument in the southern churchyard of Trinity Church. In 1804, Hamilton and his political rival Aaron Burr rowed across the Hudson River to Weehawken to face each other in a duel. Both men moved with outward nonchalance towards the stand-off. Burr shot Hamilton in the right side and was whisked away by his associates behind an umbrella to mask his identity—though socially honorable, duels were illegal. Hamilton died in New York the following morning. The city mourned a fallen patriot: black-clad, reigned-in horses clomped solemnly past thousands of mourners. The funeral oration at Trinity Church painted Burr as a black-hearted villain who had robbed the city and the nation of its hero. Burr fled New York and headed west.

Keith Haring, 1984.

© The Robert Mapplethorpe Foundation. Courtesy Art + Commerce Anthology

Keith Haring

ARTIST 1958–1990

K eith Haring moved to New York from Pittsburgh in 1978 on scholarship to the School of Visual Arts. There he expanded his small, puzzle-piece abstract drawings and paintings into ever larger formats—ultimately vibrant murals that filled walls, buildings, and other grand, blank urban surfaces. Haring's unmistakable pop iconography grew from exuberant abstract sketches, which he produced quickly on long rolls of oak-tag paper, letting the shapes metamorphose into the outlines of people, animals, and machines. Emulating the abundant, colorful graffiti lining New York's subway system, Haring began transplanting the iconic figures that had taken shape in his sketches—radiant babies, flying saucers, deified dogs—to the soft black paper backing of empty advertising frames in subway stations. Harried New York commuters stopped to watch him make fast chalk compositions, and Haring loved the impromptu art discussions that took place on the platform as he worked. Within five years, Haring's fame made the chalk sketches irresistible to collectors and dealers, who began taking the drawings for their collections. Haring shifted his focus to large-scale public work: he painted positive, political, and bright murals, enriching particularly bleak and depressed urban settings. He painted dozens of murals, legal and illegal, commissioned and unpaid, throughout New York, on the Berlin Wall, at the Children's Hospital in Paris, and in honor of Nelson Mandela. Haring learned that he was infected with HIV in 1988 and established the Keith Haring Foundation to sustain his involvement in AIDS-related and children's charities.

Pop Shop

292 Lafayette Street, between Jersey and East Houston Streets
tel. (212) 219-2784, www.haring.com/popshop/index.html

Keith Haring opened the Pop Shop in 1986 to make his artwork—prohibitively expensive once he became a sought-after artist—available to the general public. Haring's murals cover the walls and floors of the Pop Shop. Books, posters, shirts, and other Haring items are for sale. All profits go to the Keith Haring Foundation.

Carmine Street Recreation Center

1 Clarkson Street at Seventh Avenue
tel. (212) 242-5228

Haring painted this huge blue-green mural in 1987 on the outdoor wall of the recreation center overlooking the swimming pool. He populated the 170-foot by 18-foot space with swimmers, fish, mermaids, and dolphins.

Crack is wack mural

East 128th Street at Second Avenue

Painted in rust-red and black on a freestanding handball court wall, Haring's mural "Crack is wack" warns with warped skulls-and-crossbones against the dangers of addiction. Haring completed this mural without permission in 1986. On its completion, the mural was adopted by the City Department of Parks and has been preserved.

The Cathedral Church of St. John the Divine

1047 Amsterdam Avenue at West 112th Street
tel. (212) 316-7540, www.stjohndivine.org

Located in the chapel directly behind the main altar of the church is an engraved, silver triptych by Keith Haring. Though the gates to the small chapel are usually locked, the triptych can be seen clearly from the outside.

Billie Holiday

SINGER 1915–1959

B illie Holiday mastered her minimalist anthems of loneliness, betrayal, and unacknowledged pain in an organized effort to break artistic ground. Holiday, with

Louis Armstrong, is credited with inventing modern jazz singing. At the age of fifteen, Holiday joined her mother in Harlem and established herself in the jazz scene with a presence and artistic reputation that was startling in an adolescent. The jazz promoter John Hammond caught her act and arranged immediately for her first recording in New York City with an up-and-coming Benny Goodman. Holiday often appeared on stage with a signature white gardenia in her hair. Throughout her career, she was an inspiration to the most celebrated composers and instrumentalists including Duke Ellington, Teddy Wilson, Louis Armstrong, Count Basie, and many others. The poet Frank O'Hara watched Billie Holiday perform in the summer of 1957. Holiday had been relegated to performing in a movie theater because of an arrest for heroin possession that prohibited her from playing anywhere alcohol was served. She was hours late for the performance and appeared visibly wan and weak on stage. The moment she sang, however, O'Hara wrote: "everyone and I stopped breathing."

Billie Holiday, 1949.

Library of Congress Prints and Photographs Division

Lenox Lounge

288 Lenox Avenue, between West 124th and West 125th Streets
tel. (212) 427-0253, www.lenoxlounge.com

The Lenox Lounge opened its doors in 1939, and Holiday was among the first jazz legends to perform here. Through the neighborhood bar in the front room and past the double doors is the art deco "Zebra Room," named for its striped wallpaper. The Zebra Room has hosted innumerable jazz greats, including Duke Ellington, Count Basie,

Ella Fitzgerald, Miles Davis, and John Coltrane. James Baldwin and Langston Hughes met frequently at the Lenox Lounge, and Malcolm X was a regular in later years. When Billie Holiday was ready to have a seat in her favorite booth—hers was the first table on the left—she reportedly had white men cleared from her corner and moved to lesser tables. The club underwent restoration in 1999 and the art deco interiors have been faithfully restored.

. . . .

Apollo Theater

253 West 125th Street, between St Nicholas Avenue and Frederick Douglass Boulevard
tel. (212) 531-5300, www.apollotheater.com

Holiday is an Apollo legend. She sang here many times throughout her career. In 1937, Holiday performed with Count Basie on the night of his Apollo debut. Though she had made her own debut at the Apollo Theater in 1935, Holiday suffered from stage fright and reportedly required a gentle push onto the stage. She continued to sing here, and at Carnegie Hall, after she was barred from performing in cabarets because of arrests for drug possession.

. . . .

Site of Café Society

1 Sheridan Square at West 4th and Barrow Streets

Café Society was among the very first integrated nightclubs in Manhattan. Barney Josephson opened the club in 1938 to create a venue in which blacks and whites could perform and socialize together. Holiday performed at Café Society often and debuted her song, "Strange Fruit," here in 1939. "Strange Fruit," a ballad sung in protest of the lynching of African-Americans in the South, was written by a left-wing Jewish schoolteacher in the Bronx named Abel Meeropol, who became better known for adopting the orphaned sons of Julius and Ethel Rosenberg after their execution in 1953. Recording executives fought to keep the song off of Holiday's albums and club owners tried to strike it from her set list. Holiday frequently ended her shows with "Strange Fruit"—as she intended, it left audiences stunned, uncomfortable, and angry.

Harry Houdini

ESCAPE ARTIST 1874–1926

"Failure Means a Drowning Death" (tagline for Harry Houdini's signature submersion stunts)

T he world's most famous escape artist and debunker, born Erich Weiss, emigrated from Hungary with his parents in 1878; they settled in Appleton, Wisconsin where Harry Houdini's father served as the rabbi for the area's German Jewish Congregation. Houdini traveled to New York when he was thirteen, working as a garment cutter, messenger, and locksmith's apprentice, before successfully billing himself as the lock-busting "Handcuff King." Houdini's celebrity grew as he devised ever more dangerous stunts. He hung bat-like in leather strait-jackets from the peaks of skyscrapers; he leapt handcuffed into the swift East River; he strapped himself to live cannons timed to blast minutes later; he commissioned expert Belgian basket weavers to encase him; he asked Scotland Yard to imprison him; he trapped himself in glass plate boxes, bronze coffins, and zinc-lined suitcases. He escaped on every occasion. Many others, imitating him, did not and died attempting "Houdinis." Houdini's greatest illusions relied on his stamina, his high tolerance for pain, his athleticism, and his self-control, whether he was folding his muscular body into the tight space of a water-flooded milk can or wrenching himself free of chains. He was also a charismatic showman who knew that his audience was riveted by a strange alloy of feelings: a desire to see Houdini escape fused with a desire to witness a disaster. Houdini devoted much of his life to discrediting popular mediums who, he felt, betrayed the vulnerable hopes of grieving people desperate to speak with their beloved dead. He visited séances, fortune tellers, and mesmerists both as the great Houdini and disguised as a bereaved father or husband, in order to expose the tricks of the trade. Houdini died on Halloween and was sealed into the bronze coffin he had used for his underwater illusions, his head placed upon a soft stack of letters his mother had written him.

Former residence
278 West 113th Street, between Frederick Douglass and Adam Clayton Powell, Jr. Boulevards

In 1905, Houdini moved with his wife, his mother, his sister, and two brothers into this brownstone, now marked by an oval plaque. This house once contained Houdini's vast library of books about theater, magic, and the black arts. The house consisted of a dozen rooms, numerous fireplaces, and closets, one of which was fitted with an oversized tub for practicing underwater stunts.

Pier 6 on the East River
Off South Street, between Broad Street and Old Slip

Pier 6 is now the Downtown Manhattan Heliport, though not much else has changed since July 7, 1912, when hundreds of New Yorkers lined the riverfront, crowded the pier, and leaned over the railings of idling boats to watch Houdini be "thrown overboard manacled in a box." As reported by the *New York Times*, the police boarded Houdini's barge in a half-hearted attempt to stop the stunt. The delay added considerably to the suspense of the show. Once permitted to proceed, Houdini invited reporters on board to inspect the irons and the thick pine box. After another suspense-heightening turn around Ellis Island, Houdini returned, appearing on deck in a pristine white bathing suit. Assistants clicked handcuffs and heavy leg irons around his wrists and ankles; they nailed him into the solid pine box and pushed the box into the icy river. For a seemingly endless minute, a small army of reporters waited with pencils poised and the pier, "crowded to suffocation," held its collective breath. The tide was rushing out, and the assistants struggled to keep the tethered box close to the boat and the surface of the water. As the "cinematographer man cranked rapidly and the sun beat down mercilessly," Houdini bobbed to the surface smiling broadly.

Site of Heidelberg Building
West 42nd Street at Broadway

Also in July 1912, "Houdini the Handcuff King" had himself suspended off the edge of the Heidelberg Building, once opposite the Times Building. Head-down over many stories of empty air, Houdini freed himself quickly from a tightly bound leather straitjacket. Built in 1909, the Heidelberg Building was a seven-story office block crowned with an eleven-story tower—the company that leased the building conceived of a daring new advertising scheme: posting bright, flashing signs and ads along the building's then considerable height. The company went bankrupt and the unpopular building survived until 1984, when it was demolished.

Shelton Hotel (now New York East Side Marriott)
525 Lexington Avenue, between East 48th and East 49th Streets

Here Houdini broke the immersion record of Indian fakir Rahman Bey, who had attributed to supernatural powers his ability to spend one hour in a coffin submerged in water. Houdini exposed Rahman Bey by spending over an hour in a watertight, bronze coffin sunk in the swimming pool of the Shelton Hotel. Houdini attributed his success to stamina and a special technique he called "high breathing."

Harry Houdini emerging from a coffin at the Hotel Shelton, 1926.

© CORBIS

Site of New York Hippodrome
456-470 Sixth Avenue, between West 43rd and West 44th Streets

The New York Hippodrome opened in 1905, just off newly minted Times Square. Nestled among expensive Broadway theaters, the Hippodrome drew in middle-class crowds with low ticket prices and big escapist entertainment—chariot races, amusement parks rides, circuses. In 1917, Houdini organized a benefit here for the family members of the men killed in the sinking of the *Antilles*. The following year, he starred for almost five months straight in a variety show called "Cheer Up" at the New York Hippodrome. Houdini performed his classic water tank escapes here and, notably, made an elephant disappear.

New York City Police Academy
235 East 20th Street, between Second and Third Avenues

Houdini taught at the New York Police Academy, lecturing detectives and rookies on the trickery of séance and the art of handcuff escape. The Academy has changed locations numerous times.

Site of Elks Clubhouse
108 West 43rd Street, between Sixth and Seventh Avenues

Houdini often invited strongmen in the audience to punch him in the stomach. It was a remarkable display of his strength. Houdini died in Detroit on Halloween, from acute appendicitis only days after a doubting student slammed him in the stomach without warning. Two thousand mourners crowded into the ballroom of the Elks Clubhouse on November 4, 1926. Millions worldwide grieved, shocked by the sudden death of the man they had watched escape every other conceivable trap.

Langston Hughes

POET AND WRITER 1902–1967

"There is no thrill in all the world like entering, for the first time, New York harbor—coming in from the flat monotony of the sea to this rise of dreams and beauty."

P oet, playwright, and historian, Langston Hughes led the youthful second wave of the Harlem Renaissance. Like Walt Whitman—one of his poetic heroes—Hughes wrote about the up-and-down lives of "everyday people," with whom he identified. Hughes arrived in New York in 1921 from the Midwest to study at Columbia University and became deeply involved in the jazz and literary scenes of neighboring Harlem. Soon frustrated by the limitations of a university life, Hughes struck out in search of richer experience. He wrote poetry and traveled, supported by multitude of odd jobs and work as a seaman throughout Europe and Africa. By the time Hughes returned to New York, he had won acclaim for his poetry and for his 1930 novel, *Not Without Laughter*. Hughes made Harlem his home and celebrated the sound of authentic Harlem in his work: he captured the cadence and concerns of daily conversation; he animated his verse with rhythms of jazz; he wanted his poems "read aloud, crooned, shouted and sung." Hughes also created Jesse B. Semple, Harlem resident: in hugely popular newspaper columns and satirical stories, Hughes often placed rationalizing, accommodating narrators against the outraged and insistent Semple. Hughes won a Guggenheim Fellowship and went on to establish black theater groups throughout the country. His ashes are buried in Harlem beneath the floor of the Schomburg Library.

Harlem YMCA
180 West 135th Street, between Adam Clayton Powell Jr. Boulevard and Lenox Avenue
tel. (212) 281-4100, www.ymca.org

In 1921, Hughes lived here, paying $7 a week in rent, while he attended Columbia University.

Estonia House
243 East 34th Street, between Second and Third Avenues

Langston Hughes, 1958.

© Robert W. Kelly/Getty Images

When this was the Civic Club, Hughes lunched here often, once with W.E.B. DuBois soon after Hughes's arrival in the city. The two men had been corresponding for years. Bound by mutual respect and the goal of defending the rights of African-Americans, they nonetheless differed in their views of art and popular culture. DuBois advocated supporting a talented elite in Harlem while Hughes was enthusiastic about promoting jazz, free verse, and other popular art forms central to contemporary Harlem.

Site of Stage Door Canteen

216 West 44th Street, between Broadway and Eighth Avenue

Hughes worked here as a waiter from 1941 to 1942, when Carl Van Vechten was a busboy. The theater that housed the Stage Door Canteen was demolished in 1945.

Theresa Hotel
2090 Adam Clayton Powell Jr. Boulevard, between West 124th and West 125th Streets

Hughes lived here in the mid-1940s. The hotel is now an office building.

. . . .

Langston Hughes House
20 East 127th Street, between Park and Madison Avenues

Hughes lived here for the last twenty years of his life, a distinction honored by New York City's Preservation Commission, which gave the house landmark status and re-christened East 127th Street Langston Hughes Place.

. . . .

Schomburg Center for Research in Black Culture
515 Malcolm X Boulevard, between West 135th and West 136th Streets
tel. (212) 491-2200, www.nypl.org

Hughes visited the Schomburg Collection on his first day in Harlem in 1921. After his death, his ashes were buried beneath the terrazzo floor of the library, under an inscription from his poem, "The Negro Speaks of Rivers." At the point on the floor where the rivers of the world intersect, the line "My soul has grown deep like the rivers" marks the burial place.

Zora Neale Hurston

WRITER 1903–1960

Z ora Neale Hurston gained legendary status in the Harlem Renaissance for her prolific production of novels, folklore, plays, and scholarly work, as well as for her audacity and iconoclasm. She was a brilliant, lifelong observer inside the segregated, private worlds of both blacks and whites; she prided herself on her ability to draw almost anyone into a confidential relationship. Senators entrusted her with legislative secrets while she buffed their nails at the salon where she worked to put herself through Howard University; in southern backwaters, outlaw smugglers were equally forthcoming. Her life "went everywhere"—to Harlem's intellectual elite, to the rural South, to the top of academia, to the Caribbean, to fame, and to poverty. With Langston Hughes, she promoted the use of dialect and folklore, and all else that reflected authentic African-American life. Her autobiography, *Dust Tracks on a Road*, was an artful mix of personal history, lore, fact, and fiction, and remained contentious long after her death. As an anthropologist, Hurston completed invaluable fieldwork, securing for future generations a catalogue of folk tales, songs, and histories of the African-American experience. In 1937, Hurston published *Their Eyes Were Watching God*, which she had written in just two months while doing anthropological fieldwork in Haiti. At the end of her life, Hurston struggled with chronic poverty and public controversy over her stance against *Brown* v. *Board of Education*. She eventually settled in Florida, where she cultivated a lush garden and continued writing to the end. At the time of her death, Hurston was penniless and mostly forgotten—neighbors took up a collection to cover the expense of her burial in an unmarked grave. Her burial site was later rediscovered and marked by Alice Walker as "Zora Neale Hurston/A Genius of the South."

Site of "267 House"

267 West 136th Street, between Frederick Douglass Boulevard and Adam Clayton Powell Jr. Boulevard

This boarding house was home in the 1920s to leaders of the Harlem Renaissance, Langston Hughes, Aaron Douglas, Bruce Nugent, and Wallace Thurman. Hurston spent much of her time here, hanging out with friends and planning the first issue of a new literary magazine, *Fire!!*. While W.E.B. DuBois and other elders of the community emphasized that the arts should be used conservatively, and to social and political ends, Hughes, Hurston, and other members of the new guard hoped to create a venue for art for its own sake, one that would feature popular forms. The first issue of *Fire!!* was published in 1926—the high cover price dampened sales and forced the magazine to fold after a single issue. Its loss was not mourned by the old guard.

Zora Neale Hurston, 1938.

Library of Congress Prints and Photographs Division

Former residence

43 West 66th Street, between Columbus Avenue and Central Park West

Hurston moved here in 1926 with few possessions. She adapted the traditional Harlem "rent party"—thrown to raise money to meet the rent—to solve her furniture shortage, but was annoyed when guests brought too many tables and too few chairs. It was an intellectually and socially vibrant address for writers and artists who gathered here, though Hurston sometimes retreated to her room to study or write while her guests stayed on.

It was while living here that she and Hughes began their collaboration on *Mule Bone*, the play based on Hurston's story "The Bone of Contention." Both writers were committed to producing a play that drew on the folk tales, jokes, and songs that were a part of the survival strategy of African-Americans living in the segregated South. Hurston was an expert, having collected hundreds of tales during her doctoral research. Though several drafts and acts were completed, the play was never produced during their lifetimes because of a falling out between Hughes and Hurston over authorship. The dispute ended their long friendship and, in the eyes of some, signaled the end of the golden age of the Harlem Renaissance. In February 1991, Lincoln Center staged the first ever performance of *Mule Bone*.

. . . .

Barnard College
Broadway, between West 116th and West 120th Streets
tel. (212) 854-5262, www.barnard.college.edu

In 1927, Hurston earned a degree in anthropology at Barnard College, where she was the only black student. She continued her studies as a graduate student with Dr. Franz Boas at Columbia University. Hurston was among the first African-American scholars in the field of folklore and anthropology, at a time when racist assumptions about human diversity were being challenged in mainstream academia. She received many scholarships, including a Guggenheim Fellowship, and the unofficial support of patrons such as the popular writer Fannie Hurst. From the "Record of Freshman Interest," a survey given to all incoming Barnard students, Hurston answered in 1925:

"What vocations or professions have you thought of entering? (Mention in order of preference or probability.) — Writing: short story and play, Teaching, Social Work.

Reasons for this choice — I have had some small success as a writer and wish above all else to succeed at it. Either teaching or social work will be interesting but consolation prizes."

The Zora Neale Hurston '28 Lounge in Sulzberger Tower at Barnard honors one of their most illustrious alumni.

. . . .

Former residence
Graham Court Apartments
116th Street at Seventh Avenue

In 1936, Hurston lived here while pursuing her doctorate in anthropology at Columbia University.

Washington Irving
WRITER 1783–1859

F ounder of the first official school of American writers (The Knickerbocker Group), the historian, essayist, and novelist Washington Irving invented much of the mythical life of New York. He nicknamed his hometown Gotham, borrowing from the tales of an English town in which a shrewd population of tricksters throws off authorities and tax collectors by pretending to be insane. In his comic account, *A History of New York*, Irving created Dietrich Knickerbocker and provided another lasting tag for all things New York (including the NBA's Knicks). In his short stories, Irving created some of the first American bogeymen, including the headless horseman of Sleepy Hollow and the marathon sleeper Rip Van Winkle. As a lawyer, international businessman, newspaper reporter, editor, high-profile socializer, and diplomat in London and Madrid, Irving hobnobbed with eminent peers, including Henry Wadsworth Longfellow and Mary Shelley, with whom he was rumored to have had a brief affair. Irving was eminently cosmopolitan and played a major role in shaping the tastes of early Americans. He returned to New York in 1832, where he was beloved and celebrated as the first American writer to have become an international celebrity.

Washington Irving, undated.

Library of Congress Prints and Photographs Division

Colonnade Row (LaGrange Terrace)
428-434 Lafayette Street, between East 4th Street and Astor Place

This part of Lafayette Street, with the Public Theater on one side and Colonnade Row on the other, is a tiny cross section of Irving's Manhattan. Four of the original nine houses built at this address in 1833 survive. The houses were once home to some of the wealthiest New Yorkers, including John Jacob Astor.

Joseph Papp Public Theater
425 Lafayette Street, between East 4th Street and Astor Place
tel. (212) 260-2400, www.publictheater.org

In 1853, this building was home to more than a thousand books when it opened as Astor Library, the nation's first free, non-circulating library. Irving worked here as the institution's first librarian. The building now houses the Joseph Papp Public Theater.

Site of St. Thomas Episcopal Church
Northwest corner of Broadway and West Houston Street

John Jacob Astor's funeral was held here in the spring of 1848. Irving was one of Astor's honorary pallbearers. By the mid-1860s, this vaunted block had fallen into more popular use as a strip of brothels and saloons. The church moved farther uptown, and the Astor family relocated the remains of John Jacob Astor to Trinity Church Cemetery far uptown.

Salmagundi Club
47 Fifth Avenue, between East 11th and East 12th Streets
tel. (212) 255-7740, www.salmagundi.org

This is now the Greenwich Village Society for Historic Preservation and the Salmagundi Club, one of America's oldest arts societies. Irving was an original contributor to the 1807 satire, the *Salmagundi Papers*, after which the society is named. Special exhibitions on the parlor floor are open to the public.

Brevoort Apartments
Northeast corner of Fifth Avenue and 9th Street

A plaque on the 9th Street side of the Brevoort Apartments commemorates Irving's visits to this site in the 1850s when it was 21 Fifth Avenue and the custom-built home of architect James Renwick, Jr. Renwick outfitted his house with a special library for use by his frequent and illustrious guest. The plaque also commemorates Mark Twain, who lived at 21 Fifth Avenue between 1904 and 1908.

Washington Irving House
122 East 17th Street at Irving Place

True to the spirit in which Irving created a mythical life for New York, many places in the city profess connections to Irving that are likewise imaginary. Though this house is known popularly as "Washington Irving House," Irving never actually lived here. His sister lived nearby and Irving was often in this neighborhood, as commemorated by the naming of Irving Place. The developer Samuel B. Ruggles named six blocks of Lexington Avenue south of Gramercy Park in honor of his old friend.

Irving House
11 Commerce Street, between Bedford Street and Seventh Avenue

Another wishful Irving residence—this "Irving House" was the home of Irving's sister, where Irving spent much of his time.

Washington Irving High School
40 Irving Place, between East 16th and East 17th Streets

Friederich Beer sculpted this massive bust of Washington Irving in 1885. Over the years the statue migrated from Central Park, its original home, through Prospect Park and ultimately to this spot, where it was rededicated in 1935.

New-York Historical Society
2 West 77th Street at Central Park West
tel. (212) 873-3400, www.nyhistory.org

The expressive, thoughtful face of Washington Irving is represented here in idealized and idiosyncratic busts, sculptures, and paintings.

Henry James

WRITER 1843–1916

T he child of a rootless family of intellectual celebrities, Henry James was born in New York City, but eventually settled in London, believing that "it takes an old civilization to set a novelist in motion." His slow manner of speech, presumed to be an English affectation, was a willful suppression of a childhood stammer. Edith Wharton, who considered Henry James her "most intimate friend," joked that he spoke as he wrote: in long, looping sentences and lengthy parentheticals. Despite his reputation for formality, he feasted on the absurdities of parochial, local gossip. James devoted much of his fiction to American life, as it operated within the borders of his native Washington Square and as it was expressed by Americans abroad. In books such as *The Age of Innocence*, *The Bostonians*, *Daisy Miller*, and *The Portrait of a Lady*, James depicted people whose passions were constrained by rigid etiquette. In devotion to his adopted country and in protest against the American hesitation to enter the war, James became a British citizen at the outbreak of World War I. After his death, his ashes were returned to the United States, where they are entombed beside those of other eminent family members in Cambridge, Massachusetts.

Henry James, undated.

Library of Congress Prints and Photographs Division

Washington Square Park

From Washington Square North (Waverly Place) to Washington Square South (West 4th Street) and from University Place to MacDougal Street

Public hangings were carried out here until 1819: the accused were hanged from the branches of the oak in the northwest corner of the park, which still casts its shadow as (reputedly) the oldest tree in Manhattan. The executioner and gravedigger lived in traditional exile from good society in a shack at 58 Washington Square South, where an NYU building now stands. Eventually, the marshy burial grounds were filled in, and creeping Minetta Brook was forced underground, paving the way for military parades that began in 1828. The park's grisly past was hard to leave behind—the soft ground, porous with coffins, sometimes collapsed under the weight of cannons.

By the time James published *Washington Square* in 1880, the square was a more genteel setting. He writes:

"I know not whether it is owing to the tenderness of early associations, but this portion of New York appears to many persons the most delectable. It has a kind of established repose which is not of frequent occurrence in other quarters of the long, shrill city; it has a riper, richer, more honorable look than any of the upper ramifications of the great longitudinal thoroughfare—the pull of having had something of a social history."

Site of former residence
27 Washington Place, between Greene Street and Washington Square East

James was born into a house at this address. The original structure was destroyed during James's lifetime; he recorded the effect of its absence in *The American Scene*, a travel account of his visit to the United States in 1904–1905, following a quarter of a century abroad. Encountering the new building that had "ruthlessly suppressed [the] birthhouse on the other side of the Square," James lamented that the new structure had "amputated half [his] history." An NYU building now occupies the site.

Site of James's grandmother's home
18 Washington Square North at Fifth Avenue

The James family left for Europe before Henry had reached his first birthday. Whenever they were in New York, however, he and his brother William James often stayed at 18 Washington Square North, where their grandmother, Elizabeth Walsh, lived. In *Washington Square*, he wrote: "…it was here that your grandmother lived, in venerable solitude, and dispensed a hospitality which commended itself alike to the infant imagination and the infant palate." An NYU building now occupies the site.

William Kidd

PRIVATEER 1645–1701

E mpowered by the English Crown to attack French ships and colonies, Captain William Kidd sailed along smoothly for years, loading his ships with treasure. When a mutinous crew made off with everything, Kidd pursued them to New York, where he remained and married a wealthy widow. Kidd thrived as a well-to-do Manhattanite in a waterfront mansion on what is now Pearl Street, named for its luminescent bed of cracked oyster shells. He became the head of a respectable family, with a country home (in what is now the Upper East Side, 74th Street near the East River), and a pew at Trinity Church, a mark of considerable social prestige. Restless and ambitious, Kidd secured a new commission from King William III in 1695 to hunt pirates. With the blessing of the Crown, looting and raiding its enemies was deemed legal; without it, they were considered acts of piracy. In New York, Kidd assembled a crew of desperate men, including several known pirates, and spent the next few years capturing and emptying ships off the coasts of India and Madagascar. During his absence, his powerful allies spoiled his reputation with the Crown, which hanged him for acts of piracy in 1701.

. . . .

Site of former residences
86-90 Pearl Street, between Coenties Alley and Hanover Square
119-21 Pearl Street at State Street

When Kidd lived on Pearl Street it was known as River Road, the fashionable water's edge of the city. He and his wife owned property at what is now 86-90 and at 119-21 Pearl Street, and were neighbors to some of the most powerful figures in early New York. Kidd's house was a more spacious version of the Dutch-style houses facing the water on Pearl Street. Throughout the settlement in Lower Manhattan rose the steeply pitched roofs of these traditional houses, many of them fronted with glazed red and

Captain William Kidd, undated.

CAPT' KIDD

yellow Flanders tiles. As was common, Kidd's house had a six-foot stoop to keep the house clear of rising water. The house had a view of New York Harbor, and Kidd certainly would have gazed out his window to watch his crewless ship ticking back and forth in the choppy waters. As the city expanded beyond its natural borders onto landfill—the local government began selling "water lots" in the East River to underwrite building projects—Pearl Street eventually fell behind the successive streets advancing out into the water.

....

Trinity Church
Broadway at Wall Street
tel. (212)602-0800, www.trinitywallstreet.org

The Trinity Church at which Kidd worshiped was built in 1698 and expanded in 1737, before being destroyed by fires that leapt through Lower Manhattan during the British retreat of 1776. The current church was built upon the foundation of an earlier building and was consecrated on May 12, 1846. Inside, the dark pews of the chapel are marked with bronze plaques that memorialize many generations of patrons. Outside, the churchyard contains the remains of Alexander Hamilton, John Jacob Astor IV, and many others. The weathered tombstones list slightly in the trimmed yard.

....

Former Kidd real estate
56 Wall Street at Hanover Street

Wall Street was built on the site of a fence of sharpened wooden logs erected by the Dutch to keep out the British and the Indians. The wall stood for forty-six years until the British colonists took it down in 1699. Kidd and his family never lived at this address, but it turned out to be a shrewd real estate investment from which Kidd made a tidy profit—still the major preoccupation of investors in the neighborhood.

Jacob Lawrence

ARTIST 1917–2000

Jacob Lawrence's series of paintings—*Migration of the Negro*—was purchased jointly by the Museum of Modern Art and the Phillips Collection in Washington, DC, when Lawrence was only twenty-four years old. The sights and sounds of his childhood in Harlem formed his aesthetic. He recorded African-American history—both epic moments in the lives of its towering figures and otherwise invisible moments in the lives of ordinary people. Lawrence believed that in art "the human subject is the most important thing." His genius was in isolating details: a blood-red footprint in the snow, the wind lifting a curtain in Frederick Douglass's study. Lawrence captured critical moments from historical memory, making the past full of immediate consequence. Relying on color, complex geometries, and total attention to the human subject, Lawrence painted narratives of events such as the life of Harriet Tubman, Toussaint L'Ouverture's victory in Haiti, and the Great Migration of African-Americans out of the South.

....

Site of Utopia Children's House
170 West 130th Street, between Adam Clayton Powell Jr. Boulevard and Lenox Avenue

Lawrence's mother, who had left the South in pursuit of greater safety and opportunity, struggled alone to support her children in New York. She enrolled Lawrence in Utopia House, the after-school arts program where he met his mentor, Charles Alston, then a student at Columbia University. Years later, Alston recalled how the discovery of Lawrence's originality and talent—Lawrence was only ten at the time—prompted him to keep Lawrence apart and thus free from influence of the styles of his teachers and peers.

Schomburg Center for Research in Black Culture
515 Malcolm X Boulevard, between West 135th and West 136th Streets
tel. (212) 491-2200, www.nypl.org

After Lawrence dropped out of high school in order to work to support his mother and siblings, he continued his studies on his own at this library. In 1932, he trained here with Charles Alston when the library housed the Works Progress Administration Harlem Art Workshop, and researched his narrative series, *The Life of Toussaint L'Ouverture*, which he completed in 1938. Lawrence returned here to research his later series, *The Migration of the Negro* and *Struggle…From the History of the American People*.

Apollo Theater
253 West 125th Street, between St Nicholas Avenue and Frederick Douglass Boulevard
tel. (212) 531-5300, www.apollotheater.com

After Lawrence moved with his mother and siblings to Harlem from Atlantic City, New Jersey, he recalled, "Going to the Apollo Theater was a ritual of ours." In 1951, he began a series exploring the life of people on the stage, inspired by productions at the Apollo and by vaudeville. Lawrence was a teenager in 1934 when the Apollo, formerly a whites-only establishment, opened its doors to integrated audiences.

Abyssinian Baptist Church
132 Odell Clark Place (West 138th Street), between Lenox Avenue and Adam Clayton Powell Jr. Boulevard
tel. (212) 862-7474, www.abyssinian.org

In his youth, Lawrence attended services and Sunday school here. He listened to sermons delivered by Adam Clayton Powell, Jr., and in 1933 received a church honor for his painting of the life of the Apostle Peter.

Site of Harlem Art Workshop
306 West 141st Street, between Bradhurst Avenue and Frederick Douglass Boulevard

Here, in the mid-1930s, the adult Lawrence continued to paint with Alston and the artist Gwendolyn Knight, whom he would marry and with whom he would spend the rest of his life. The developments in the Harlem arts world during the Depression were discussed and debated in "306," whose members included Ralph Ellison, Romare Bearden, and Richard Wright. Lawrence rented studio space in "306" and exhibited his early work here. Alston, Lawrence, and other painters at "306" were influenced by socialist artists like the Mexican muralist Diego Rivera. Alston had watched Rivera at work on his Rockefeller Center mural, which was destroyed within a year for its heroic depiction of Lenin.

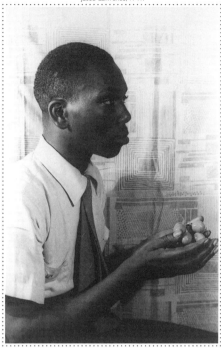
Jacob Lawrence, 1941.

Harlem YMCA

180 West 135th Street, between Adam Clayton Powell Jr. Boulevard and Lenox Avenue
tel. (212) 281-4100, www.ymcanyc.org/harlem

In February of 1938, Lawrence had his first solo exhibition here, which was underwritten by the James Weldon Johnson Literary Guild.

Former residence

33 West 125th Street, between Lenox and Fifth Avenues

Lawrence moved into an unheated apartment in this building in 1940. He paid $8 a month in rent and shared the building with other artists, including Romare Bearden and Claude McKay.

Former residence

72 Hamilton Terrace, between West 141st Street and West 144th Street

Lawrence and his wife moved here in 1942. They were settled for only a year before Lawrence was inducted into the US Coast Guard. In 1944, he was assigned to the first racially integrated ship in the history of the US Navy. Lawrence painted scenes of naval life during his tour, and in October 1944, his Coast Guard paintings were exhibited together with the *Migration* series at the Museum of Modern Art.

New York in Transit mural

Times Square subway station

This mural depicts life in New York as if watched through subway windows: artists, shoppers, and workers stand and sit together, their bags full of papers, produce, and tools. It is one of Lawrence's last commissioned public works. Lawrence's wife, artist Gwendolyn Knight Lawrence, supervised the fabrication of the glass mosaic in Murano, Italy after her husband's death. The mural is installed over the steps that lead passengers down from the shuttle platform towards the N/Q/R/W subway lines.

Studio Museum of Harlem
144 West 125th Street, between Lenox Avenue and Adam Clayton Powell Jr. Boulevard
tel. (212) 864-4500, www.studiomuseum.org

Founded in 1968, the Studio Museum of Harlem promotes work by artists of African descent and, more generally, national and international works that reflect African and African-American influence. In 1979, the collection moved into its current home, donated by the New York Bank for Savings. In 2004, the museum underwent extensive renovations, including the addition of 3,000 square feet of exhibition space for the permanent collection, which includes works by Jacob Lawrence.

The Metropolitan Museum of Art
1000 Fifth Avenue at East 82nd Street
tel. (212) 535-7710, www.metmuseum.org

In the permanent collection here is Lawrence's painting *Pool Parlor*, for which he won an award at the museum's 1942 "Artists for Victory" exhibition.

Museum of Modern Art (MoMA)
11 West 53rd Street, between Fifth and Sixth Avenues
tel. (212) 708-9400, www.moma.org

MoMA purchased the even-numbered panels of Lawrence's *Migration of the Negro*. Also in the collection is Lawrence's *Street Shadows* (1959).

Emma Lazarus

POET AND ACTIVIST 1849–1887

"Send these, the homeless, tempest-tost to me, I lift my lamp beside the golden door!"

E mma Lazarus is best known for her poem, "The New Colossus," which is inscribed on the pedestal at the base of the Statue of Liberty. At a time when political activism was not expected from young women born, as Lazarus was, into New York's upper class, she became an advocate of Jewish immigrants and committed herself to defending what she called the "colossal experiment" of the United States. She came of age writing poetry and studying English, Greek, French, and German literature in the private library of her father, a prosperous sugar refiner, who published his daughter's first collection of poems when she was seventeen. Having abandoned the strict religious observance of the extended Lazarus clan, who were members of the Sephardic Jewish community, Emma's family focused their social energies in elitist strongholds such as the Union Club, the Newport summer-house circuit, and the Knickerbocker Club, of which her father was a founding member. By the time Lazarus reached adulthood, however, such private clubs, hotels, and professional associations had instituted policies that excluded Jews. Angered by this betrayal by her country and moved by the plight of impoverished Jewish immigrants fleeing Eastern Europe and Russia, Lazarus devoted her writing and her time to aiding immigrants and defending the rights of the Jewish community. She was a talented linguist, and translated the German Jewish poet Heinrich Heine and the work of medieval Spanish Jewish scholars from Hebrew. She also wrote essays, commentary, and a novel imagining the formative scenes in the early life of Goethe; and she corresponded with poetic elders Emerson, Browning, and Longfellow. Joking that her society friends would be shocked to find her there, Lazarus spent much of her time on Ward's Island aiding Russian immigrants.

Emma Lazarus, ca. 1878–1900.

Library of Congress Prints and Photographs Division

Statue of Liberty
Liberty Island
tel. (212) 363-3200, www.nps.gov/stli

Lazarus published "The New Colossus" in 1883 to raise money for a pedestal to support the Statue of Liberty. The statue, "Liberty Enlightening the World," was planned as a gift from France. Lady Liberty's torch-bearing arm arrived in Philadelphia in 1876. Curious visitors could climb inside the massive arm and wind their way up steep stairs to the torch. Sculptor Frederic-Auguste Bartholdi hoped that this and other special exhibitions (her head was displayed at the Paris World's Fair in 1878) would excite the Amercian and French publics into donating money. The statue was completed in July 1884. Americans were expected to match France's contribution by providing a dignified pedestal, but they proved to be unenthusiastic patrons at first. Newspaperman Joseph Pulitzer almost single-handedly raised the funds by promising to print the names of every single donor on the front page of *The New York World*. By the late nineteenth century, the Statue of Liberty had evolved from a symbol of French-American friend-ship into the beacon sought by immigrants as they entered New York Harbor. In 1903, officials mounted a bronze plaque bearing Lazarus's poem:

The air-bridged harbor that twin cities frame.
"Keep ancient lands, your storied pomp!" cries she
With silent lips. "Give me your tired, your poor,
Your huddled masses yearning to breathe free."

JFK Airport, International Terminal
JFK Expressway
Jamaica Bay, Queens
tel. (718) 244-4444, www.kennedyairport.com

The present busy port of entry for immigrants to the United States arriving in New York, the International Terminal at JFK Airport bears the words of the "New Colossus."

The Jewish Museum
1109 Fifth Avenue at 92nd Street
tel. (212) 423-3200, www.thejewishmuseum.org

The Jewish Museum houses one of the world's largest collections of Jewish art and ar-tefacts. The collection has been in its current location in the former Warburg mansion across from Central Park since 1947.

The Center for Jewish History
15 West 16th Street, between Fifth and Sixth Avenues
tel. 212 294-8301, www.cjh.org

Lazarus's handwritten original copy of "The New Colossus" is among the relics in the center's permanent collection.

Sephardic Shearith Israel
99 Central Park West at West 70th Street
www.shearith-israel.org

Lazarus's extended family had long belonged to the Shearith Israel, the only Jewish con-gregation in New York City between 1654 and 1825. The congregation was founded by two dozen men and women who had fled Recife, Brazil, when the Portuguese (and the Inquisition) took control of the region. Governor Stuyvesant made life difficult for the fledgling community, but they persevered and eventually gained a comfortable status within the upper class of early New York. Members of Shearith Israel participated in the founding of the New York Stock Exchange and fought in the Revolutionary War.

In 1897, the congregation settled in its current location. Objects and furnishings from the original Mill Street synagogue of 1730 connect generations of worshippers to one another and to the history of the city: the two millstones, now located at the entrance, once milled grain in colonial New York on the eponymously named street (now South William Street). "The Little Synagogue" at the present location is furnished with the reader's desk, railing, candlesticks, a tablet of the Ten Commandments, benches, and Sabbath lamp from the Mill Street synagogue.

Site of former residence
36 West 14th Street, between Fifth and Sixth Avenues

Lazarus's childhood home, where she studied assiduously in her father's library, once stood on this spot.

. . . .

Former residence
18 West 10th Street, between Fifth and Sixth Avenues

This 1856 house was once the home of Lazarus. A plaque honors her as a "poet, essayist and humanitarian."

John Lennon
MUSICIAN 1940–1980

J ohn Lennon grew up in Liverpool, England—his father abandoned the family three years after Lennon's birth, and his mother was struck down in 1958 by an off-duty policeman driving drunk. Following years of truancy, Lennon, then living with an aunt, enrolled at Liverpool Art College where he formed the Quarrymen in 1957; the band eventually became the Beatles. With Paul McCartney, Lennon was the main singer and songwriter. After the dissolution of the Beatles in 1970, Lennon began a new life with his wife, the artist Yoko Ono, in New York City, which he loved as the "new Rome" and the "toy box." In his later years, Lennon was the contra-pop icon—a peace activist, political contrarian, riler of talk show hosts, gadfly, and composer, who used his celebrity in muscular and radical ways. Fans and the press were sometimes put off by Lennon's stunts but to the end he was a sincere and moody champion of peace. In the midst of the success of his album "Double Fantasy," Lennon was murdered outside his apartment building by a deranged fan, whose copy of the album he had autographed hours before.

. . . .

Dakota Apartments
1 West 72nd Street at Central Park West

John Lennon and Yoko Ono spent artistically and domestically fruitful years here, in upper apartments overlooking Central Park. The building is morbidly famous as the site of Lennon's murder on December 8, 1980.

Built in 1884, the Dakota was the city's first apartment building designed with luxurious living and social exclusivity in mind; previously apartments had been living places for those who could not afford a private home. The imposing chateau-inspired apartment house towered over acres of old-growth trees, a wilderness in the minds of Lower Manhattanites. Newspapers of the time mocked the far-flung architectural folly, so remote that it might as well be in the Dakota territories. Doubters were soon traveling north away from the crowds and expensive land downtown. The Dakota led, in part, to the building boom that finally drew rapid transit and New Yorkers north of West 50th Street.

. . . .

Strawberry Fields
Enter Central Park at West 72nd Street and Central Park West

Named for the Beatles song, the triangular memorial to John Lennon begins at the park entrance across from the Dakota. A round mosaic, donated by Naples, Italy, and a re-

production of a mosaic from Pompeii, encompass the word "IMAGINE." The mosaic is usually strewn with flowers and lit by candles, and is visited by people from around the world. A symbolic garden of peaceful coexistence, it contains more than 160 species of plants and flowers.

St. Regis Hotel

2 East 55th Street at Fifth Avenue
tel. (212) 753-4500, www.stregis.com

John Lennon and Yoko Ono's first address in New York. They lived on the seventeenth floor before living briefly in a sublet at 105 Bank Street.

Ear Inn

326 Spring Street, between Greenwich and Washington Streets
tel. (212) 226-9060

Lennon liked to meet friends in this cozy pub where, in the nineteenth century, sailors on liberty ambled in from the water's edge. Dunes and wetlands predominated when James Brown, believed to be an ex-slave and a soldier in the Revolutionary War, built this house in 1817. The neighborhood had flourished and tanked repeatedly through the decades and was desolate in 1973 when students and artists rented upstairs rooms in the landmark James Brown House. They began making repairs and taking inventory of centuries of detritus in the house and cellar. They eventually bought the derelict house and altered the "Bar Inn" sign to "Ear Inn" to mark a fresh start for the building. Antique liquor and medicine bottles, found in the cellar of the building, sit on top of the bar. The Ear Inn drew artists such as John Lennon, Salvador Dalí, and Allen Ginsberg, all of whom became regulars, sometimes sleeping in the upstairs rooms. A painted line on the side of the Ear Inn marks the pre-landfill waterline of the Hudson, when the building was a dockside pub and brothel for sailors.

Abraham Lincoln

US PRESIDENT 1809–1865

P ortraits of the sixteenth president almost always emphasize his famously lugubrious physiognomy: stooped, rumpled, and melancholy. Audiences who attended his lectures and speeches remarked with surprise and delight that once Lincoln spoke, his clouded face suddenly lit with a passion, wit, and enthusiasm that made him among the most charismatic speakers of the age. In youth, Lincoln "the rail splitter" awed all with his physical strength. His reputation for fairness earned him the nickname "Honest Abe," but it was his ambition, his odd charm, and his talent for persuasion that ensured his success as a lawyer and politician. As president, Lincoln dealt the fatal blows to the institution of slavery. On the first day of 1863, he signed the Emancipation Proclamation and later in the same year he delivered the Gettysburg Address at a dedication ceremony for the battlefield's cemetery. On April 14, 1865, in the waning days of the Civil War, Abraham and his wife Mary Todd Lincoln settled in their box at Ford's Theater in Washington, DC to watch the play *Our American Cousin*. The actor John Wilkes Booth, younger brother of the celebrity Edwin Booth, crashed in behind them during the play and shot and killed Lincoln to avenge the humiliated Confederacy.

Cooper Union

7 East 7th Street at Cooper Square
tel. (212) 353-4100, www.cooper.edu

Lincoln's address in the Great Hall in the basement of this building on February 27, 1860 made him a serious contender for the Republican presidential nomination. Lincoln was opposed to slavery in all states, but he gained broad support by putting forth a "reasonable" compromise: slavery would not be abolished where it existed nor would it be extended to free states.

An audience member recorded his impression of Lincoln: "When Lincoln rose to speak,

I was greatly disappointed. He was tall, tall,—oh, how tall! and so angular and awkward that I had, for an instant, a feeling of pity for so ungainly a man." Then, as Lincoln addressed the crowd, "his face lighted up as with an inward fire; the whole man was transfigured. I forgot his clothes, his personal appearance, and his individual peculiarities. Presently, forgetting myself, I was on my feet like the rest, yelling like a wild Indian, cheering this wonderful man."

Abraham Lincoln photographed by Mathew Brady before his Cooper Union speech, 1860.

Library of Congress Prints and Photographs Division

Former St. Denis Hotel
Southwest corner of East 11th Street and Broadway

Abraham and Mary Todd Lincoln stayed at the St. Denis Hotel as guests on trips to New York. Two years after Lincoln's assassination, Mrs. Lincoln returned to New York and stayed here once again. The widowed former first lady was on a mission to sell clothes and jewelry for desperately needed cash, but she was taken in by con men. Planning to profit from the sale of authentic Lincoln items, her contacts stole everything, and she reaped only public embarrassment from the incident. The building is now home to offices and retail shops.

New-York Historical Society
2 West 77th Street at Central Park West
tel. (212) 873-3400, www.nyhistory.org

The New-York Historical Society has several images and sculptures of Lincoln on display. Some of the most unusual are the colossal clay head of Lincoln used as the model for the Lincoln Memorial in Washington DC; a maquette of an earlier version of the memorial, in which Lincoln stands, his hands clasped comfortably; and bronze casts of Lincoln's face and hands.

Brooks Brothers
Several locations in Manhattan
tel. (212) 267-2400, www.brooksbrothers.com

When Lincoln was assassinated, he was wearing a Brooks Brothers coat, which had been created for him only a few weeks earlier in honor of his second inauguration. It was made of fine wool, lined in silk, and hand-stitched with the image of an American eagle holding a banner that read "One Country, One Destiny." After Lincoln's death, his widow gave the coat to her husband's footman, Alphonse Donn, who reputedly rejected P. T. Barnum's offer of $20,000 for it. A later generation sold the coat to the Lincoln Museum in the basement of Ford's Theater.

Brooks Brothers, America's oldest clothier, was founded in New York in 1818 on the busy waterfront near Cherry and Catherine Streets in present-day South Street Seaport. During Lincoln's time, it was located on the corner of Broadway and Grand Street. Brooks Brothers supplied uniforms for Union soldiers, and was among the first establishments ransacked during the draft riots in 1863. Today, branches are located at 1 Liberty Plaza between Broadway and Cortland Street, 346 Madison Avenue at 44th Street, and 666 Fifth Avenue at 53rd Street.

City Hall
City Hall Park, between Broadway and Park Row

Mourners lined miles of track as the train bearing Lincoln's body headed for New York. The casket and funeral entourage stopped first in Jersey City, where the clocks had been stopped to the hour of the President's death, and continued across the Hudson River by ferry to a landing at Debrosses Street. On April 24, 1865 the body of Lincoln lay in state on a black dais under the rotunda of City Hall. According to newspaper reports, 500,000 people waited in line to view the President's body. Before a City Hall draped in black and under a large sign proclaiming "THE NATION MOURNS," grieving New Yorkers crowded adjoining City Hall Park.

Irene Hayes Wadley & Smythe Le Moult
1 Rockefeller Plaza
(212) 247-0051, www.irenehayes.com

Irene Hayes (the expanded moniker reflects the acquisition of several flower shops over the decades) supplied the flowers for Lincoln's funeral cortège.

Robert Mapplethorpe
PHOTOGRAPHER 1946–1989

R obert Mapplethorpe was born in Floral Park, Queens, into a conservative, tightly knit family. His father, a devout Catholic, discouraged early signs of his son's talent, stressing the practice of Catholicism as the antidote to artistic decadence. Though his father's efforts to inhibit Mapplethorpe's artistic ambitions were unsuccessful, the rites and symbols of the Church figured prominently in Mapplethorpe's work. Mapplethorpe left Long Island, where he was a member of the Reserve Officers Training Corps honor society, to attend Pratt Institute. Soon after earning his BFA, Mapplethorpe began exploring photography as a way of incorporating Polaroid self-portraits into paintings and collages. He became a staff photographer for Andy Warhol's *Interview* magazine, though he continued to work on self-portraits and portraits of others, most notably the poet, singer, and artist Patti Smith, with whom he lived. As Mapplethorpe relied more on photography as his sole means of making art, he moved on to large format cameras and expanded his portraiture to include friends, artists, outcasts, and sex workers, frequently selecting extreme subject matter in search of the outer boundaries of art. His homoerotic and sadomasochistic photographs made him the target of broad censorship. Before his death, Mapplethorpe established a foundation in his name; the foundation continues his efforts to promote photography and provide support to HIV/AIDS research.

Chelsea Hotel

222 West 23rd Street, between Seventh and Eighth Avenues
tel. (212) 243-3700, www.hotelchelsea.com

Mapplethorpe and Patti Smith lived here together during the raucous heyday of the

Robert Mapplethorpe, self-portrait, 1980.

hotel in the 1970s. Members of the Andy Warhol contingent were residents, as were Janis Joplin, William Burroughs, and many other transient artists, musicians, and celebrities. While living here, Mapplethorpe photographed Smith for the cover of her first album, *Horses*. The album cover is iconic of the age: Smith before a blank wall in a slant of sunlight, wearing a man's tie and hooking a jacket over her shoulder. The photograph was taken in a friend's empty apartment at One Fifth Avenue, which Mapplethorpe had been using as a temporary studio. Never before had a female singer appeared unsmiling, disheveled, and without makeup on the cover of a successful album, and the record company tried hard to dissuade Smith from using the cover, offering to rephotograph her with a bouffant hairdo. She declined.

Site of Max's Kansas City
213 Park Avenue South, between East 17th and East 18th Streets
www.maxskansascity.com

Soon after its opening in 1965, Max's Kansas City became the hub of pop art and affiliated scenes. Unknowns Mapplethorpe and Smith hung out on the curb outside and in the bar hoping to get in with the Warhol crowd, which ruled the back room. The tables turned when Smith played the first of many shows here in 1973.

Former residence
24 Bond Street, between Lafayette Street and the Bowery

Mapplethorpe lived and worked in an apartment and studio in this building in the 1980s. The building is, incidentally, also home to the Eulenspiegal Society, a social club and educational center dedicated to sadomasochism.

F.A.O. Schwarz
767 Fifth Avenue at East 58th Street
tel. (212) 644-9400, www.fao.com

Mapplethorpe worked here as a window designer—briefly—when the store was located across the street at 745 Fifth Avenue. Frederick Schwarz, an immigrant from Germany, founded the toy store in 1862.

Solomon R. Guggenheim Museum
1071 Fifth Avenue at East 89th Street
tel. (212) 423-3500, www.guggenheim.org

In 1993, a gift from the Robert Mapplethorpe Foundation established the Robert Mapplethorpe Gallery and helped to found the Guggenheim Museum's photography department. The largest single collection of Mapplethorpe's work is at the Guggenheim Museum. Highlights include *Ken and Tyler* (1985); *Calla Lily* (1986); and *Self-Portrait* (1988).

Harpo Marx
ENTERTAINER 1888–1964

S alvador Dalí presented Harpo Marx with a harp strung with barbed wire; it was a surrealist token of admiration for Harpo's brilliant, wordless, comic contribution to the Marx Brothers. Harpo and his three brothers grew up in an affectionate, crowded, and impoverished immigrant family on New York's Upper East Side. While Harpo's father, a tailor, took care of the cooking and cleaning, his ambitious mother charged out into the world promoting her sons in show business. Marx left school at the age of eight and spent his time either hustling on the street or hanging out with his grandfather. In 1908, the brothers' vaudeville act, The Three Nightingales, grew to Four Nightingales when young Harpo joined them onstage for the first time. He experimented with small speaking roles early on but discovered his comic genius as the physically expressive, mute foil to his brothers. The Marx Brothers appeared in the first of thirteen films in 1929 in *The Cocoanuts*, based on their successful Broadway play. Harpo played Silent Sam. The Marx Brothers came to great Broadway success in 1924 with *I'll Say She Is*, which the cynical drama critic Alexander Woollcott hailed as the funniest evening in the history of his theatergoing. In his review of the play, Woollcott recommended it as a "splendacious and reasonably tuneful excuse for going to see that silent brother, that shy, unexpected, magnificent comic among the Marxes, who is recorded somewhere on a birth certificate as Arthur [sic] but who is known to the adoring two-a-day as Harpo Marx. Surely there should be dancing in the streets when a great clown comic comes to town, and this man is a great clown."

Harpo Marx on his Bar Mitzvah day, 1901.

Photo courtesy of William Marx

Former residence

179 East 93rd Street, between Third and Lexington Avenues

This section of the Upper East Side, Yorkville, was a small Jewish neighborhood boxed in by larger Irish and German areas when Marx lived here with his four brothers, a cousin, parents, and grandparents, from 1895 to 1910. Cousins, aunts, and uncles dropped in often to share in the meals that Marx's father made from meager supplies. His father cut cloth on the dining room table all day, and bundled up his needles and thread and patterns every night to lay dinner on the table.

Tammany Hall politicians sent a well-appointed hansom cab to this address each election day, to deliver Marx's father and grandfather to the polls—sometimes three times in a single day. On those nights, Tammany Hall distributed free beer and firecrackers, and children, who had hoarded flammable scraps in their basements, built great bonfires in the streets throughout Manhattan. Firemen and trucks raced through the chaos of firecrackers and drunken crowds to extinguish the blazes.

Central Park

From Central Park South (59th Street) to Central Park North (110th Street) and from Fifth Avenue to Central Park West (Eighth Avenue)

In the Upper East Side at the turn of the last century, Irish, Italian, German, and Jewish neighborhoods were clearly delineated. Marx had to bribe the boys of surrounding neighborhoods with a "dead tennis ball, an empty thread spool, a penny" for safe passage through "foreign blocks." Marx spent a lot of his time in Central Park, a neutral zone, watching the players on the tennis courts, occasionally snagging a stray ball for his collection. In winter, he waited for the Ice Flag to be flown over Central Park, so that he could skate. His family owned only one ice skate, so Marx became in his words "the best single-foot skater in New York City."

Algonquin Hotel

59 West 44th Street, between Fifth and Sixth Avenues
tel. (212) 840-6800, www.algonquinhotel.com

Marx was a core member of the Algonquin Round Table. He was a regular at meetings of the Algonquin's "Thanatopsis Inside Straight and Literary Club," the Round Table's weekly poker game. His elder brother Groucho called the Algonquin an "intellectual slaughterhouse."

Palace Theater

1564 Broadway, between West 46th and West 47th Streets

Every actor in vaudeville dreamed of playing the Palace, and its shuttering in 1932 was seen by many as the death knell of vaudeville. The Marx Brothers appeared here in 1915 in *Home Again*. The Palace became a movie theater until its renovation in 1951.

Former residence

87-48 134th Street, between 89th and Jamaica Avenues
Richmond Hill, Queens

The Marx Brothers lived in this house during their Broadway success in the 1920s. A plaque on the house commemorates the famous brothers' days here, and the house is a featured stop on the East Richmond Hill Walking Tour sponsored by the Richmond Hill Historical Society.

Herman Melville

I n 1891, *The New York Times* alone noted the death of "the author of…sea-faring tales, written in earlier years." Within the week, the *Times* eulogized him at greater length: "*There has died and been buried in this city, during the current week, at an advanced age, a man who is so little known, even by name, to the generation now in the vigor of life that only one newspaper contained an obituary account, and this was but of three or four lines. Yet forty years ago the appearance of a new book by Herman Melville was esteemed a literary event, not only throughout his own country, but so far as the English-speaking race extended.*"

From early life, Herman Melville was both a beneficiary and victim of his mother's social ambitions. He attended the best schools and lived in a succession of ever finer Manhattan houses, until Allan Melvill's (Herman's mother later added the final "e" because she believed it suggested refinement) business failed, forcing the family to the remote outpost of Albany. Young Melville escaped by finding work on whaling ships. He jumped ship in the Marqueses and spent a year among the Typee, whose rumored cannibalism thrilled New Yorkers. Melville's accounts of his adventurous, apparently happy, years at sea became bestsellers (*Typee* and *Omoo*). Controversial and intensely popular, Melville entered the literary salons of New York in 1847 on the heels of Edgar Allan Poe. Despite the considerable success of his novels, Melville struggled to support his wife and children, unhappily churning out more adventure books. Describing himself as "damned by dollars," Melville wrote *Moby Dick*, which turned out to be a commercial and critical flop. Disenchanted and increasingly dependent on his wife's unimpressed family, Melville worked for two decades as a clerk for the New York Customs House.

. . . .

Site of former residence

6 Pearl Street, between State Street and Broadway

Melville was born in the house that once stood on this site.

. . . .

Site of former residence

104 East 26th Street, between Park Avenue South and Lexington Avenue

Melville spent his last twenty-eight years here. The intersection of East 26th Street and Park Avenue South was named Herman Melville Square in honor of the author's long residence in a yellow brick house, which has since been replaced by the building adjacent to the 69th Regiment Armory at 68 Lexington Avenue.

. . . .

Gansevoort Market Area

From Ninth Avenue to the Hudson River and from Gansevoort to West 14th Streets

After the Revolutionary War, New York City renamed this market district to honor General Peter Gansevoort, hero of the Revolution and the maternal grandfather of the future Herman Melville. The family connection continued many decades later, when Melville found work here as an outdoor customs inspector, a post he held for twenty years. He spent his days in his office at 507 West Street and his evenings at home writing.

In the 1840s, Greenwich Village remained mostly the domain of rural farmhouses, though busy markets had begun to spring up near the water. By 1900, the docks and warehouses were dominated by slaughterhouses and meatpacking plants. Carcass-lugging workers can still be seen delivering fresh meat to local merchants and restaurants. Though the neighborhood has never been kinder to diners and evening strollers, its long history as a shipping dock and meat-processing zone remains an aesthetic and olfactory force. Strangely angled streets opening onto cobblestone squares, creaking metal awnings overhanging broad dark sidewalks, hulking warehouses, abandoned piers, and the absence of normal traffic—all give the neighborhood the atmosphere of an old industrial city.

As the sea-bound narrator of *Moby Dick* walks the shore of Manhattoes [sic], he sees: *"Posted like silent sentinels all around the town, stand thousands upon thousands of mortal men fixed in ocean reveries. Some leaning against the spiles; some seated upon the pierheads; some looking over the bulwarks of ships from China; some high aloft in the rigging, as if striving to get a still better seaward peep. But these are landsman; of week days pent up in lath and plaster—tied to counters, nailed to benches, clinched to desks."*

Herman Melville, 1885.

Private collection

The Museum of the City of New York

1220 Fifth Avenue at East 103rd Street
tel. (212) 534-1672, www.mcny.org

Melville crewed aboard whaleships, battle frigates, clipper ships, steamboats, and other commercial vessels. The maritime world of Melville's New York can be visited in an ongoing exhibit of the city's shipping history on the second floor of the museum. Detailed dioramas show the bustle of South Street Seaport and the East River in miniature. Also on display are relics from Manhattan's sail-powered days—spiked iron whaling hooks, figureheads, and the wooden head of Andrew Jackson that once stared out from the prow of the ship, "Old Ironsides."

Grace Church
800-804 Broadway at East 10th Street
tel. (212) 254-2000, www.gracechurchnyc.org

In 1848, with the financial help of his brother-in-law, Melville moved his family into 103 Fourth Avenue, then a townhouse across from Grace Church. Melville had an intense distaste for social ambition and status, both of which were conspicuous features of the elite congregation of Grace Church in the mid-nineteenth century. In letters to friends, Melville complained about the oppressive proximity of the church and the fashionable socializing that took over the neighborhood on Sundays.

Designed by James Renwick, Jr. and built upon the cornerstone of the original Grace Church in Lower Manhattan, the church is a small-scale gothic structure, edged by private gardens, a school, and parish buildings. Grace Church started simply, but its patrons and donors over the years have sponsored stained-glass windows, stonework, and other embellishments that have resulted in an ornate exterior of ash-gray stone.

Snug Harbor Cultural Center
914-1000 Richmond Terrace, between Tysen Street and Kissel Avenue
New Brighton, Staten Island
tel. (718) 448-2500, www.snug-harbor.org

Like his older brother Herman, Thomas Melville spent much of his life at sea. The brothers sailed together on Thomas's ship, the *Meteor*, traveling around Cape Horn to San Francisco as part of a three-year lecture circuit that Herman Melville undertook in 1857. Ten years later, Thomas Melville retired to land living and settled on Staten Island as the administrator of Sailors' Snug Harbor, where Herman Melville was often his visitor. During his seventeen-year tenure, Thomas Melville became the most despised administrator in the history of the sailors' retirement home.

In 1801, heirless Robert Richard Randall had asked his lawyer, Alexander Hamilton, to redraft his will to provide for the establishment of a home for "aged, decrepit and worn-out seamen" on Randall's family farm. Fifteen years after Randall's death, the value of the land—which included present-day Washington Square Park—had already doubled in value. Fearing the displeasure of well-to-do residents if the neighborhood were infiltrated by decrepit seamen and worried that the sailors would be "exposed to many temptations" in Manhattan, the New York Supreme Court allowed the retirement center to open on Staten Island in 1831.

Within the high stone walls of Snug Harbor, worn-out sailors strolled elegant grounds and lived in a row of handsome Greek Revival buildings. For their leisure (and edification), sailors had use of beautifully equipped reading rooms—an innovation based on the new notion that convalescent or retired people required books, activities, and interests in order to maintain good health.

In the main hall, now a museum and art gallery, are maritime details meant to put lifelong sailors at ease on land. The domed ceiling contains a colorful mural of ships, swells, and mystical sea creatures. Orienting constellations, such as Orion, glimmer in white on panels of deep blue glass. Also abundant are comforting sayings: "Port After Stormy Seas"; "The Cross is my Anchor"; "Rest After Dangerous Toil."

Snug Harbor is now a collection of maritime museums, an antique rose garden, a hedge maze, art galleries, and a Chinese Scholar's Garden, all set within eighty-three acres of waterfront property.

Woodlawn Cemetery

Entrances: East 233rd Street at Webster Avenue; Jerome Avenue north of Bainbridge Avenue
Woodlawn, The Bronx
tel. (718) 920-0500

Melville is buried here. His tombstone is a four-foot slab of stone sunk in a bed of ivy and engraved with a plume stylus resting on a blank scroll of paper. Visitors paying their respects leave rocks, coins, and pencils on the top of his gravestone.

Edna St. Vincent Millay, 1933.

Library of Congress Prints and Photographs Division

Edna St. Vincent Millay

POET 1892–1950

Famous from an early age, Edna St. Vincent Millay was said to mesmerize listeners with the rich timbre of her voice, and her poetry readings drew the largest audience of any American woman of her generation. In 1923, she became the first woman to be awarded the Pulitzer Prize for poetry, and her books remained bestsellers throughout the Great Depression. She was among the first bohemian celebrity residents of Greenwich Village, where she wrote, acted in the Provincetown Players, and burned "the candle at both ends"—a phrase she invented. Men and women confessed to her, to each other, and to their diaries that they had been desperately in love with the pale, slight redhead from the instant she spoke. True to the free love ideal of early Greenwich Village, Millay had affairs with men and women throughout her life, and throughout her later marriage to Eugen Boissevain (whom she said she loved most "after poetry"). In 1925, Millay and Boissevain started spending most of their time at their home in Austerlitz, New York, where the couple wrote and sank, in the end, into alcohol and morphine addiction. Millay fell to her death from the top of the stairs, a year after Eugen's death.

Former residence
75-1/2 Bedford Street, between Morton and Commerce Streets

Millay lived here with Boissevain in 1924 and 1925. They paid $200 a month in rent and were practically across the street from Chumley's. Chronicler of Village life, Jessie Tarbox Beals, photographed Edna and Eugen standing by their little house, well known as the narrowest in the Village, stretching only nine-and-a-half feet in width and occupying a former alley between two older houses. The odd space had once been used as a cobbler's shop. A plaque commemorating Millay's time here can be read from the street.

Chumley's
86 Bedford Street, between Barrow and Grove Streets
tel. (212) 675-4449

When Millay was in the city, she and her artistic coterie made Chumley's their social hub. In 1926, itinerant writer and laborer Lee Chumley rented the second story of this building to publish his radical workers' rights journal and to host clandestine meetings of the IWW (Industrial Workers of the World, or Wobblies). Two years later, Chumley converted the street-level blacksmith's studio into a speakeasy that soon became a favorite of the Village literati. Founder Chumley asked his patrons to bring in dust jackets of their books, and they still line the walls over the well-worn wooden booths. Patrons—including John Dos Passos, Eugene O'Neill, Ernest Hemingway, William Faulkner, Allen Ginsberg, Dylan Thomas, E.E. Cummings, Edmund Wilson, Dorothy Parker, Dawn Powell, and many others—passed through the unmarked entrance. Though the crowd has expanded and the need for secrecy has long-since passed, Chumley's remains a cozy bastion of literary history.

Cherry Lane Theater
38 Commerce Street at Bedford Street
tel. (212) 989-2020, www.cherrylanetheater.com

In 1924, Millay and others established the Cherry Lane Theater as an alternative to the increasingly successful and commercial work at the Provincetown Playhouse, of which she was an early member. The Cherry Lane Theater—a wishful name propped up by a lone cherry tree—was built as a brewery in 1836. By the time the radical thespians took over, it was being used as a box factory. Cherry Lane Theater produced plays by Samuel Beckett, Gertrude Stein, Edward Albee, and John Dos Passos, among others.

Former residence

139 Waverly Place, between Sixth Avenue and Gay Street

Millay lived here with her sister in 1918 while having an affair with Floyd Dell, editor of *The Masses.*

Marianne Moore

POET 1887–1972

A fter a visit to Marianne Moore's apartment at 260 Cumberland Street in Fort Greene, Brooklyn, Elizabeth Bishop described "a bushel basket, the kind used for apples or tomatoes, filled to overflowing with crumpled papers"—Moore's drafts and numerous redrafts of a single book review (a book of poems by Wallace Stevens). Championed by Ezra Pound, W. H. Auden, and T. S. Eliot, Moore awed people with her erudition, integrity, and undiminishing curiosity about the world. Moore was a veteran suffragist and a socialite who attended Truman Capote's Black and White Ball; she was a pious Presbyterian and a modernist; she helped the Ford Company dream up car names, and she wrote the liner notes to "I Am the Greatest" by Muhammed Ali. In her later years, the public knew Moore by her serious face, her black tricorn hat, and her colonial cape. On the occasion of her eightieth birthday, Auden wrote: "we see you sitting, / in a wide-brimmed hat beneath a monkey-puzzle, / at your feet the beasts you animated for us / by thinking of them."

··

Former residence

14 St. Luke's Place, between Seventh Avenue and Hudson Street

The Moore family lived in the basement apartment of 14 St. Luke's Place from 1918 to 1929. Moore lived continuously with her mother—an aged doppelganger who looms in the background of photographs of Moore—until her mother's death in 1947. The elder Moore raised Marianne and her brother alone, and the three became a loyalty-bound triumvirate, which no outsider could crack. Mrs. Moore read and edited her daughter's poems, exerted influence over which pieces should be published in *The Dial*, and generally enforced modesty and piety in the house. Mother and daughter were so tightly bound that when serious illness kept her mother from eating, Marianne refused food.

··

Hudson Park branch of the New York Public Library

66 Leroy Street, off Seventh Avenue South
tel. (212) 243 6876, www.nypl.org/branch/man/hp.html

Moore worked across the street from her St. Luke's apartment at the Hudson Park branch of the New York Public Library from 1921 to 1925. Her career as a librarian provided ample opportunity to bulk up her encyclopedic familiarity with everything from the natural sciences to baseball statistics.

··

Former offices of *The Dial*

152 West 13th Street, between Sixth and Seventh Avenues

Founded in 1840 as a Transcendentalist showcase, and edited for a period by Ralph Waldo Emerson, the original *Dial* folded in 1844. It was brought back to life in 1880 and sailed to 1916 as a polite and predictable critical review. After a period of flux, it reemerged in New York as one of the most important little magazines of the period under the editorial guidance of Scofield Thayer. Its pages were filled mostly with criticism and analysis of the arts, with about a fourth devoted to publication of poems, stories, and artwork. Many criticized *The Dial*, but almost everyone acknowledged that it had been the best of its type and generation. T. S. Eliot, for one, wrote a scathing critique of the magazine's editorial decisions, but he first published *The Waste Land* in its pages.

Moore contributed scrupulously researched and written pieces and poems for the magazine, and edited *The Dial* from 1925 until its demise in 1929. By the end, editing *The Dial* had become a drain for Moore. Though she kept at the exhausting and largely thankless work of dealing with contributors and critics, she was dismayed by what she perceived to be new forms of obscenity creeping into literature. The Berg Collection at the New York Public Library maintains an archive of letters, papers, and issues of *The Dial*.

Marianne Moore, 1948.

Library of Congress Prints and Photographs Division

Former residence
260 Cumberland Street, between DeKalb and Lafayette Avenues
Fort Greene, Brooklyn

Weary of Manhattan and its preoccupation with "making a fashion of itself," Moore and her mother moved here to be near the Brooklyn Navy Yard, where her brother worked. They spent the next thirty-seven years in Brooklyn. She loved what she called its "tame excitement." Institutions central to her life in Brooklyn included the Brooklyn Institute and the Pratt Free Library. She worshipped on Wednesday evenings and at Sunday service at the Lafayette Presbyterian Church (Lafayette Avenue at South Oxford Street). Moore left the neighborhood when Fort Greene began its temporary decline into a crime-ridden area. A plaque to the right of the entrance commemorates Moore's long residency here, her pioneering modernism, and her love of the Brooklyn Dodgers.

Former residence

35 West 9th Street, between Fifth and Sixth Avenues

Moore lived in Apt. 7B from 1966 until her death in 1972. Her apartment was populated by the statues, drawings, and carvings of elephants she had collected her entire life.

Yankee Stadium

East 161st Street at River Avenue
Grand Concourse, The Bronx
tel. (718) 293-6000, www.yankees.com

Moore, a serious baseball fan, threw out the first pitch in Yankee Stadium in 1968.

Isamu Noguchi

ARTIST 1904–1988

I samu Noguchi forged a new aesthetic that merged elements from Japanese and American art. In his sculpture, Noguchi emulated harmonious Japanese garden arrangements of stone, water, and earth, but he believed equally in providing evidence that an individual artist was at work (a trait he considered American). His Akari lamps, lunar ceilings, and low tables—characterized by softened corners and boomerang shapes—created a sleek profile for modern living. He was the illegitimate son of an eminent Japanese poet; he and his American mother lived in Japan until his father settled into a separate, strictly Japanese family life with a new wife. Noguchi attended high school in the United States and studied medicine at Columbia University for a year in 1922, after which he began his formal artistic training on the Lower East Side at the Leonardo da Vinci School. Noguchi's sculptures ranged from small, carved abstractions to large, sculpted landscapes. When Parks Commissioner Robert Moses sneered at his designs for a public playground in 1934, Noguchi was dropped from the Public Works of Art Project. The following year, Noguchi completed the first of many abstract set designs for Martha Graham's *Frontier*; the collaboration lasted for decades and revolutionized the staging of modern dance. When Japanese residents and Japanese-Americans were imprisoned in internment camps during World War II, Noguchi attempted to improve conditions at the Colorado River Relocation Center in Poston, Arizona. He was soon disillusioned, realizing that none of his plans for the center would be adopted by military commanders; he had to battle authorities for permission to leave the camp he had entered voluntarily.

Isamu Noguchi Museum

9-01 33rd Road, between Vernon Boulevard and 10th Street
Long Island City, Queens
tel. (718)204-7088, www.noguchi.org

In 1961, Noguchi moved his studio and home to a defunct factory in Long Island City, Queens. Over the years, he bought up adjoining buildings and established a complex of work and exhibition space, gardens, and storage. The complex has been the home of the Isamu Noguchi Foundation since 1980 and remains one of the great, serene havens in the busy city. For the last fifty years, the Noguchi Museum Store has sold masterful reproductions of Noguchi's original furniture and lamp designs. Noguchi adapted his now stylishly ubiquitous Akari lamps—translucent paper molded onto flexible bamboo frames—from traditional Japanese lanterns.

Rockefeller Center Associated Press Building
50 Rockefeller Plaza at West 50th Street

Journalists are idealized in relief on the front of this building: heroic figures armed with typewriters, cameras, pencils, and telephones seem to reach into space in their search for news. The stainless steel relief, which was selected as the winner in a sculpture competition, is inscribed "Isamu Noguchi 1940."

Red Cube
140 Broadway at Liberty Street, in front of Marine Midland Bank

Isamu Noguchi, 1984.

Noguchi created this piece in 1968. This massive, bored-through red steel cube is balanced on one of its corners. It was commissioned by Marine Midland Bank.

Office building
666 Fifth Avenue at West 53rd Street

From 1956 to 1958, Noguchi created the ceiling and a waterfall-wall for the lobby of this building. The ceiling of softly lit, evenly spaced slats, arranged to give the impression of depth, is reminiscent of a topographer's map of a gentle, hilly landscape.

Solomon R. Guggenheim Museum
1071 Fifth Avenue at East 89th Street
tel. (212) 423-3500, www.guggenheim.org

Highlights of the collection include *Lunar* (1959–1960), and *The Cry* (1959).

The Metropolitan Museum of Art
1000 Fifth Avenue at East 82nd Street
tel. (212) 535-7710, www.metmuseum.org

Noguchi's sculpture *Kouros* (1944–1945) is in the permanent collection here.

Frank O'Hara

POET 1926–1966

A major New York School poet, Frank O'Hara made his mark with eccentric, quickly dispatched chronicles of life in New York—parties, music, weather, high and low culture, haughty and rough characters, coffee bars, long walks. In his New England youth, he had wallpapered his attic room with movie posters, album covers, and maps. He had helped with the haying, read voraciously, loved swimming, and played the piano to ward off his sense of provincial isolation. O'Hara enrolled at Harvard to study music after serving on the destroyer USS *Nicholas* during World War II. At Harvard, he formed important friendships with John Ashbery, Kenneth Koch, and Edward Gorey (his roommate). His first book of poetry, *A City in Winter*, came out in 1952, though he gained more attention initially for his brilliant essays on painting and sculpture in *ArtNews* and for his role as the inexhaustible extrovert who brought together the Beat poets and Abstract Expressionist painters. His later books, *Meditations in an Emergency* and *Lunch Poems* brought him wider acclaim, though many critics remained unsure of how to rate or place such rebellious material. O'Hara came to wield great influence in the art world as a critic and curator at the Museum of Modern Art. At the age of forty, he was struck down by a jeep on Fire Island, while he waited by the road for a flat tire to be repaired.

Museum of Modern Art (MoMA)
11 West 53rd Street, between Fifth and Sixth Avenues
tel. (212) 708-9400, www.moma.org

At the front desk of the museum, O'Hara sold postcards and souvenirs while chatting with artist friends and writing poetry and essays for *ArtNews*. MoMA hired him again in 1955 as temporary help for an exhibition of French masterpieces. It was largely

© John Jonas Gruen/Getty Images

administrative work, but O'Hara was organizationally gifted despite his apparently casual attitude. He was promoted to a permanent position in the International Program, where he continued to write poems during lunch hours. His eminence among rising painters, tenacity, and smart ebullience moved him through the curatorial ranks, until he graduated to his own office, cluttered with books and catalogues. He selected the Jackson Pollock paintings and drawing for the Bienal de São Paulo in 1959 and was given special commendation by the judging committee. He only regretted that he was forced to reign in his enthusiasm for new painters once his curatorial status gave his praise new weight and responsibility.

Cedar Tavern

82 University Place at East 11th Street
tel. (212) 741-9754

O'Hara's friendships with Larry Rivers, Willem de Kooning, and Isamu Noguchi often led him to the Cedar Tavern. He spent most of his time here among painters, fleeing once from a drunken Jackson Pollock who was on a violent, homophobic rampage. Despite such scenes, O'Hara insisted on Pollock's genius and revered his work. The Cedar Tavern was originally located at 24 University Place.

Site of San Remo
93 MacDougal Street, between Bleecker and West Houston Streets

The former San Remo became a Village watering hole of the Beats and the Abstract Expressionists, with O'Hara frequently in their company. The San Remo was predominantly a working-class bar dating back to 1925. Regular patrons and bartenders alike initially tried to fend off the colonizing intellectuals by heaving them off the property and beating them up at the bar, though the Beats kept coming back. Finally, curious tourists arrived at the bar and scared the Beats off.

P.J. Clarke's
915 Third Avenue at East 55th Street
tel. (212) 759-1650, www.pjclarkes.com

O'Hara lived and worked in this neighborhood periodically, and he patronized P.J. Clarke's, a historic establishment that has somehow held its ground in the land of skyscrapers for more than 130 years. Bartender P.J. Clarke purchased this long-running saloon in 1912 from his boss and lent his name to the establishment. Successive owners have shored up the interiors and replaced the floorboards, but the old-world atmosphere of this Midtown bar has never been disturbed.

Plaza Hotel
768 Fifth Avenue at Central Park South
tel. (212) 759-3000, www.fairmont.com

O'Hara spent much of his time here at the bar here and at other gay bars in the Village and in the Upper East Side. In the 1950s and 1960s, plainclothesmen from the police department regularly infiltrated and shut down these bars around the city, arresting and harassing patrons. The Oak Room at the Plaza evolved quietly into a de facto gay bar, until the hotel noticed the trend and banned men unescorted by ladies.

Former residence
791 Broadway at East 10th Street

In May 1963, O'Hara moved into a loft here, across from Grace Church. O'Hara filled the spacious, white walls of his apartment with the work of his famous painter friends.

World Financial Center Plaza
In Battery Park City, bordered by West Street, the Hudson River, Vesey, and Liberty Streets
tel. (212) 945-2600, www.worldfinancialcenter.com

Along the Hudson River, just south of North Cove, there is a public marina between Liberty and Vesey Streets. Incorporated in bronze into the steel fence overlooking the river are fragments of love poems to New York by Walt Whitman and Frank O'Hara.

*One need never leave the
confines of New York to get all the greenery one wishes—I can't
even enjoy a blade of grass unless I know there's a subway
handy, or a record store or some other sign that people do not
totally regret life—Frank O'Hara*

Georgia O'Keeffe

ARTIST 1887–1986

Georgia O'Keeffe lived and painted in Manhattan for thirty years. From the vantage point of the hotel apartment she shared with photographer Alfred Stieglitz, O'Keeffe painted landscapes of Midtown Manhattan office buildings and the dark valleys between them. She also completed her flower series while living in the city. Her

Georgia O'Keeffe, 1936.

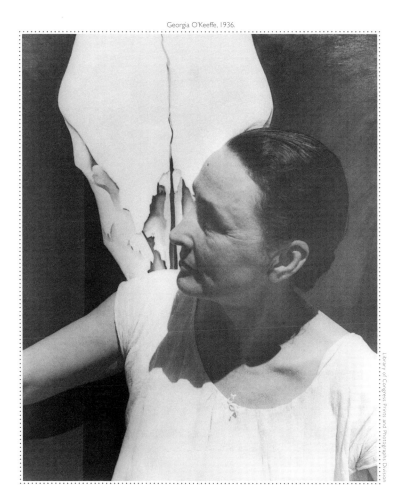

last New York painting was of the Brooklyn Bridge in 1949. O'Keeffe, the daughter of Wisconsin dairy farmers, claimed her first memory was of the brightness of light. She was vehemently opposed to interpretations of her work and claimed to care only for the thing itself—a dark, windy tree, a pale flower. O'Keeffe was teaching in Texas when a friend showed her work to Stieglitz, and he, increasingly obsessed with O'Keeffe and her work, exhibited her paintings at his famous 291 gallery without her consent. She eventually returned to New York to settle, and she and Stieglitz were married in 1924. On New Year's Eve, 1916, O'Keeffe decided to start fresh with her painting and disposed of all her previous work in the garbage cans outside the Shelton Hotel. She and Stieglitz returned home that night to find her paintings, studies, and drawings blowing through the streets. O'Keeffe started spending summers in New Mexico in 1929; she moved there permanently three years after Stieglitz's death in 1946.

Shelton Hotel (now New York East Side Marriott)
525 Lexington Avenue, between East 48th and East 49th Streets

O'Keeffe and Alfred Stieglitz moved into rooms on the upper floors of this hotel after their wedding in 1924 and stayed for ten years. His photographs and her paintings were often done in their apartment here; both also made portraits of the hotel and surrounding buildings from the street. O'Keeffe asserted that New York could only be painted as "it was felt"—rows of pale, lit windows that line the sides of mountainous Midtown buildings, symmetrical dark gorges, dazzling sunspots, all of the extreme lights and darks of Manhattan. The hotel is now the New York East Side Marriott. O'Keeffe worked on her flower paintings here, and an otherwise generic banquet hall in the basement of the hotel, called the O'Keeffe Room, is enlivened slightly by reproductions of O'Keeffe flowers on the wall.

Site of Little Galleries of the Photo-Secession
291 and 293 Fifth Avenue, between East 30th and East 31st Streets

O'Keeffe described "the 291 gallery" as "the loveliest place I ever saw." The galleries were filled with diffused light and the stone-green walls were hung with pieces by Picasso, Rodin, Matisse, and Cézanne.

The Art Students League
215 West 57th Street, between Seventh Avenue and Broadway
tel. (212) 247-4510, www.theartstudentsleague.org

O'Keeffe was a student here in 1907–1908. During her tenure, she won the "Still Life Scholarship" for her pieces, *Dead Rabbit* and *Copper Pot*.

The Metropolitan Museum of Art
1000 Fifth Avenue at East 82nd Street
tel. (212) 535-7710, www.metmuseum.org

Alfred Stieglitz made hundreds of photographic portraits of O'Keeffe over the decades. He photographed her hands obsessively, and focused on her particular moods, stances, and expressions in an effort to create a total portrait of a human being. The Metropolitan Museum's Department of Photographs has several hundred images by Stieglitz and by other prominent photographers displayed in his 291 gallery, all of which were donated to the Museum by Stieglitz before his death. The Museum acquired seventy-three of the O'Keeffe portraits in 1997. Highlights of the collection include O'Keeffe's pastel *A Storm* (1922) and her oil painting, *Red, White, and Blue* (1931).

Whitney Museum of American Art
945 Madison Avenue at East 75th Street
tel. (800) 944-8639, www.whitney.org

O'Keeffe's *Music—Pink and Blue II* (1919) is in the collection here.

Museum of Modern Art (MoMA)
11 West 53rd Street, between Fifth and Sixth Avenues
tel. (212) 708-9400, www.moma.org

O'Keeffe's *Evening Star III* (1917) is in the collection here.

Frederick Law Olmsted, 1893.

Library of Congress Prints and Photographs Division

Frederick Law Olmsted
LANDSCAPE ARCHITECT 1822–1903

T here is no plaque or monument in Central Park commemorating the work of its designers, Frederick Law Olmsted and Calvert Vaux. Olmsted described the role of landscape architect as the making of "a picture so great that Nature shall be employed upon it for generations, before the work he arranged for her shall realize his intentions." Olmsted began his work on the land as a "scientific farmer" on Staten Island. He had shipped out to China and the East Indies in his youth, setting a pattern of intelligent roving and writing for which he became famous. He toured the gardens of Europe and wrote *Walks and Talks of an American Farmer* in England, and in 1856 published *A Journey Through the Seaboard Slave States, With Remarks on Their Economy*, in which he critiqued the economic rationale for slavery and argued for its abolition. Olmsted wrote successive travel books and worked for a while as an editor at *Putnam's Magazine*. In 1857, thwarted in his pursuit of a literary career by the failing economy, Olmsted partnered with English landscape architect Calvert Vaux; they won the design competition for Central Park with their "Greensward" plan, which created the illusion of natural, ambling countryside in the middle of the city. Olmsted oversaw every detail of the park's construction and, with Vaux, fought to keep commerce and compromise out of the park. In 1895, Olmsted, failing physically and mentally, was consigned to the McLean Hospital in Waverly, Massachusetts, the grounds of which he had designed years before.

Central Park

From Central Park South (59th Street) to Central Park North (110th Street) and from Fifth Avenue to Central Park West (Eighth Avenue)

Olmsted joined well-established landscape architect Calvert Vaux in developing the winning plan for New York's proposed Central Park. In the mid-1850s, affluent New Yorkers and public leaders called for the creation of a public park on par with those that enriched the best European cities. A great park—like the other public institutions taking shape in New York in the mid-nineteenth century—was considered a necessary ingredient for a world-class city. It was also agreed that a parcel of "open" country would provide recreational zones for both the carriage-racing rich and for the poor living in crowded downtown Manhattan.

In 1853, the state of New York granted the city the right to take over 700 acres of land, though the domain of the park eventually expanded to incorporate land owned by Seneca Village, an established African-American community. Irish immigrants had also settled on the site of the future park to escape the suffocating conditions downtown. By the 1850s, all residents had been cleared off the land, and 20,000 workers began fifteen years of blasting, digging, paving, and planting. In the completed park, the classes mingled, and men courted their future wives on long public walks. There were nighttime ice carnivals on the frozen pond lit by calcium lights. The disorienting landscape of foot bridges, snaking paths, and sloping meadows were intended by Olmsted and Vaux to pull city dwellers into a wilderness—one in which it became impossible to determine one's precise location on the grid, or the exact hour of the city clocks.

Prospect Park

From Prospect Park West to Flatbush Avenue and from Prospect Park Southwest to Ocean Avenue and Parkside Avenue Prospect Park, Brooklyn

Organized around a mile-long meadow, a lake, and ravine in the relative peace and quiet of Brooklyn, Prospect Park is regarded by many as the greatest achievement of Olmsted and Vaux. Trees and flowers native to Brooklyn lean over wide carriage paths, and a carousel, one of the few still in use from the golden age of carnivals, turns a herd of vibrant horses carved by carousel legend Charles Carmel in 1912. The Prospect Park Zoo—originally a turn-of-the-century menagerie—may be as close as some New Yorkers ever come to the wild. Visitors are permitted to feed goats, cows, and horses, to crawl through human-size prairie dog tunnels (in order to spy on the prairie dogs from within clear plastic domes), and to leap between giant lily pads on the pond. When the park opened in 1868, an estimated two million people visited in its first year.

. . . .

Riverside Park
From West 72nd to West 153rd Streets and from Riverside Drive to the Hudson River

Secured for public use by Olmsted and Vaux, Riverside Park is meant to look like a continuation of the Hudson River Valley. The waterfront from West 68th to West 155th Streets is banked with terraced walks, community gardens, picnic slopes, and a scattered regiment of heroic statuary. Olmsted and Vaux's subtle and sinuous designs ensure that the end is never in sight for urbanites in the park—in places, Riverside Park looks as if it goes on forever in sunny, cobblestone walks and mild green slopes.

Eugene O'Neill

PLAYWRIGHT 1888–1953

E ugene O'Neill was born in a hotel room on Broadway at West 43rd Street, the son of James O'Neill, a popular theater actor. Until the age of seven, O'Neill traveled constantly with his itinerant parents; his father led his troupe of actors from city to city and his mother followed unhappily—she was wary of actors, especially in groups. O'Neill passed through Princeton, Harvard, a first marriage, years as a gold prospector in the West, a life at sea, numerous short-lived jobs, roles on the vaudeville stage, and a stint as a reporter, before ending up in New York in flophouses and derelict pubs. While recovering from tuberculosis in a sanatorium, O'Neill began to write plays in the fall of 1913. In 1935, he began a cycle of plays tracking the material ambitions, flush years, and catastrophes of several generations of an American family. In 1944, a degenerative neurological disease slowed O'Neill's progress until the disease stopped his work altogether. Only two of the proposed eleven plays emerged after his death—*The Iceman Cometh* and *Long Day's Journey into Night*. He was awarded the Nobel Prize for literature in 1936.

. . . .

Site of former residence
38 Washington Square South, between MacDougal and Sullivan Streets

In 1916, O'Neill lived in a boarding house on the corner now occupied by the NYU Law School building. While he lived here, O'Neill's first play, *Bound East for Cardiff*, was in production at the Provincetown Playhouse, and he was carrying on an affair with Louise Bryant, the wife of radical journalist John Reed.

. . . .

Golden Swan Garden
Sixth Avenue at West 4th Street

O'Neill loved the volatility of Greenwich Village in the years before World War I. He drank with Edna St. Vincent Millay, Dorothy Day, and Emma Goldman at bohemian dives such as the Golden Swan Café, formerly on the site of present-day Golden Swan Garden. The three-story pub was named for the gilded statue of a swan that stood out front, but it was known locally as the Hell Hole or the Bucket of Blood. O'Neill based characters in *The Iceman Cometh* on the denizens of the Golden Swan, which was home

Library of Congress Prints and Photographs Division

to the members of the Hudson Dusters, a gang of young Irish men whose criminal glory days had passed and who were reduced to petty theft and the destruction of ballot boxes in city elections. Gangsters and roughs stayed at one end of the bar, the anarchists, poets, painters, novelists at the other: the two crowds eyed each other uneasily. After a long night at the Hell Hole, O'Neill retreated to Jimmy the Priest's, a flophouse on Fulton Street, which also figured prominently in the play.

. . . .

Provincetown Playhouse
133 MacDougal Street at West 3rd Street
tel. (212) 998-5867

The Provincetown Playhouse was founded in Provincetown, Massachusetts in 1915 and moved to Greenwich Village the following year. Eugene O'Neill had his debut here with *Bound East for Cardiff*. The Playhouse produced almost all of O'Neill's short plays over the years. In 1920, his first long play, *Beyond the Horizon*, appeared on Broadway and garnered him his first of four Pulitzer Prizes, the last given posthumously in 1957 for *Long Day's Journey into Night*. The Playhouse was originally located at 139 MacDougal, between West 3rd and West 4th Streets.

. . . .

Former residence
45 Grove Street, between Bleecker and Bedford Streets

In the 1981 movie *Reds*, this 1830 Federal-style house stood in as the home of Eugene O'Neill, friend of radicals John Reed and Louise Bryant, on whom the film is based. The poet Hart Crane actually did live here in 1923, and John Wilkes Booth planned his assassination of Abraham Lincoln here.

Former residence

Milligan Place, off Sixth Avenue, between West 10th and West 11th Streets

One of O'Neill's Village addresses. Like its neighbor Patchin Place, Milligan Place is an unexpected alcove off a busy downtown thoroughfare and is open to residents only. Cast-iron molded into script on the gate marks the entrance. The alley and the 1850s buildings, which housed workers from the Brevoort Hotel, were owned by Samuel Milligan, whose daughter married Aaron Patchin.

Site of Brevoort Hotel

15 Fifth Avenue, between Washington Square North and East 8th Street

Now displaced by the Brevoort Apartments, the Brevoort Hotel was once home to O'Neill and other Villagers, including Edna St. Vincent Millay. The hotel's cafe became famous as a hangout for the Villagers and regularly made cameo appearances in articles, gossip pieces, and novels set in Greenwich Village. The Brevoort Hotel hosted a banquet for Margaret Sanger after she was convicted for speaking in public about the of use contraception. The cafe handed out free whisky on the first day of Prohibition.

The Museum of the City of New York

1220 Fifth Avenue at East 103rd Street
tel. (212) 534-1672, www.mcny.org

The Theater Collection maintains a collection of Eugene O'Neill Papers, including original play scripts annotated by the playwright.

Elisha Graves Otis

INVENTOR 1811–1861

With his invention of the elevator safety break, Elisha Graves Otis granted New York verticality. Without a reliable passenger elevator, buildings could spring no higher than six stories. With verticality came millions of square feet of new real estate, stacked high on small lots, and the dozens of towering and angular buildings that defined the modern city. By the 1850s, cargo elevators had been in use for years, but the prospect of a failed cable and a crash into the well of the shaft made passenger elevators untenable as public transport. At the Crystal Palace exposition of 1854, Otis built a full-scale open elevator, raised himself to a height of a few stories, and then ordered his assistants to cut the elevator cable. The crowds cried out, then sighed with relief as Otis's safety break locked the platform and held him safely in place. He installed the first passenger elevator in New York City in 1857. In the elapsing 150 years, the skyline of New York has grown from dark and hilly to gleaming and mountainous. Until the completion of Joseph Pulitzer's World Building in 1890 (309 feet), the spire of Trinity Church had been the highest point in New York. Elevators are central to the city's circulatory system: pumping residents, workers, and visitors higher and higher. Otis Elevators claims that its elevators circulate the equivalent of the world's population every seventy-two hours.

Haughwout Building

488-492 Broadway at Broome Street

In the spring of 1857, Otis installed the first passenger elevator in this landmark five-story cast-iron building, then E.V. Haughwout & Co. Store. Haughwout's consolidated fashionable housewares under one roof for the first time, making it a prototype of modern department stores. New Yorkers could buy silver table settings, gas chandeliers, tea sets, mirrors, and hand-painted porcelain then descend safely and speedily to the street.

On May 16, 1861, Mary Todd Lincoln, given the task of refurbishing the dilapidated White House, visited Haughwout's to commission a full set of china. The old lobby of the building is now an office supply store. The original elevator lobby, now a private entrance, is immediately north of the intersection of Broadway and Broome Street at 490 Broadway.

Elisha Graves Otis, undated.

Private collection

Site of Equitable Building
120 Broadway, between Pine and Cedar Streets

Built in 1868, the seven-story Equitable Building, since demolished, qualifies as the first "skyscraper." It was the first building in New York City to incorporate passenger elevators into its design.

Flatiron Building
Fifth Avenue, between East 22nd and East 23rd Streets

In 1888, Otis Elevators—run by Otis's son—broke into the international market by designing the elevators for the Eiffel Tower. It was the first of many triumphs. Beginning in 1902, Otis elevators ferried occupants up and down the record-breaking height of the Flatiron Building, the most famous and longest standing of the original skyscrapers. Otis Elevators supplied the elevators for the next three record-breaking skyscrapers: the Woolworth Building in 1912, the Empire State Building in 1931, and the World Trade Center Towers in 1973.

The Skyscraper Museum

39 Battery Place at the foot of Battery Park City
tel. (212) 968-1961, www.skyscraper.org

The Skyscraper Museum opened in a new, permanent home in the ground floor of this downtown building in March 2004. It celebrates New York City, as "the world's first and foremost vertical metropolis" and examines the visionaries, innovations, and urban demands that have shaped modern skylines.

Thomas Paine, 1793.

Library of Congress Prints and Photographs Division

Thomas Paine

REVOLUTIONARY AND WRITER 1737–1809

T homas Paine's pamphlets—*Common Sense, The Age of Reason, The Rights of Man, The American Crisis* among them—were read aloud in streets and in pubs, and fomented popular support for the American Revolution. He argued against slavery, for social security, and, catastrophically, against organized religion (he was a devout deist). Paine's words were debated everywhere, at home and abroad, in high and low public halls, yet he died a drunken pauper in the city of his Revolutionary glory. The Founding Fathers, concerned with stabilizing the new nation, had no intention of allowing Paine the chance to exercise his gift for inciting rebellion. In France, he went through a dizzying cycle of reputations: as a father of the American Revolution, Paine was made an honorary French Citizen

(*The Rights of Man* was written in defense of the French Revolution), and he was given the key to the Bastille. When he entered Paris during the Reign of Terror, however, he was imprisoned and nearly executed. President Washington refused to bail him out and denied he was an American citizen. A decade after Paine's death in New York City, radical Englishman William Cobbett opened Paine's grave in New Rochelle, New York, and removed his remains, planning to bury them in English soil as a symbol of democratic reform. Paine's bones disappeared soon after; rumors have placed them in Australian attics, unmarked graves, and on an English coat as tooled buttons.

Site of former residence
85 Church Street, between Barclay and Vesey Streets

Paine, thoroughly disliked and exiled from post-Revolutionary governmental affairs, lived here in 1806. Though an ailing old man, Paine's enemies gave him no reprieve. As long as he could speak or write, he was deemed a threat. Once very ill, Paine moved to the countryside of Greenwich Village and is said to have passed away in the backroom of a friend's house on the land now occupied by 59 Grove Street.

Barrow Street
From West Side Highway to Washington Place

Named Reason Street in Paine's honor soon after his death. The influential members of Trinity Church, rankled by a memorial to Paine, engineered the change to Barrow Street.

Marie's Crisis Café
59 Grove Street, between Bleecker Street and Seventh Avenue South
tel. (212) 243-9323

Paine died in the backroom of a house formerly on this site. The current structure, built thirty years after Paine's death, houses a café named for Paine's *Crisis Papers*, in which he wrote his best-remembered words ("These are the times that try men's souls"). A plaque on the exterior of the building commemorates Paine's last days.

Christopher Street / Sheridan Square subway station
Christopher Street at Seventh Avenue

Three small mosaic and glazed murals are midway along the Uptown 1/9 platform in the Christopher Street Station. The murals are a tribute to the rebels of Greenwich Village. Thomas Paine is a central figure, wearing a coat of red, white, and blue mosaic tiles and holding a torch in his right hand.

Dorothy Parker
WRITER AND CRITIC 1893–1967

I conic of the vicious wit and sad glamour of the Prohibition era, Parker was an early and constant contributor to *The New Yorker* until 1957—she is credited with having invented, by example, "*The New Yorker* Short Story." Dogged at cocktail parties by people desperate to be insulted cleverly, Parker sometimes obliged. Her unrelenting, stinging critique was a genuine, difficult search for truth—

she cast a cold eye on all, including members of the Algonquin Round Table, of which she was a founding member. Despite a string of deeply miserable relationships, famously self-destructive pursuits, and more to the point, several attempts to take her own life, Parker lived to be seventy-three. She bequeathed her entire literary estate to the Rev. Dr. Martin Luther King, Jr., whom she had never met.

When he was assassinated the following year, the rights to her estate transferred to the NAACP.

Algonquin Hotel

59 West 44th Street, between Fifth and Sixth Avenues
tel. (212) 840-6800, www.algonquinhotel.com

Always a hub for glamorous and arty crowds, the hotel was immortalized by the Algonquin Round Table—the famously quick-witted, long-lunching crowd of artists, thinkers, and personalities who gathered in the Oak Room from 1919 to 1929. The group assembled for the first time in the Rose Room to welcome drama critic Alexander Woollcott back from World War I. The crowd returned devotedly to the hotel for boozy, argumentative lunches, and the early issues of *The New Yorker* were filled with post–Round Table gossip and repartee. Parker lived in the hotel during 1924, after her first marriage crumbled. The hotel marked its 100th anniversary in 2002 with the unveiling of a new painting of Round Table members.

Biltmore Theatre

261-265 West 47th Street, between Broadway and Eighth Avenue

Parker wrote theater reviews for many years as the drama critic for *The New Yorker*. (Parker had previously been the drama critic at *Vanity Fair*, where her barbed reviews did not conform to established style; her editor told her over lunch at the Plaza Hotel that she would be famous one day, then fired her.) On the Broadway of the 1920s, many new theaters were going up, and plays, rather than musical extravaganzas, became trendy. Built in 1925, at the peak of the Round Table days, the Biltmore had been shut down and was fast decaying by 1987. In 2003, the Biltmore reopened as a performance venue for the Manhattan Theatre Club.

Waldorf-Astoria Hotel

301 Park Avenue at East 49th Street
tel. (212) 355-3000, www.waldorfastoria.com

Parker's devotion to political justice (she acted as national chairman of the Joint Anti-Fascist Refugee Committee) and her involvement in public protests landed her in front of the House Un-American Activities Committee in 1951. Her Federal Bureau of Investigation file was one thousand pages thick. In a lighter episode of civil unrest, Parker joined Alexander Woollcott and Robert Benchley on February 6, 1934 in a protest to support the striking waiters of the Waldorf-Astoria who were trying to unionize. Hotel detectives sat tensely among the diners waiting for the scene to develop. When protest leader Selden Rodman stood on his chair to speak, he was tackled before making it past a few introductory remarks. Hotel detectives dragged him out to the street, while mayhem unfolded in the dining room. According to *New York Times* coverage the next day, Dorothy Parker and Robert Benchley "gibed at the detectives with a running fire of extemporaneous bon mots and 'wisecracks' as [Selden] Rodman and friends were mauled." Parker and Benchley, the paper added, "escaped unscathed."

Former *New Yorker* offices

412 West 47th Street, between Ninth and Tenth Avenues

Harold Ross had started *The New Yorker* in 1925 in his house at 412 West 47th Street in Hell's Kitchen—a dangerous and depressed neighborhood deserving of its name in the 1920s. During a party to celebrate the launch of the magazine, Dorothy Parker and Harpo Marx hired a carousel to entertain neighborhood kids. A red plaque on West 47th Street commemorates the work of Harold Ross, and notes Parker's tenure here.

....

Former *New Yorker* offices
25 West 43rd Street, between Fifth and Sixth Avenues

The New Yorker was edited and published in this building from 1935 until 1991, when Condé Nast purchased the magazine. The office was moved across West 43rd Street for several years before settling in its current home in the Condé Nast building at 4 Times Square.

Edgar Allan Poe

WRITER 1809–1849

E dgar Allan Poe was a prolific and ambitious poet, journalist, critic, and editor who is credited with inventing the modern detective story. He cultivated a gothic public persona, wearing his silk-black hair brushed back to emphasize his gray eyes and going around town in a black frock coat buttoned to the top and stuffed with a black cravat. When he called on friends, he left a calling card bordered in mourning black. As an adolescent, he had disrupted his stepfather's social evenings by walking through the room with a sheet over his head. Later in life, he proposed to a woman in a graveyard and confided to friends that he believed he was being stalked. He wrote light pieces, including "The Philosophy of Furniture," and was nicknamed the "Tomahawk Man" for his brutal reviews during the same period. In 1844, Poe, nearly penniless, moved his family—his cousin, whom he had married when she was thirteen, and her mother—to New York City. The publication of "The Raven" in a local paper boosted him to immediate celebrity. He was drawn into the exclusive company of Manhattan's literary salons and, with their support, took over as editor-in-chief of *The Broadway Journal* in 1845. Within months, he was ruined by its failure. He made ends meet by writing hoax pieces and venomous sketches of local personalities for the newspapers. The local personalities retaliated by spreading rumors of his drunkenness, debts, and madness. In October of 1849, he was found in Baltimore, delirious, in cheap, ill-fitting clothes. He died within days of unknown causes (officially "congestion of the brain").

....

Poe Cottage
2640 Grand Concourse at Kingsbridge Road
Fordham, The Bronx
tel. (718) 881-8900, www.bronxhistoricalsociety.org

This part of the Bronx was a sleepy village of church chimes and grazing livestock in 1846, when Poe lived in the house with his wife and mother-in-law for $100 yearly rent paid to a Mr. Valentine. Jasmine and honeysuckle grew in the yard, the shingles were cut from dark pine, and the walls washed with lye. Poe gardened, read poetry aloud, and discussed ideas with the students and professors at nearby St. John's College, now Fordham University.

The poet worked well in the still atmosphere of the countryside—nearby orchards had the hush of low winds cutting through the tree branches and the smell of fallen apples on the ground. Poe wrote "The Cask of Amantillado," "Annabel Lee," "The Bells," and "Eureka" here. Poe hoped that the country air would strengthen his ailing wife Virginia, but she succumbed to tuberculosis in January of 1847, and Poe's life defaulted to its chaotic state. Poe and his mother-in-law, Mrs. Clemm, were gravely poor again: she foraged dandelion roots from the side of the country road so that they could eat. Poe set out on a money-making lecture tour, which he deemed a success, though observers found him in a seriously nervous condition. He collapsed in Baltimore and died under mysterious circumstances a few days later.

Poe enthusiasts first proposed making Poe's last home a historic site in the 1870s. Rights to the surrounding land were secured, and Poe Park opened officially in 1902. In 1913, New York bought the cottage and moved it inside the boundaries of the Park. Curators have preserved Poe's rocking chair and the bed in which Virginia died—both are on display with other period furniture and a fully set table, meant to convey the eerie sense that the poet will return to the room any moment.

Edgar Allan Poe, 1848.

Library of Congress Prints and Photographs Division

Edgar Allan Poe Way

West 84th Street from Amsterdam Avenue to Broadway

Poe finished his poem "The Raven" while living at a boarding house in the countryside at what is now 84th Street and Broadway. Poe, his wife, and mother-in-law lived here from about June 1844 to January 1845 in a farming family's boarding house on what was then Bloomingdale Road (which had been laid over an Indian trail). Poe enjoyed a rare serenity while living in Upper Manhattan—he strolled through the wild countryside, crisscrossed farmlands, and looked out upon the Hudson River from the rocky height at the island's edge. He wrote gloomily to friends that he feared the city would engulf his lovely wilderness one day. Horse-drawn streetcars would not travel as far as 84th Street for another twenty years; the elevated train stretched to 104th Street in 1879 and set off a mini-building boom that began drawing Lower Manhattanites north.

Former residence of Anna Charlotte Lynch Botta
116 Waverly Place, between MacDougal Street and Sixth Avenue

During the 1840s, Anna Charlotte Lynch Botta hosted her literary salon at this address. Widowed, bright, and serious, she was a critic and editor who cultivated some of the most promising writers of the day, including Poe and Herman Melville. It has been claimed that the first public reading of "The Raven" took place here, during one of Lynch's evenings, though Poe sometimes "debuted" his work in person and in print more than once.

Former Northern Dispensary
165 Waverly Place at Christopher Street

This 1831 triangular building has been made into an island by the intersections of Grove, Christopher, and Waverly Streets. In the late 1830s, when the dispensary was a clinic for the indigent, Poe was treated here for a severe head cold. The Northern Dispensary has been the Hostel for the Disabled since 1997.

Jackson Pollock
ARTIST 1912–1956

J ackson Pollock, who made revolutionary advances in painting, started out as a mediocre art student of realistic forms under the tutelage of Thomas Hart Benton, a hard-drinking, man's man whom Pollock emulated. Shy, melancholy, and gifted, Pollock came into his own as an artist when he shifted to abstraction. Peggy Guggenheim recognized his brilliance when he was unknown and she became his most ardent supporter and promoter. She commissioned a vast Pollock mural for her East 61st Street apartment and hosted a reception for the unveiling, during which, notoriously, a drunken Pollock urinated in the lit fireplace. In his most important works, Pollock set his canvas on the floor and dripped tributaries of paint onto it, allowing the paint to trail beyond the edges. In these drip paintings, the brush never touched the canvas, but Pollock rejected adamantly the claim that there were accidents in art. Pollock and his wife, the artist Lee Krasner, left New York for East Hampton in the fall of 1945. On August 11, 1956, Pollock died behind the wheel of his car. Two women were in the car with him: his girlfriend at the time, Ruth Kligman, who survived with serious injuries, and her friend Edith Metzger, who was killed.

Cedar Tavern
82 University Place at East 11th Street
tel. (212) 741-9754

The Abstract Expressionists, including Jackson Pollock, Willem de Kooning, Larry Rivers,

© Martha Holmes/Getty Images

and Franz Kline, met here regularly to test each other, their limits, and the patience of the establishment. On one occasion, Pollock, in a drunken rage, kicked in the door of the men's room and was banished from the bar for a month. Patrons reported that the bar was like a "funeral parlor" in the weeks after Pollock's death. The bar was originally located at 24 University Place.

New York Central Art Supply

62 Third Avenue at East 11th Street
tel. (212) 473-7705, www.nycentralart.com

Pollock was a devoted patron of this historic art supply store. New York artists have shopped here for almost a century.

Former residence

46 East 8th Street at Waverly Place

Pollock lived here from 1934 to 1942—first with his brother and sister-in-law, who characterized him as sullen, moody, and lazy, and then on his own, managing the $35 monthly rent.

General Sheridan statue

Christopher Park
Waverly Place at Christopher Street and Seventh Avenue

In 1935, Pollock worked for the city as a monument polisher. He buffed the statue of stalwart General Sheridan and later the bronze relief by Attilio Picirilli at Riverside and West 100th Street.

Former residence
9 MacDougal Alley, between Washington Square North and West 8th Street

Pollock lived here in 1949 and 1950. No. 8 West 8th Street had earlier housed the first incarnation of the Whitney Museum. The row houses were built in 1833 as stables for the houses lining Washington Square North.

Whitney Museum of American Art
945 Madison Avenue at East 75th Street
tel. (800) 944-8639, www.whitney.org

Pieces in the permanent collection include *Number 27* (1950).

The Metropolitan Museum of Art
1000 Fifth Avenue at East 82nd Street
tel. (212) 535-7710, www.metmuseum.org

The Metropolitan Museum of Art provided one of Pollock's first public exhibitions of his work in the group show, "Artists for Victory" in 1942—he showed his painting *The Flame* (circa1934–1938). Paintings now in the museum's collection include *War* (1947) and *Autumn Rhythm (Number 30)* (1950).

Solomon R. Guggenheim Museum
1071 Fifth Avenue at East 89th Street
tel. (212) 423-3500, www.guggenheim.org

Pieces in the permanent collection include: *The Moon Woman* (1942), *Circumcision* (January 1946), *Eyes in the Heat* (1946), *Alchemy* (1947), *Enchanted Forest* (1947), and *Ocean Greyness* (1953).

Museum of Modern Art (MoMA)
11 West 53rd Street, between Fifth and Sixth Avenues
tel. (212) 708-9400, www.moma.org

Pieces in the permanent collection include *Untitled* (circa 1950); *One (Number 31, 1950)* (1950); *Shimmering Substance* (Sounds in the Grass Series) (1946); *Number 1* (1948); and *Full Fathom Five* (1947). In the late 1990s, MoMA exhibited a retrospective of Pollock's work, which proved to be one of the museum's most popular shows. More than 300,000 people attended.

Dawn Powell

WRITER 1897–1965

D awn Powell, the great comic novelist of Prohibition-era New York, wrote novels about the ambitious, fraternizing Greenwich Villagers she knew so well. She strove for a comic realism that encompassed all of the light and dark impulses of human nature. About her characters Powell said: "I give them their heads. They furnish their own nooses." Powell's satires about life in New York and Ohio followed characters down the path she had taken—she fled home after her vindictive stepmother burned all of her writing and stayed with relatives in other small Ohio towns before reaching Manhattan in 1918. In New York, Powell found her city and her permanent home; in the Village, she developed close friendships with John Dos Passos, E.E. Cummings, and Edmund Wilson. Powell's novels are both funny and cutting; she believed that "true wit should strike at the exact point of weakness and it should scar." In Greenwich Village, she was famous among her friends for clever retorts—she and Dorothy Parker were often held up for comparison—and for a rare compassion and tolerance in caring for others. Powell wrote novels, short stories, plays, book reviews, and scripts—churning out thousands of words a week to make ends meet.

El Faro Restaurant

823 Greenwich Street at Horatio Street
tel. (212) 929-8210

El Faro was one of Powell's Village favorites and dining mainstays in the 1940s, when the neighborhood was known as "Little Spain." Since opening in 1927, El Faro has stayed true to the authentic Spanish fare and to the original ambiance: warm, umber light, flamenco murals, and old wooden booths.

Cedar Tavern

82 University Place at East 11th Street
tel. (212) 741-9754

Powell established this as a new favorite drinking and meeting spot after her beloved Café Lafayette was demolished. She called her last novel, *The Golden Spur*, her "Cedar novel." After a dinner at the Cedar Tavern on December 10, 1958, Powell wrote in her diary: "Decided Village is my creative oxygen." The bar was originally located at 24 University Place.

Former residence

106 Perry Street, between Hudson and Bleecker Streets

Powell lived here between 1928 and 1934, while she wrote *Dance Night* and *Turn, Magic Wheel*.

Former residence

35 East 9th Street, between University Place and Broadway

Powell and her husband, Joseph Roebuck Gousha, moved to this duplex in the early 1940s, riding on the success of her novel *A Time to Be Born*. Powell had been involved in an affair with magazine editor Coburn Gilman for many years, an arrangement accepted by an increasingly disengaged and alcoholic Gousha. The couple never stopped caring for their autistic son together, but they were otherwise apart. Gousha lived upstairs, coming and going through his own door, while Powell lived on the street level, where she hung out with Gilman and Village friends. Across the street was Powell's favorite restaurant, Café Lafayette in the Lafayette Hotel (since demolished). Powell joked that from her apartment she could "look out the window and watch [her own] checks bouncing there." In *The Wicked Pavilion*, Powell referred to Café Lafayette as Café Julien, in which the waiters were "forthright self-respecting individuals who felt their first duty was to protect the café from customers." Powell and her husband lived here until 1958, when resurgent money troubles forced them into a routine of temporary lodging in sublets and hotels.

Dawn Powell, 1940.

Library of Congress, Prints and Photographs Division

Empire State Building

350 Fifth Avenue, between West 33rd and West 34th Streets
tel. (212) 736-3100, www.esbnyc.com

Powell marveled at the Empire State Building when it went up in 1931, calling it: "The most magical spot in the world. Bizarre, theatrical—it is impossible to believe in it and people jumping off are (I'm sure) caught on rubber mattresses a few feet below their jumping off place."

New York Public Library

Fifth Avenue at West 42nd Street
tel. (212) 930-0830, www.nypl.org

In 1922, Powell began work on *Whither,* an autobiographical novel about her first years in New York. Powell wrote much of the novel in Central Park and the New York Public Library, spending most of her time in the Children's Reading Room, then one of thirteen special reading rooms. The Children's Reading Room has since moved to the Donnell Library Center at 20 West 53rd Street.

Hart Island

East of City Island in Long Island Sound

Powell died destitute and was buried on Hart Island, the city's potter's field, maintained by inmate labor and closed to the public. Since 1868, Hart Island has provided burial grounds for the indigent and unclaimed—from Confederate Army POWs to victims of yellow fever. In the tradition of Manhattan's small satellite islands, Hart Island has done many municipal turns: as a prison, quarantine center for epidemic victims, charity hospital for women, insane asylum, a missile base, narcotic rehabilitation center, and a housing center for "male derelicts." A thirty-foot monument, proposed and built by inmates, honors the nameless dead. The Corrections Department attributes the term "Potter's Field" to the Bible (Gospel of St. Matthew 27:3-8)—Judas has repented and returned the thirty pieces of silver to the chief priests, who take the coins and buy "with them the potter's field to bury strangers in."

Tito Puente, undated.

© Craig Lovell/CORBIS

Tito Puente

MUSICIAN 1923–2000

T ito Puente's parents were among the early Puerto Rican immigrants to New York City who settled in Spanish Harlem. His father found work as a foreman in a razor blade factory, while his mother nurtured her son's musical ability. Puente's first ambition was professional dance (he started competing at five), but an injured ankle changed his plans. By age twelve, Puente was already a "star of the future," a title given to him by the head of a local funeral home who organized talent competitions. He began to work as a drummer in a New York big band at the age of thirteen. He drummed while serving in the Navy in World War II and, on the GI bill, studied at the Julliard School of Music. Over decades, Tito Puente and His Orchestra developed Latin Jazz and led audiences through big band, mambo, cha-cha, and salsa. He was crowned again and again: King of the Kettledrums, King of Mambo, King of Latin Music, until he was known definitively and simply as "El Rey." Inexhaustible and prolific, Puente recorded more than one hundred albums and received five Grammies.

Tito Puente Way
110th Street from Fifth to First Avenues

This stretch of 110th Street was named in honor of Puente. He lived with his family in a tenement on the block of 110th between Madison and Park Avenues until 1938.

. . . .

El Museo del Barrio
1230 Fifth Avenue at 104th Street
tel. (212) 831-7272, www.elmuseo.org

This building was an orphanage beginning in the 1920s, hence the murals of toadstools, gnomes, and other staples of children's literature, which fill the walls, ceiling, and proscenium of this active theater in El Museo del Barrio. The Teatro Heckscher housed Broadway auditions in the 1930s. A tribute to Tito Puente was held here during the 39th Grammy Awards.

. . . .

Palladium Dance Hall
140 East 14th Street, between Third and Fourth Avenues

In the 1950s, Puente and the Palladium made each other famous by providing the venue and music for the 1950s obsession with the mambo and cha-cha. New Yorkers from all neighborhoods and backgrounds gathered at the Palladium (and spin-off dance studios) to learn the steps. In the 1970s, salsa—an umbrella term for mambo, cha-cha, merengue, and other dance music with Caribbean origins—developed in New York City. Puente collaborated with Celia Cruz, the "Queen of Salsa," on many albums. Two current salsa venues in the city are Sounds of Brazil (SOB's) at 204 Varick Street at Houston and Studio 145, at 3534 Broadway at 145th Street. SOB's features salsa lessons and an orchestra that plays Puente and other salsa masters on Monday nights.

. . . .

Tito Puente's
64 City Island Avenue
City Island, The Bronx
tel. (718) 885-3200

Puente founded his namesake restaurant on City Island, which is connected to the Bronx by a small, two-lane bridge. Though City Island is no longer necessarily quaint, neither does it feel like the rest of New York. Boats are everywhere; houses outnumber apartment buildings; city people eat fried fresh seafood and look out over Long Island Sound and wooded Hart Island. A former fishing, oyster harvesting, and boat building village, City Island attracts visitors with a string of restaurants along its main street. Tito Puente's is decorated with vibrant murals, memorabilia, and many photographs of Puente with fellow greats such as Duke Ellington. The bar stools are conga drums. Puente spent much of his time here dining with friends, speaking with customers, and hosting benefits for the Tito Puente Scholarship Fund, which supports young musicians studying Latin Jazz.

Joey Ramone

MUSICIAN 1951–2001

T all, ungainly, and soft-spoken, the young man from Forest Hills, Queens, was not obvious rock star material. In 1974, the innovator of punk rock changed his name from Jeff Hyman to Joey Ramone and founded a band—all four members of whom adopted "Ramone" as their last name. At venues throughout New York, most notably CBGB's, Joey Ramone, in black leather jacket and sunglasses, led the band through jagged, upbeat anthems such as "I Wanna Be Sedated," "Teenage Lobotomy," and "Blitzkrieg Bop." The Ramones's minimalist, agitated lyrics backed up by fast, spare instrumentals became hallmarks of the underground music scene in the 1970s. The Ramones took their new album—thirty-plus songs compressed into an hour and a half—to London in 1976, where their performances influenced the Sex Pistols and other English punk bands. Ramone battled lymphoma for seven years, and died at forty-nine of complications from the disease.

CBGB-OMFUG

315 Bowery, between East 1st and East 2nd Streets
tel. (212) 982-4052, www.cbgb.com

When The Ramones debuted here, owner Hilly Kristal, who had hoped to attract Country Bluegrass Blues bands and fans, was not impressed by The Ramones's chaotic, aggressive performance. As the band improved and a scene developed around CBGB's, it became the premiere venue—some said the birthplace—of punk rock. Won over by The Ramones and the punk scene, Kristal tagged on a second acronym: Other Music for Uplifting Gormandizers. Ramone lived down the street from CBGB's and, after his death, the front of the club became a shrine to him. For weeks after, photos, candles, flowers, and letters spilled onto the sidewalk.

Continental

25 Third Avenue, between St. Mark's Place and East 9th Street
tel. (212) 529-6924, www.continentalnyc.com

Continental has been open for over a decade and has hosted legends like the Ramones and Patti Smith as well as unknown and young bands emerging on the punk scene. Ramone performed his last show here on December 11, 2000.

Joey Ramone Place

Corner of Second Street and Bowery

Close to his muscial headquarters, CBGB, to the "Ramones Loft" where he lived for many years, and to the brick wall that provided the backdrop to the Ramones's first album cover, this intersection has been given the honorific name of Joey Ramone Place.

Jacob Riis

REFORMER AND PHOTOGRAPHER 1849–1914

J acob Riis emigrated from Denmark in 1870. Despite his best efforts to find work and safe lodging, he was soon swamped by the poverty that overtook most immigrants arriving in the midst of a citywide economic depression. For seven years, Riis struggled, often sleeping in doorways. A writer by trade, he eventually found work as a crime reporter for *The New York Tribune*, working from offices located in notoriously violent, crowded Mulberry Bend. Determined to expose middle-class readers to the plight of immigrants and the poor, Riis wrote poignant profiles of people in the slums, but later turned to photography to provide incontrovertible evidence of the squalor and degradation. Through his life of total engagement with the problem of the slums, Riis's attitude evolved: he initially supported the toughest bootstraps remedies and theorized about the cultural inferiority of different immigrant groups, but he ultimately pressured the state to clear slums and provide affordable, safe housing for the poor. His campaign to reform New York City culminated in his photodocumentary, *How the Other Half Lives*. The police commissioner Theodore Roosevelt walked with Riis through the worst-off neighborhoods of the Lower East Side. He called Riis "the most useful citizen of New York" and offered him positions in his administration after becoming president. Riis declined and worked on his reform-minded books and photographs until his death in 1914.

Jacob Riis, 1903.

The Museum of the City of New York

Former site of *The New York Tribune* office
303 Mulberry Street at East Houston Street

Riis worked out of a house at this address from 1877 to 1889. From the stoop of their two-story, rundown office, Riis and fellow reporters watched for activity at Mulberry Street Police Headquarters across the street. They listened for the buzz of reported crimes along the crudely strung telegraph wires that linked police stations in the city. Riis remembered as the fondest time in his life his all-night walks with police commissioner Teddy Roosevelt, as they paced the gaslit streets together, collars turned up against the cold and anyone who might recognize them. "It is long since, I have enjoyed anything so much as I did those patrol trips of ours in the 'lost Hour' between midnight and sunrise…I had at last found one who was willing to get up when other people slept—including too often the police—and see what the town looked like then. He was more than willing."

Columbus Park
Mulberry Street, between Bayard and Worth Streets

This community park has taken root at the former "foul core" of the slums, Mulberry Bend, the local name for the intersection of Mulberry, Bayard, and Worth Streets. Dangerously overpopulated, disease-ridden, and composed of twisting back alleys and ramshackle houses, the mostly Irish "Bloody Sixth" Ward came to represent crime and depravity to nineteenth-century New Yorkers. In addition to overcrowding, filth, and crime, the neighborhood was overrun by gangs like the Dead Rabbits, who waged violent street battles against the Plug Uglies and others. Riis led the fight to have the Mulberry Bend slums destroyed and replaced by community centers and safe housing. This former heart of darkness is now a serene neighborhood where Chinatown residents play chess and mahjong.

Lower East Side Tenement Museum

90 Orchard Street at Broome Street
tel. (212) 431-0233, www.tenement.org

The Lower East Side Tenement Museum is the best portal into tenement life through the decades. The story of the Gumpertz Apartment, restored to a domestic scene from 1874, touches the economic and family troubles that befell immigrants, whose only support came from within their own communities.

The Museum of the City of New York

1220 Fifth Avenue at East 103rd Street
tel. (212) 534-1672, www.mcny.org

Roger William Riis donated the 326 glass lantern slides, 191 vintage prints, and other materials produced by his father to the Museum of the City of New York in 1946. Riis published his photographs in *How The Other Half Lives* in 1890. He had learned to take and develop photographs just two years earlier. Riis quit photography and journalism to follow the lecture circuit after the book made him a sought-after speaker. In his speeches, he used his own slides, as well as those by Jessie Tarbox Beals and others who had documented tenement life.

Greenwich House Community Center

27 Barrow Street, between Bleecker and West 4th Streets
tel. (212) 242-4140, www.greenwichhouse.org

Riis was among the social reformers who founded this community center in 1902, opening its doors on Thanksgiving Day to provide services for the immigrant population in New York's most crowded zone. Greenwich House created the country's first tenants' manual, first neighborhood association, and the Greenwich Village Improvement Society. The affiliate settlement house opened in 1917.

Site of former residence

84-47 120th Street, between 85th and Myrtle Avenues
Richmond Hill, Queens

Riis lived in a white Victorian house with a broad front porch at this address in Queens. A plaque on the contemporary apartment building commemorates his long residence here. Riis wrote most of his pieces, including *How The Other Half Lives*, in a tiny cottage behind the house. Other Victorian houses remain in the neighborhood and are listed at www.richmondhillhistory.org.

Church of the Resurrection

85-109 118th Street, between Hillside and 85th Avenues
Kew Gardens, Queens
tel. (718) 847-2649

Riis's daughter had her wedding here in 1900. Among the guests was Riis's old friend President Theodore Roosevelt. The church has been here since 1874.

··

International Center for Photography

1133 Sixth Avenue at West 43rd Street
tel. (212) 857-0000, www.icp.org/weegee

Riis's photograph, *Bandits' Roost* (1888), of rough-looking men lining a narrow alley in slums of New York, is in the collection here.

Diego Rivera

ARTIST 1886–1957

D iego Rivera was gregarious, pear-shaped, and politically principled. He devoted his art to the elevation of the poor and the politically oppressed by glorifying workers, factories, and socialist leaders in his paintings and murals. An ideologically resolute Marxist, Rivera was less consistent in his personal life and tormented his wife Frida Kahlo with his womanizing. John D. Rockefeller, Jr. commissioned him to paint a mural for his new Rockefeller Center—material opposites, the men shared a belief in "human intelligence in control of the forces of nature," in the words of Rockefeller's commission. Rivera and Kahlo moved to New York in the spring of 1933. Rivera's mural, *Man at the Crossroads*, resembled the engineered interior of a society-bettering machine: interlocking people inventing, building, lifting, and supporting the integrity of the whole. Manual and intellectual workers appeared healthy and courageous, with perfect limbs and smooth, symmetrical faces. Outraged to see Lenin depicted as a heroic figure at the center of the "crossroads," Rockefeller ordered workers to destroy the mural, while Rivera and Kahlo watched from the floor. Supported by outraged artists, writers, and activists in New York, Rivera remained in the United States to finish a series of panels, a "portrait of America," at the New Workers School as a gift to the people of the United States. The panels were taken down and dispersed when the institution shut down.

··

GE Building (formerly RCA Building)

570 Lexington Avenue at East 51st Street

The site of the public standoff between John D. Rockefeller, Jr. and Diego Rivera. Though Rivera's mural is, obviously, no longer in place, other murals by painters of the same period survive throughout the complex.

John D. Rockefeller, Jr. was rightly famous as a philanthropist, whose huge contributions provided the United Nations with its New York headquarters, restored Colonial Williamsburg, and aided many other civic institutions. In 1928, Rockefeller entered into an agreement to develop a new Metropolitan Opera House. When the crash of 1929 dashed those plans, Rockefeller dreamed up a new kind of skyscraper—a self-contained entertainment and retail complex—for the land that had been set aside for it. Now a

Library of Congress Prints and Photographs Division

landmark iconic of New York, Rockefeller Center was first derided by many, particularly artists who remained angry over the destruction of Rivera's mural and who considered the center a monument to capitalism. In *Panorama*, a WPA–sponsored book of essays about New York written in 1938, the caption under a photo of the sunken plaza reads: "Rockefeller Center's Sunken Plaza—for those who can afford it."

While Rivera and Rockefeller were celebrating the machine as America's most beautiful object, *The New York Times* editorialized that: "People are pretty well-agreed that humanity is in such a sorry pass today because we have been unable to maintain control of the elaborate machines we have invented," and the WPA writers described Rockefeller Center itself as a kind of nefarious machine, one that "sucks tenants out of a large area of smaller obsolescent buildings into one close-packed super-center….The jagged rhythm of the buildings appears to endow them with motion."

Union Square

From 14th to 17th Streets and from Union Square West (Broadway) to Union Square East (Park Avenue South)

Rivera and Kahlo passed much of their New York visit in the Union Square area—traditionally a site of social activism and political protest. In the 1930s, Union Square was rich soil for labor unions and socialist organizations. The New Workers School, where Rivera painted his series Portrait of America, was located at 51 West 14th Street, a few blocks west of Union Square; it is now a retail space that fails to evoke much feeling for the past. Rivera and Kahlo also lived and worked earlier in their visit at 8 West 13th Street, now part of the Parsons School of Design/New School complex.

The square marks the union of Fourth Avenue and Broadway and was saved from further development by the city in 1811. Soon after the park's creation, it became the natural and automatic gathering point for many rallies, protests, and marches in support of workers' rights. A quarter of a million people filled the neighborhood for a pro-Union Army rally in 1861; in 1882, ten thousand workers marched through Union Square to support the proposal for a national Labor Day. In 1908, an unsanctioned rally for the unemployed was quashed by hundreds of police. When two anarchists were killed by their own bomb, the police scattered the crowd (which was reportedly singing the "Marseillaise" defiantly) with clubs. Protesters against the conviction of Sacco and Vanzetti marched through in 1927. By the 1930s, when Rivera and Kahlo spent time in the area, Union Square had a solidly "red" reputation—many labor unions had opened offices around the park and rallies were held often. Shop owners tried to overshadow the park's reputation as a haven for socialists, anarchists, and leftist artists by draping the park in American flags. The history of social awareness and activism is remembered at the southwest corner of the park with a statue of Ghandi, pensive and in mid-stride.

· ·

El Museo del Barrio

1230 Fifth Avenue at 104th Street
tel. (212) 831-7272, www.elmuseo.org

El Museo hosted major exhibits of work by Rivera and Frida Kahlo in 2002. The museum's permanent collection is rich with pre-Colombian, traditional, and contemporary pieces from Puerto Rican, Caribbean, and Latin American artists.

· ·

Barbizon-Plaza Hotel

106 Central Park South at Sixth Avenue

In 1933, Rivera and Kahlo stayed here. The Barbizon-Plaza Hotel had debuted just three years earlier as New York's "first fully equipped music-artist residence center." In New York, Kahlo filled her room with the prints of Mexican artist Jose Guadalupe Posada—traditional folk art depictions of skeletons dancing, talking, playing—and sketched self-portraits on Barbizon-Plaza Hotel stationary. This building has since been converted to pricey condominiums.

· ·

Museum of Modern Art (MoMA)

11 West 53rd Street, between Fifth and Sixth Avenues
tel. (212) 708-9400, www.moma.org

Included in the permanent collection of the museum are drawings by Rivera, including *Two Figures* (circa 1925). Frida Kahlo's *Self-Portrait with Cropped Hair* (1940) is also here—she painted the portrait of herself dressed in a man's suit, scissors in hand, shorn locks at her feet after her divorce from Rivera. At the top of the painting is an excerpt from a Mexican song: "Look, if I loved you it was because of your hair. Now that you are without hair, I don't love you anymore."

Sugar Ray Robinson

BOXER 1921–1989

S ugar Ray Robinson remains the only boxer to have won five middleweight championships; he had an almost perfect record, losing only a handful of bouts during his career. His boxing nemesis, Jake "the Raging Bull" LaMotta from the Bronx, beat Robinson in only one of their six standoffs. In their last match in 1951, dubbed the St. Valentine's Day Massacre, Robinson pummeled LaMotta through thirteen rounds until referees finally called the match. After retiring from the ring, Robinson opened a string

Sugar Ray Robinson, 1947.

of successful businesses in Harlem. He toured the country and Europe with a tap dance revue that was a hit for more than two years—when he returned, he found his Harlem ventures floundering in the hands of an inept business manager. Robinson was thereafter under constant pressure to earn money to keep the businesses open and to fend off the IRS, which began collecting his prize money to cover overdue taxes. He was forced to stay in the ring to make a living, and he fought professionally until the age of 44. In 1965, Madison Square Garden saluted Robinson's long, illustrious boxing career with lavish ceremony, though Robinson himself was living with very little in a Manhattan apartment. Throughout his career, Robinson donated many of his winnings to charity, and in 1969, he established the Sugar Ray Robinson Youth Foundation in Los Angeles. Forty thousand children in need have passed through the center since 1969. It has no boxing program.

Site of Sugar Ray Robinson's Café

West 124th Street at Seventh Avenue

Robinson practically owned this stretch of Harlem's Seventh Avenue in the 1950s—he ran a café, his wife's lingerie shop, a barbershop, and dry cleaners in the neighborhood. He parked his fuchsia Cadillac, which he called the "Hope Diamond of Harlem," in front of his café and held court inside. Robinson was a resident of Sugar Hill and spent most of his time in the community, looking in on his businesses, sparring affectionately with kids on the street, and helping many young athletes, including Althea Gibson.

Apollo Theater

253 West 125th Street, between St Nicholas Avenue and Frederick Douglass Boulevard
tel. (212) 531-5300, www.apollotheater.com

Dance was Robinson's first love, and before he began boxing, he took tap dancing lessons. Years later, Robinson (and, after him, Muhammad Ali) learned footwork from Sandman Sims, the legendary resident tap dancer at the Apollo Theater who died in the summer of 2003. Sandman Sims's twenty-five-night winning streak at the Apollo's Amateur Night forced the theater to place a four-win limit on contestants.

Salem-Crescent Athletic Club

Salem United Methodist Church
211 West 129th Street at Adam Clayton Powell Jr. Boulevard

Robinson first learned to box in the basement of this building. A friend took Robinson to the community athletic center then located in the church's basement and introduced him to George Gainford, who would be Robinson's trainer for life.

Site of Stillman's Gym

919 Eighth Avenue, between West 54th and West 55th Streets

Robinson was the charismatic prince of Stillman's Gym, once located on this block in a converted union hall. From the moment he arrived in his decked-out convertible Cadillac, Robinson was the center of attention. He did most of his professional training here, and when he sparred in the ring or pounded the speed bag, all of the other boxers left their own routines to watch him work, awed by his elegant footwork. Stillman's Gym originally opened as a rehabilitation organization for ex-convicts. Lou Ingber (who changed his name to Stillman) took over the gym in the 1920s. Though Stillman's closed in 1959, the atmosphere of the classic New York boxing gym can be experienced at Gleason's Gym (83 Front Street, almost under the Brooklyn Bridge), which has been operating since 1937.

Yankee Stadium

East 161st Street at River Avenue
Grand Concourse, The Bronx
tel. (718) 293-6000, www.yankees.com

In the summer of 1952, Robinson faced light heavyweight champion Joey Maxim at Yankee Stadium. The fighters lasted thirteen rounds in the 103 degree heat—the referee had quit in the tenth—but Robinson failed to come out of his corner when the bell sounded for the fourteenth, and Maxim remained champion.

Franklin Delano Roosevelt speaking at Hunter College before a speech at the Democratic Rally at Madison Square Garden, undated.

The Museum of the City of New York

Franklin D. Roosevelt

US PRESIDENT 1882–1945

F ranklin D. Roosevelt's casual public manner belied a fierce pride in his august lineage. He claimed hereditary ties to Queen Elizabeth and Winston Churchill, and was famously related to Theodore Roosevelt, his fifth cousin. He married another fifth cousin, Eleanor Roosevelt, in 1905. At age thirty-nine, FDR the voluminous speaker and restless extrovert, was struck down with polio. With Eleanor Roosevelt's support, arduous physical therapy, and twelve pounds of metal bracing to scaffold his large-framed body, FDR pushed on to win the presidency in 1932. He remains the only president to have served beyond the now constitutional two-term limit (he was elected to office four times). Jubilantly aware of the power of the office of the presidency, and mindful of the fragility of his own political power, FDR immediately launched a torrent of government programs designed to pull the country out of the Depression. His fast work—the suspension of the gold standard, the creation of Social Security, and vast public works programs—alarmed the banking and governing elite, who railed against the New Deal. At the end of World War II, FDR called upon "the United Nations" (those unified against the Axis Powers) to form a world-governing body to promote peace and justice. FDR died in the spring of 1945, just months before fifty nations signed the United Nations charter and before the US dropped atomic bombs on Hiroshima and Nagasaki.

Site of Roosevelt wedding

8 East 76th Street, between Fifth and Madison Avenues

FDR and Eleanor Roosevelt were married here in 1905, when it was the home of Mr. and Mrs. Henry Parish, Jr., cousins to bride and groom. President Theodore Roosevelt had invited his beloved niece to stage the ceremony at the White House, but she opted for New York City. Because both of her parents had died when she was young, the president accompanied Eleanor Roosevelt down the aisle.

Former residence

47-49 East 65th Street, between Madison and Park Avenues

In 1908, Eleanor and FDR took possession of 47 East 65th Street, a wedding gift from Franklin's mother, Sara D. Roosevelt, who continued to live next door at 49 East 65th Street. For Eleanor, it proved a difficult arrangement; her formidable mother-in-law, separated from their lives by a matter of feet, critiqued all marital, housekeeping, and child-rearing decisions. This is the home in which FDR worked to overcome polio. In 1941, Sara D. Roosevelt died and FDR sold the joint home to Hunter College. Hunter College has undertaken a $15 million renovation of the building, which will be used by the school's public policy institute.

The United Nations

First Avenue, between East 41st and East 42nd Streets
tel. (212) 963-8687, www.un.org

"We cannot live alone, at peace…our own well-being is dependent on the well-being of other nations—far away…We have learned to be citizens of the world, members of the human community…We can gain no lasting peace if we approach it with suspicion and mistrust—and with fear."—Roosevelt's Inaugural Address, January 20, 1945

The League of Nations, created in 1919 by the Treaty of Versailles, had collapsed after failing to avert World War II, but Roosevelt insisted on the need for a world-governing body to promote the sanctity of human rights and the cessation of war. FDR coined the term "United Nations" to describe the solidarity of the twenty-six nations allied against the Axis Powers. He and Winston Churchill drafted the "Atlantic Charter" (signed somewhere in the Atlantic on the HMS *Prince of Wales*) in August 1941, with the rest of the twenty-six allied nations ratifying the Declaration of United Nations on January 1, 1942. In 1945, fifty nations signed the founding charter. In recognition of Eleanor Roosevelt's civic leadership, President Harry Truman appointed her to the United States Delegation to the United Nations General Assembly, a post she held from 1945 to 1953. She rose to chairman of the UN Human Rights Commission during her tenure and played a central role in drafting and securing the Universal Declaration of Human Rights.

....

McSorley's Old Ale House

15 East 7th Street, between Cooper Square and Second Avenue
tel. (212) 473-9148

McSorley's has served its light and dark ale to many presidents, including FDR. Lore has it that Abraham Lincoln stopped in while campaigning for the presidency in 1860, that Theodore Roosevelt relaxed here after a day's work at the office at the Police Commission, and that John F. Kennedy followed his father's footsteps through these doors.

....

New-York Historical Society

2 West 77th Street at Central Park West
tel. (212) 873-3400, www.nyhistory.org

Portraits, busts, manuscripts, and political campaign props of Roosevelt's are on display here.

Theodore Roosevelt

US PRESIDENT 1858–1919

T heodore Roosevelt, whose barrel-chested physique, all-terrain bravery, and military adventures made him a national symbol of strength, began life as the asthmatic and sickly son of socially conscious, affluent parents in New York. Despite his frailty, young Roosevelt was delighted by life in all its forms: he collected animals, flowers, and insects from an early age, and filled his parents' house with specimens. As an adolescent, Roosevelt overcame his physical weakness with an obsessive, painful routine of weight-lifting and exercise. In 1895, he became president of the New York Police Commission. During one of New York's most corrupt and politically shady periods, he alone was considered beyond fear, pressure, or bribery. Roosevelt led the charge up Kettle Hill in the Battle of San Juan and returned to New York as a celebrity candidate in his successful gubernatorial race and later as running mate to presidential candidate William McKinley. He ascended to the presidency in 1901, after McKinley's assassination, and was elected to a second term in 1904. He strong-armed the Panama Canal into existence and was a naturalist and prolific writer who coined many Americanisms, including "lunatic fringe" and "bully pulpit." He is memorialized at the entrance to the American Museum of Natural History as "Author, Patriot, Statesman, Soldier, Conservationist, Ranchman, Naturalist, Scholar, Scientist."

....

Theodore Roosevelt Birthplace

28 East 20th Street, between Broadway and Park Avenue South
tel. (212) 260-1616, www.nps.gov/thrb

The birthplace and childhood home of Roosevelt. He remembered that his mother had filled the house with "everything that was beautiful." Destroyed in 1916, the house was rebuilt in 1922 as a museum. Roosevelt's wife and sisters provided furniture and ob-

jects from his early life to fill the childhood home and to evoke his early years. Visitors are taken through the house on hourly tours that include the upstairs gym in which Roosevelt built up his strength. In the long, narrow exhibition room on the ground floor of the house are relics from all stages of Roosevelt's life: personal items, such as his baptismal gown and wedding clothes are on display, as are photographs, letters, and political cartoons from his public life. The last shovelful of the Panama Canal excavation is kept in a glass jar.

Also on display is a bullet-pierced, red-leather bound manuscript. Roosevelt had his speech in his breast pocket when he rose to address a crowd in Milwaukee in 1912 as the Progressive Party presidential candidate. A would-be assassin charged the podium and shot him at close range in the chest. Roosevelt did not lose his composure or allow anyone to examine his wound. He spoke for ninety minutes, his white vest soaked with blood, before consenting to be rushed to the hospital.

Theodore Roosevelt Rotunda and Memorial Hall

American Museum of Natural History
Central Park West at West 79th Street
tel. (212) 769-5100, www.amnh.org

The charter for the American Museum of Natural History was signed by Roosevelt's father in the family home in 1869. Decades later, Theodore Roosevelt collected specimens for the museum and, as president, cultivated national policies and a national spirit in defense of natural resources.

At the Central Park West entrance to the museum, a statue of Theodore Roosevelt looks deep into the trees of Central Park. Surrounding the Theodore Roosevelt Rotunda, dedicated in 1936, are murals of Roosevelt, New York, and world events, often intersecting. Scenes from Roosevelt's life commemorated on the rotunda include: the brokering of the Russo-Japanese peace; a hunting Roosevelt over an alert lion; Roosevelt in spectacles and white suit overseeing the completion of the Panama Canal: "The Land Divided. The World United."

Downstairs from the rotunda is the Memorial Hall, built between 1929 and 1935. It has the thick columns and stillness of a tomb. Four dioramas and glassed-in bookshelves contain relics and photographs of the remarkably full stages of Roosevelt's life. Things to see there: a Snowy Owl "collected" and mounted by Roosevelt himself in 1876; Roosevelt's buckskin suit; the political cartoons that followed Roosevelt's famous refusal to shoot a bear cub that inspired the "Teddy Bear" craze; nature drawings by young Teddy; a replica of the Nobel Peace Prize he was awarded for having mediated the peace between Russia and Japan; and dioramas of taxidermied birds scavenging among the leaves at a virtual Oyster Bay, the Roosevelt Long Island retreat.

National Arts Club

15 Gramercy Park, between Park Avenue South and Irving Place
tel. (212) 475-3424, www.nationalartsclub.org

Roosevelt was an active member of the National Arts Club, which was founded in 1898 by Charles DeKay, the literary critic of *The New York Times*, as a meeting place for artists, writers, and others active in the arts community. The National Arts Club was the first arts club to include women as members from its inception. The club moved into this building, the former mansion of Samuel J. Tilden, in 1906. Though the club is only open to members, the public is free to visit the art galleries on the lower level. (The galleries close every July and August.) Through the entrance and down a shallow set of marble stairs is the old billiards room, lined with examples of patriotic embroidery. Overlooking the old-fashioned pool table are a portrait and a carved bust of Theodore Roosevelt.

Former police headquarters

300 Mulberry Street at East Houston Street

Each morning at 8:30 between 1895 and 1897, Police Commissioner Roosevelt ran up the steps of the police headquarters formerly at this address. His mania for police work was observed with interest by the group of police reporters, including Jacob Riis, who loitered on the stoop of 303 Mulberry across the street waiting for news to break. In 1895, the police department was plagued by corruption and scandals. Policemen rarely bothered to patrol, except to collect protection money from citizens. They were also known to club New Yorkers without provocation or consequence, and generally did Tammany Hall's bidding. Roosevelt created the ideal of the modern police department with his requirements—uniform appearance, duty-bound service, and civil treatment of the public. Accompanied by his friend Riis, Roosevelt prowled the streets of the Lower East Side incognito and caught his on-duty officers napping, drinking, or absent from their beats. Fearful of an unannounced visit from Roosevelt, police resumed their patrols until they were as regular as clockwork. Unafraid of controversy, Roosevelt instituted a police bicycle patrol and put New Yorkers through a summer hell of dry Sundays when he shut down all saloons (of which there were an estimated 15,000) to starve Tammany Hall out of liquor racketeering.

Wave Hill

Entrance at: 675 West 252nd Street
Riverdale, The Bronx
tel. (718) 549-3200, www.wavehill.org

Roosevelt spent the summers of his twelfth and thirteenth years with his family at Wave Hill. They lived in the main house, but young Teddy spent most of his time outside, exploring the grounds and adding its flora and fauna to his collection.

Alice Roosevelt's townhouse

217 East 61st Street, between Second and Third Avenues

In 1906, Roosevelt delivered ownership of this townhouse to his daughter Alice as a wedding present.

Onieal's Grand Street Bar and Restaurant

174 Grand Street at Baxter Street
tel. (212) 941-9119, www.onieals.com

Roosevelt is rumored to have reached this bar through an underground tunnel leading from the police headquarters directly across the street. This is highly suspect, since the old police headquarters on Centre Street did not appear until a decade after Roosevelt's tenure as police commissioner. Whether or not Roosevelt met reporters here for off-the-record chats, this elegant restaurant evokes its 1930s life as a speakeasy, when New Yorkers gathered downstairs at the hidden bar. The tunnel between Onieal's—which has operated as a pub under many different names for over a century—and the former police headquarters has since been sealed off. Onieal's uses the truncated passage as a wine cellar.

Bronx Zoo

Fordham Road at the Bronx River Parkway
Bronx Park, The Bronx
tel. (718) 367-1010, www.bronxzoo.com

Roosevelt was a founding member of the New York Zoological Society, established in 1895, and its flagship, the Bronx Zoo, which opened to the public in 1899. Though the look of the Zoo has changed dramatically in the last century, the World of Reptiles looks just as it did in 1899, which seems appropriate.

George Herman "Babe" Ruth

BASEBALL PLAYER 1895–1948

B abe Ruth started out as a left-handed pitcher. He went on to break hitting records that stood for seventy years and to lead the formerly losing Yankees to seven pennants and four World Championships. Even at the pinnacle of his celebrity, he remained a good-natured and grateful public figure, whose affability and soft looks belied his athleticism. Ruth grew up the first of eight children, only three of whom survived, on the dicey Baltimore waterfront. His mother and father were consumed by the upkeep of a tavern, so Ruth fended for himself until his parents gave up entirely in 1902 and signed custody of their son over to the Jesuit order. At St. Mary's Industrial School for Boys, Ruth pitched and hit impressively on the walled-in baseball diamond. At nineteen, he joined the Baltimore Orioles but was soon in Boston playing for the Red

Babe Ruth, 1926

© Bettmann/CORBIS

Sox and living with his young bride. Traded by the Red Sox in 1919, Ruth began his career with the New York Yankees, drawing the largest crowds in the history of baseball. Ruth excelled at all sports, and loved golf, fishing, and hunting. He prized the attention of young fans and was happiest in the midst of a mob of children. April 27, 1946 was declared "Babe Ruth Day" in all ballparks—Ruth was frail from his battle with throat cancer, but he returned to Yankee Stadium for the honor.

Former Ansonia Hotel
2109 Broadway, between West 73rd and West 74th Streets

Built between 1899 and 1904, the Ansonia Hotel was home to many illustrious New Yorkers. It opened its doors at the dawn of the twentieth century as the grandest of the residential hotels in the city. The Ansonia was full of innovative and traditional pleasures for its guests—there were pneumatic arteries snaking through the hotel, so that tenants could exchange messages from within their rooms; there were six passenger elevators and two swimming pools; there were Turkish baths and pet seals splashing in the ornate lobby fountain. The Ansonia was Babe Ruth's first home in New York after joining the Yankees. Though he returned briefly in later years to share an eleven-room suite with his first wife, he spent his bachelor days in pursuit of ladies in the lobby and in the halls. He also tried to learn the saxophone while staying here. The Ansonia is now an apartment building.

Gramercy Park Hotel
2 Lexington Avenue at East 21st Street
tel. (800) 221-4083, www.gramercyparkhotel.com

Babe Ruth frequented this hotel and was a rambunctious presence in its famous bar—he was thrown out often for excessive reveling, but he was a devoted patron and always came back. The bar has recently undergone a major refurbishment. The Kennedys lived here briefly when the future president was eleven, and Humphrey Bogart married Helen Mencken on the roof.

St. Gregory's Roman Catholic Church
224 Brooklyn Avenue at St. John's Place
Crown Heights, Brooklyn

On April 17, 1929, widowed Ruth married for the second time here. In the Yankees Opening Day Game (which was the very next day), Ruth hit a homerun in Yankee Stadium—he called it a wedding present for his wife.

McSorley's Old Ale House
15 East 7th Street, between Cooper Square and Second Avenue
tel. (212) 473-9148

Ruth was a patron of McSorley's. On the west wall of the backroom is a photograph of Ruth, in tuxedo, and fellow sports stars at the Graphic All Sports Dinner in 1929.

Yankee Stadium
East 161st Street at River Avenue
Grand Concourse, The Bronx
tel. (718) 293-6000, www.yankees.com

Ruth's ability to fill the Polo Grounds with more than one million fans during the 1920 season had angered the resident Giants and inspired the Yankees to bankroll a home of their own. In 1923, the "House that Ruth Built" opened in the Bronx boasting 70,000 seats. It was the first sports venue to market itself as a "stadium." Babe Ruth hit the first home run in Yankee Stadium, and years later, on June 13, 1948, he donned his uniform (Number 3) for the last time to retire his number. He had been battling throat cancer since 1946. After his death, his body lay in state at the entrance to Yankee Stadium for two days. Hundreds of thousands of people (many times the capacity of Yankee Stadium) filed past to pay their respects. Monument Park, behind the centerfield wall, is populated with statues honoring Babe Ruth and other baseball greats.

St. Patrick's Cathedral
Fifth Avenue at 51st Street
tel. (212) 753-2261

Babe Ruth's funeral was held here on August 19, 1948.

Frank Sinatra
ENTERTAINER 1915–1998

F rank Sinatra was the only son of doting parents in a rundown section of Hoboken, New Jersey. As a teenager, he cruised around town in his convertible and belted out lyrics through a megaphone, creating in his hometown the kind of pop idol hysteria he would soon bring to the nation. Taking the path later romanticized in his hit, "New York, New York," Sinatra came to the city to make it big. He was soon a standout performer with Tommy Dorsey's band; Sinatra's voluble, fanatical fans seemed to aggravate everyone but Sinatra. During World War II, he was questioned in the press for his failure to go overseas, and critics even suggested that Sinatra was exploiting a nation of lonely ladies. Sinatra, however, made the rare transition from teen idol to great artist. He had studied the voice of Billie Holiday assiduously and developed his own unique phrasing for romantic songs, imbuing them with intensity and autobiographical immediacy. In addition to his fifty-year singing career, Sinatra performed with Sammy Davis, Jr. and other members of the "Rat Pack." He acted in more than sixty films and won an Oscar in 1953 for his role in *From Here to Eternity*. From Franklin D. Roosevelt, from whom a young Sinatra accepted an invitation to tea during the War, to John F. Kennedy, Jr. and Ronald Reagan, Sinatra worked to stay close to legitimate seats of power, though he denied frequent allegations of closeness to others, such as the mafia. When Apollo 11 touched down on the surface of the moon, astronauts listened to Sinatra's recording of "Fly Me to the Moon," making his the first singing voice in outer space.

Paramount Building
1505 Broadway, between West 43rd and West 44th Streets

This theater went up in 1926 as the New York Headquarters for Paramount Motion Pictures. Here in Times Square, Sinatra first met his army of fanatical teenage followers, when he was a featured solo act in a December 30, 1942 Benny Goodman show. He returned to the Paramount Building on October 12, 1944 headlining his own show. An estimated 30,000 fans crowded Times Square for the afternoon performance, disrupting traffic, undone by their proximity to their idol. The Police Department had to call

in reinforcements. As Sinatra's New York fame grew, parents and authorities grew distressed over an epidemic of truancy that they believed he inspired.

The Paramount Building was converted to office space in the 1950s.

Mare Chiaro
176-1/2 Mulberry Street, between Broome and Grand Streets
tel. (212) 226-9345

Once known in the neighborhood as "Sinatra's Bar," Mare Chiaro is a great Little Italy relic—sawdust on the floors, classic jukebox in the front bar, a partitioned back area with wooden coat hooks and lace curtains, and "Mare Chiaro" painted in an old-fashioned arc on the plate glass window. Photographs and paintings of Sinatra adorn the walls.

Patsy's Restaurant

236 West 56th Street, between Eighth Avenue and Broadway
tel. (212) 247-3491

Sinatra's favorite restaurant has been in the Scognamillo family since its founding in 1944. Sinatra's connection to Patsy's ran deep—the restaurant once opened on Thanksgiving just for Sinatra—and the legacy of his affection for Patsy's continues on the menu. Diners can still enjoy Sinatra's favorite dish, Clams Posillipo, and read about Sinatra's days at the restaurant in the introduction to *Patsy's Cookbook* written by Sinatra's daughter, Nancy Sinatra. Once Frank Sinatra made Patsy's part of his routine, the Rat Pack soon followed. Dean Martin and Sammy Davis, Jr. often joined Sinatra at his table here for the traditional Neapolitan cuisine.

P.J. Clarke's

915 Third Avenue at 55th Street
tel. (212) 317-1616, www.pjclarkes.com

Table 20 at P.J. Clarke's belonged to Sinatra, who is fondly remembered as an "extremely generous tipper." In his high-stamina roving through Manhattan bars and nightclubs, Sinatra usually started at Sardi's (234 West 44th Street) and ended up at P.J. Clarke's.

Empire State Building

350 Fifth Avenue, between West 33rd and West 34th Streets
tel. (212) 736-3100, www.esbnyc.com

To celebrate Sinatra's eightieth birthday in December 1995, the crown of the Empire State Building was illuminated blue, in honor of "Ol' Blue Eyes."

Valaida Snow

MUSICIAN 1903–1956

I n her lifetime, Valaida Snow was billed as "Little Louis" and the "Queen of the Trumpet." She spoke several languages, acted, sang, danced, and played a dozen instruments including the cello, the banjo, the clarinet, and the trumpet. Stunning and elegant, at fifteen she began performing in revues and cabarets throughout Harlem, before joining the early expatriate wave of African-American artists escaping racial persecution and exclusion in the United States. She was adored in Europe, where she ruled Paris with Josephine Baker and Maurice Chevalier; the queen of the Netherlands presented her with a gold trumpet. Snow exuded fabulousness: dressed in shimmering evening gowns, she rolled through town in an orchid-colored limousine that matched the uniform of her chauffeur and the costume of her pet monkey. In a world that expected jazz musicians, especially trumpeters, to be men, Snow was often relegated to appear as a novelty act on the entertainment circuit. She toured Europe during World War II with her all-women band. While she was in Copenhagen, German warplanes dropped leaflets over the city proclaiming, "This is now Germany." Snow's money and instruments were confiscated; she and other Americans were arrested by the Nazis and imprisoned at a concentration camp at Wester-Faengle for more than a year. She was released in poor health in a prisoner exchange program with Allied forces and returned to New York. She continued to perform and to tour, though she never recov-

ered physically from her imprisonment. She died backstage after her last performance at the Palace Theater in New York in 1956.

Apollo Theater

253 West 125th Street, between St. Nicholas Avenue and Frederick Douglass Boulevard
tel. (212) 531-5300, www.apollotheater.com

Snow headlined often at the Apollo Theatre. She appeared here shortly before returning to Europe, in the early days of World War II, where she was imprisoned for eighteen months.

Site of Small's Paradise

2294 Adam Clayton Powell Jr. Boulevard at West 135th Street

This is the site of Small's Paradise, the legendary Harlem nightclub owned by Ed Small.

Snow performed here often and was featured on April 20, 1950 in a "Salute to Show Business," during which honorary scrolls were given to Lena Horne, Cab Calloway, Ethel Waters, and Snow, in praise of their contributions to the performing arts.

Many of Snow's better-remembered contemporaries, including a deeply impressed Louis Armstrong (Snow was often billed as the "Little Louis" on her tours) were in awe of Snow's talent. In addition to speaking several languages, singing, and mastering several musical instruments, she was an accomplished dancer who lined the stage with several pairs of shoes—from clogs to Russian boots—and made her way through a tap revue, changing her shoes throughout. Though her many talents were well appreciated, some of her fellow artists mused that Snow could have been one of the greatest trumpeters in the world had she focused her talents solely on that instrument.

Theresa Hotel

2090 Adam Clayton Powell Jr. Boulevard, between West 124th and West 125th Streets

On May 8, 1950, Snow was here for the first recording of "Uptown Skyline," a WLIB radio show that profiled the leading figures of Harlem. She appeared with Nat King Cole, Ray Robinson, and Billy Eckstine.

Town Hall

123 West 43rd Street, between Sixth Avenue and Broadway
tel. (212) 840-2824, www.the-townhall-nyc.org

On May 20, 1949, Snow performed at this landmark theater, built between 1919 and 1921. She was billed as a "dramatic contralto" and performed with Wen Talbert's All Male Choir.

Palace Theater

1564 Broadway, between West 46th and West 47th Streets

Snow died backstage here on May 30, 1956, following her performance. She had topped the bill here two years earlier in a vaudeville-style show of comedy, music, and singing.

Alfred Stieglitz

PHOTOGRAPHER 1864–1946

A lfred Stieglitz, photographer and father of the modernist movement in American art, was first a student of science, preoccupied by the chemistry, physics, and optics of creating photographs. Just as his photographs eventually inducted the "machine art" (the derisive tag offered by traditionalists) of photography into the pantheon of the fine arts, his support of European abstract art helped launch the so-called invasion of modern art in the United States. He introduced Pablo Picasso and discovered Georgia O'Keeffe, and he further enlivened the staid art scene with the definitive modern art journals *Camera Work* and *Camera Notes*. As an artist, he concentrated on the peculiar depth of and profound interconnection among ordinary things—trees, clouds, the hands of women. In 1918, Stieglitz left his marriage to live with Georgia O'Keeffe, whose work he had introduced at his 291 Gallery. An avid outdoorsman, Stieglitz, as a young man, had walked hundreds of miles in the Alps honing his landscape portraiture. In New York City, his huge appetite for images and interconnections drove him through the streets of Lower Manhattan, and he exalted to friends that he wanted to capture all of it: "the Tombs, the old Post Office, Five Points…. I wanted to photograph everything I saw."

Site of Little Galleries of the Photo-Secession
291 and 293 Fifth Avenue, between 30th and 31st Streets

Stieglitz created a haven for new, challenging art at his Little Galleries of the Photo-Secession. In *Panorama*, the 1938 Works Progress Administration writers remembered the 291 as "a center of authentic novelty in art." Here Stieglitz mounted Picasso's first one-man show in America and debuted work by O'Keeffe and many others. His progressive writing, eye, and efforts introduced America to modern art. Before the Armory Show in 1913, of which Stieglitz was a driving force, 291 was the only place in the country to see abstract art and European avant-garde art.

Site of An American Place
509 Madison Avenue at East 53rd Street

Housed on the seventeenth floor from 1929 until 1946 was Stieglitz's successor to his "little galleries" at 291 and 293 Broadway.

National Arts Club
15 Gramercy Park, between Park Avenue South and Irving Place
tel. (212) 475-3424, www.nationalartsclub.org

Stieglitz helped to launch the Photo-Secession movement at the National Arts Club in 1902. The movement represented an organized effort to present photographs as works of art and to push serious discussion of photography's contributions into debates about modernist art.

Flatiron Building
Fifth Avenue, between East 22nd and East 23rd Streets

One of Stieglitz's photographic preoccupations. On a foggy, gray day in 1903, he photographed the building in the background of a dark tree in sharp focus, giving the building an ethereal, unreal appearance.

Site of Photochrome Engraving Company
162 Leonard Street, between Lafayette and Centre Streets

At the urging of his father, Stieglitz had trained as a graphic artist. Stieglitz, Sr. bought his son an interest in a printing enterprise here to encourage him to return from Europe, where he had been studying and exploring.

Former Residence
114 East 59th Street, between Park and Lexington Avenues

Stieglitz and O'Keeffe lived in his niece's fifth floor studio here in 1918, after Stieglitz had left his first wife.

The Jewish Museum

1109 Fifth Avenue at East 92nd Street
tel. (212) 423-3200, www.jewishmuseum.org

Stieglitz's 1907 photograph, *The Steerage*, of immigrants returning to Europe is in the museum's permanent collection. Stieglitz took the photograph while he was an up-per-deck passenger aboard the luxury liner *Kaiser Wilhelm II*. He claimed to have been particularly moved by the composition of the scene—the slung chains and heavy ma-chinery of the ship contrasted with the soft, rounded lines of the human activity below. He was captivated by the "simple people; the feeling of ship, ocean, sky; a sense of re-lease that I was away from the mob called 'rich.'"

The Metropolitan Museum of Art

1000 Fifth Avenue at East 82nd Street
tel. (212) 535-7710, www.metmuseum.org

In 1928, the Met accepted a gift of twenty-three Stieglitz prints from David Schulte and other unnamed donors; it was the first time the Met acquired photographs as works of art for its permanent collection. Included in the collection are portraits of Georgia O'Keeffe spanning several years and images of New York such as *From the Back Window, 291*, taken in 1915 from the back window of his gallery at night.

Dylan Thomas, undated.

Dylan Thomas

POET 1914–1953

Born in Wales and nurtured on a private world of reading and writing poetry, Dylan Thomas published his first poems to acclaim at the age of twenty. In his celebrated readings, Thomas set audiences afloat on the rolling cadence of his speech. At odds with the brainy modernism of many of his peers, Thomas explored life through the emotional importance of elemental and earthy details—sea-slicked rocks, sleeping towns, "the birds of the winged trees." Thomas was a hard drinker and publicly bellicose, behavior that struck many Americans as proof of his authenticity as a romantic, rogue poet from an enchanted land. Legendary by the time of his final tour in New York, Thomas frequented Greenwich Village bars and read publicly for the last time at City College of New York. Within a month, the poet collapsed at the Chelsea Hotel, in the wake of ill health and a sustained drinking binge.

Chelsea Hotel

222 West 23rd Street, between Seventh and Eighth Avenues
tel. (212) 243-3700, www.hotelchelsea.com

Thomas and his wife, Caitlin, stayed here on trips to New York. On their last visit in

November of 1953, Thomas was rushed from his room unconscious to nearby St. Vincent's Hospital, where he passed away. A plaque beside the main entrance memorializes the poet's association with the hotel.

Gotham Book Mart
16 East 46th Street, between Fifth and Madison Avenues
tel. (212) 719-4448

Thomas is among the many authors celebrated in photographs and memorabilia in the foyer of this famous bookstore. In 1920 Frances Steloff opened the Book Mart at 128 West 45th Street; when Steloff moved the operation to 51 East 47th Street the legendary period of the Gotham Book Mart began. Steloff sold little magazines, literary journals, and first editions of young unknown authors. Gotham Book Mart was the site of a literary lark funeral held in honor of the publication of *Finnegan's Wake*. T.S. Eliot bought the first membership to the James Joyce Society, which was founded at the Book Mart. Steloff also gave desperately needed financial and other help to many artists, including John Dos Passos, Edmund Wilson, Martha Graham, and Henry Miller—a charitable habit that was formalized as the Writer's Emergency Fund in 1941.

White Horse Tavern
567 Hudson Street, between West 11th and Perry Streets
tel. (212) 243-9260

Thomas did not collapse in the White Horse Tavern as legend has it, but at the Chelsea Hotel at the tail end of a drinking marathon that included a stop at the White Horse. He was a frequent patron of the bar, however, and spoke often in conversations and interviews of his love of the place. The White Horse is still dim and cool. The worn wooden angles of the bar have the soft finish of long use, and paintings and photographs of Thomas hang on the walls. The tavern has a long literary history and has counted James Baldwin, Norman Mailer, and Allen Ginsberg among its patrons.

Sojourner Truth
CIVIL RIGHTS ACTIVIST 1797–1883

Born into slavery, Sojourner Truth spent her childhood in the cellar of a Dutch planter's home. Upon his death, Truth was sold to a succession of plantation owners, ending up at age fourteen with John and Sally Dumont, who abused her for seventeen years. For Truth, the only escape was private prayer. In secret, she addressed God, the only one in whom she said she had perfect trust, and sought solace in the natural world. Truth escaped the Dumonts in 1826 and eventually sued successfully for the return of her son, who had been sold illegally in Alabama. In New York, Truth rose to prominence as a speaker and activist in the abolitionist and women's movements. Preaching that human justice was God's will, Truth lectured sympathetic white audiences on the evils of slavery. In 1843, she felt called by God, renounced her slave name, christened herself Sojourner Truth, and set out across the country to spread her word. She left New York, which she called "the second Sodom," on June 1, 1843. On her national travels she shared the platform with Frederick Douglass and was received at the White House by Abraham Lincoln. After the Civil

War, Truth lobbied Congress for land distribution to African-Americans and aided recently emancipated slaves.

Site of Mother African Methodist Episcopal Zion Church
156 Church Street at Leonard Street

Truth was a member of this congregation, founded in 1796, from 1829 until she left New York in 1843. She joined the church with her son, whose freedom she had won in the courts, and was reunited in the congregation with other family members. This was the first church in New York built by African-Americans for their own congregants, who were otherwise forced to worship from the back pews or stifling closed balconies of white churches. Even in death, black congregants were barred from the sanctified ground of the city's churchyards and forced to conduct their own funeral rites outside of the city proper. Mother African Methodist Episcopal Zion Church was founded by Peter Williams, who had bought his freedom from the trustees of the John Street Methodist Episcopal Church. Mother African Methodist Episcopal Zion Church was attacked by pro-slavery rioters in 1834 and was destroyed by fire six years later. Ultimately the congregation began to head north in the 1920s and its church is now located at West 137th Street and Lenox Avenue. A plaque on the sidewalk in front of 158 Church Street commemorates the founding of Mother AME Zion Church at this site, believed to be an important refuge along the Underground Railroad.

Sojourner Truth, ca. 1864.

Library of Congress Prints and Photographs Division

Site of Broadway Tabernacle

340-44 Broadway at State Street

On September 7, 1853, Truth, Susan B. Anthony, Lucretia Mott, and other leaders of the Women's Rights Movement Convention gathered in a building formerly at this site. In the afternoon session, Truth rose to roaring applause before being interrupted by insults shouted by young white men who had come to disrupt the proceedings and to present the Old Testament case for withholding rights from women. A *New York Times* reporter quoted her as respsonding: "But we'll have them, see if we don't, and you can't stop us neither, see if you can! Oh, you may hiss as much as you please, like any other lot of geese, but you can't stop it; it's bound to come."

Mark Twain

WRITER AND HUMORIST 1835–1910

M ark Twain arrived in New York as a young typesetter, barely surviving on the "villainous wages" he was offered. About New York, he admitted in the cantankerous voice that would become his trademark, "I have taken a liking to the abominable place." He became a celebrity with *The Innocents Abroad*, a satirical account of his travels with fellow Americans in Europe and the Middle East. Returning to New York in 1900 after years of roving and wry reportage, Twain complained that the city had changed for the worse. Though the absence of chivalry, the trashing of manners, and the crass machinery of city life disappointed him, he stayed. Two charmed decades of fame and family harmony gave way to destructive debt, the sickness and death of his daughters, and the loss of his beloved wife. In public, he remained a bright, resilient wit; privately he was ever more convinced of the depravity and wickedness of humankind. In his last socially vibrant years, the iconic author of *Tom Sawyer* and *Huckleberry Finn* strolled Broadway in his white flannel suit, his head wreathed in a cloud of unruly white hair.

. . . .

Site of the Crystal Palace

In Bryant Park; from West 42nd to West 44th Streets, and from Fifth to Sixth Avenues

Twain visited the Crystal Palace in 1853 and was awe-struck: "the lofty dome, glittering jewelry, gaudy tapestry…with the busy crowd passing to and fro—'tis a perfect fairy palace—beautiful beyond description."

New Yorkers watched Bryant Park, a former potter's field, for months while the palace, modeled after the great exhibition hall of the same name built in London in 1851, was being constructed. The vast ironwork of arcades, arches, and the dome were paneled entirely with luminous glass panels. On July 11, 1853, *The New York Times* devoted many of its columns to describing the final preparations and opening ceremonies. According to the paper, the grounds crowded with "presidents, lords, generals, counts, barons, knights, squires, b'hoys, gentlemen, scholars, loafers, philosophers." Veterans of the War of 1812 paraded past Mayor Westervelt and President Franklin Pierce in the opening ceremonies. "All children, with visitors from remote rural abodes, unaccustomed to behold city sights, will have their credulity and wonder as strongly incited by the curious things of the outside world, as they will by the things inside the Crystal Palace." Things inside the Crystal Palace included: an ice cream parlor; observatory; dome of the Crystal Temple; a 200-foot "spyglass platform;" Lilliputian cows; mammoth oxen; twelve automaton wax bell ringers; giant sheep and crocodiles; a maze garden; and a "View of the Universe," a miniature representation of cityscapes and landscapes that could be studied through magnifying glasses. The Crystal Palace was, in the end, as illusory as it seemed: on an autumn night in 1858, the fragile structure caught fire and melted in less than an hour.

Site of St. Nicholas Hotel
521-523 Broadway, between Spring and Broome Streets

In 1867, two days after Christmas, Twain met his future wife, Olivia Langdon, the only daughter of a wealthy Elmira coal dealer, among the beveled mirrors and gold brocade curtains of the St. Nicholas Hotel. Twain had befriended Livy's brother Charley aboard ship during his trip to the Middle East; during the trip, Twain had studied a miniature portrait of Livy that Charley kept with him. In love with her even before their first meeting, Twain happily accompanied Livy and her family from the St. Nicholas to a reading by Charles Dickens from his new novel *David Copperfield* at Steinway Hall.

A portion of the former St. Nicholas Hotel still stands on Broadway just below Spring Street.

Cooper Union
7 East 7th Street at Cooper Square
tel. (212) 353-4100, www.cooper.edu

In the Great Hall on May 6, 1867, Twain delivered one of his humorous accounts of travel, in this case through the Hawaiian islands and along the West Coast. The lecture series minted his literary fame and expanded his reputation as a humorist. Twain mesmerized the audience with a novel mix of false modesty and outrageously exaggerated tales about the outside world. He would spend the rest of his life as a lecturer and performer, relying on the excellent money to recover from periods of bankruptcy.

Peter Cooper, operator of the first railroad and the inventor of gelatin dessert, established Cooper Union in 1859 to provide free education to working class people—Cooper Union was the country's first free, non-sectarian school to admit both men and women. The building itself is distinguished by Cooper's novel use of structural wrought-iron beams, which later made the engineering of skyscrapers possible. Anticipating the development of a passenger elevator, Cooper also installed a round elevator shaft in the building.

C.O. Bigelow Chemists
414 Sixth Avenue at West 9th Street
tel. (212) 533-2700, www.bigelowchemists.com

Twain was a regular customer at this venerable pharmacy when he lived in the neighborhood. Bigelow's occasionally displays the 1905 ledger bearing Twain's signature.

Former Residence
14 West 10th Street, between Fifth and Sixth Avenues

"We were very lucky to get this big house furnished. There was not another one in town procurable that would answer us, but this one is all right—space enough in it for several families, the rooms all old-fashioned, great size."

Twain returned from Europe in 1900 and settled into the house still at this address. Once the newspapers announced that he had moved in, people made a point of passing up and down the street in the hope of spotting the celebrity. Newspapers fought for interviews with him and gossip about him; they were assured excellent sales if any utterance by Twain appeared in their pages.

Mark Twain, ca. 1907.

Library of Congress Prints and Photographs Division

Wave Hill

Entrance at: 675 West 252nd Street
Riverdale, The Bronx
tel. (718) 549-3200, www.wavehill.org

"I believe we have the noblest roaring blasts here I have ever known on land; they sing their hoarse song through the big tree-tops with a splendid energy that thrills me and stirs me and uplifts me and makes me want to live always."

The jurist William Lewis Morris built Wave Hill on a promontory overlooking the Hudson and the wooded Palisades across the river. Twain lived here from 1901 to 1903. He built a "treehouse parlor" in a chestnut tree on the lawn of the main house. Wave Hill is now a hilly complex of fieldstone houses, an art gallery, nature paths, greenhouses, Japanese and English gardens, cottages, and trellises crowded with colorful blooms nodding towards the Hudson River. Sleepy city people sit quietly in Adirondack chairs and take in the view.

Chelsea Hotel

222 West 23rd Street, between Seventh and Eighth Avenues
tel. (212) 243-3700, www.hotelchelsea.com

Twain is numbered among the eminent artists who lived here after its conversion to a hotel in 1905.

Delmonico's

56 Beaver Street, betweeen William and Broad Streets
tel. (212) 509-1144, www.delmonicosny.com

Twain celebrated his seventieth birthday here to great fanfare. Nearly two hundred illustrious guests gathered in the Red Room. A *New York Times* account of the evening noted: "Even the presence as the guest of honor of the world's foremost fun maker could not drive away the serious reflection that never before in the annals of this country had such a representative gathering of literary men and women been seen under one roof."

President Theodore Roosevelt sent his congratulations by letter, which was read aloud:

Nov. 28, 1905

My Dear Col. Harvey: I wish it were in my power to be at the dinner held to celebrate the seventieth birthday of Mark Twain—it is difficult to write of him by his real name instead of by that name which has become a household word wherever the English language is spoken. He is one of the citizens whom all Americans should delight to honor, for he has rendered a great and peculiar service to America, and his writings, though such as no one but an American could have written, yet emphatically come within that small list which are written for no particular country, but for all countries, and which are not merely written for the time being, but have an abiding and permanent value. May he live long, and year by year may he add to the sum of admirable work that he has done.

Sincerely yours,
Theodore Roosevelt

At the end of the evening, each guest took home a foot-tall bust of Twain as a souvenir.

Delmonico's, established in 1827, is officially the oldest restaurant in New York City. It evokes Old New York with etched glass, a mural of turn-of-the-nineteenth century highlife, a wood-paneled dining room, and culinary classics like Oysters Rockefeller and Lobster Newburg.

. . . .

The Players

16 Gramercy Park South, between Park Avenue South and Irving Place
tel. (212) 475-6116, www.theplayersnyc.org

Twain was a founding member of this theatrical social club. According to club lore, he smoked cigars and played pool until the wee hours. His retired pool cue hangs over an oil painting of the author, which overlooks the pool table. The club is open to members only.

William Marcy "Boss" Tweed

POLITICAL BOSS 1823–1878

W illiam Marcy "Boss" Tweed was the founder and chief of the influential and corrupt political machine of Tammany Hall, whose emblem was the tiger. While Tweed's predatory approach to the public trust during his tenure as New York mayor suited his tiger totem, his appearance did not—his personal corpulence made him seem like Greed personified. Tweed and his cohorts pocketed an estimated $75 million during their tenure, keeping an iron grip on power through voting fraud and intimidation. Tweed's supporters, paid hooligans, and operatives swarmed the polling booths in their bright red shirts, crushing the honest vote for many years. Finally, in 1870, new federal legislation was enacted to combat election-day fraud. President Grant ordered federal troops quartered in the city and warships anchored around Manhattan Island to secure the polls. Tweed and his machine were brought down eventually, thanks in large part to an exposé in *The New York Times* and the relentless, fierce satirical treatment of Tweed by cartoonist Thomas Nast in the pages of *Harper's Weekly*. Nast drew Tweed with a moneybag head or Tweed in a closed circle of his cronies each pointing to blame the man to his left. Tweed passed in and out of jail, where he usually enjoyed all of the comforts of home (including a grand piano). Facing serious consequences at last for his misappropriation of public funds, Tweed escaped to Spain in 1875, where he was arrested and extradited by Spanish officials. He died in Ludlow Street Jail, which he had built during his reign as Mayor.

William Marcy "Boss" Tweed, undated.

Private collection

Tweed Courthouse

52 Chambers Street, between Broadway and Centre Street

The courthouse that shares the grounds of City Hall is now engraved with its unofficial name—Tweed Courthouse—as a reminder to future governments to resist the temptations of power. Tweed illegally filtered millions of dollars through the construction budget of his courthouse, which ultimately cost taxpayers fifty times the amount originally promised. The Courthouse has, despite its criminal origins, hosted decades of corruption-busting inquiries into the lives of criminals, some of them mayors—in 1932, Mayor Jimmy Walker stood trial for corruption and fraud here.

Site of Ludlow Street Jail

350 Grand Street, between Ludlow and Essex Streets

This was once the site of the Ludlow Street Jail, built in 1859 adjoining the Essex Street Police Court already on the site. Tweed died here in 1878 after his thwarted escape to Spain. Seward Park High School now stands on this site.

....

New-York Historical Society

2 West 77th Street at Central Park West
tel. (212) 873-3400, www.nyhistory.org

On display here is a stoneware jug presented as a gift from the Kirkpatrick brothers of Illinois to political cartoonist Thomas Nast—the jug seethes with scaled, tangled snake bodies, each ending in the head of Tweed or one of his associates.

....

Green-Wood Cemetery

Entrance: Fifth Avenue at 25th Street
Sunset Park, Brooklyn
tel. (718) 768-7300, www.green-wood.com

Once-bucolic Green-Wood Cemetery was founded in 1838 and became the place where many prosperous and prominent New Yorkers, including Tweed, were buried.

Carl Van Vechten

PHOTOGRAPHER 1880–1964

C arl Van Vechten, by his own account, fled small town life in Iowa, where even as a child his eccentricities had made a strong impression on the townspeople of Cedar Rapids. He moved first to Chicago before settling eventually in New York. Van Vechten found success as a dance critic, music critic, "Jazz Age" novelist, publisher, benefactor, and social organizer, before beginning, in the 1930s, his most illustrious career, as a photographer. As a novelist, Van Vechten usually celebrated the social decadence, fun, and excess of the Twenties. Like some of his characters, Van Vechten dressed outrageously (in bright, clashing colors), socialized tirelessly, drank heartily, and carried on numerous homosexual affairs despite his long marriage to the Russian émigré actress Fania Marinoff. Van Vechten's diaries from the Twenties are lists of parties attended, hangovers suffered, and significant people met—almost every figure of importance from Harlem to Greenwich Village to Paris crossed Van Vechten's path. In his most famous novel, *Nigger Heaven,* Van Vechten aimed to create full, complex African-American characters. Some, including his close friend Langston Hughes defended the ambition of the book, while many others, including W.E.B. DuBois, were fiercely critical of its caricatures of black life. Van Vechten's lasting contribution to the Harlem Renaissance, beyond his patronage and support of many of its artists, is his series of photographic portraits of celebrated artists, including Ella Fitzgerald, Paul Robeson, Billie Holiday, Bessie Smith, Josephine Baker, and dozens of others.

....

Former residence

151 East 19th Street, between Third Avenue and Park Avenue South

A Jazz Age party hub beginning with Van Vechten's move to the top floor in 1914. A startling number of luminaries from Harlem and beyond gathered here in moments of rare social and racial integration. After three of his novels became best sellers, Van Vechten and Marinoff moved to more posh environs at 150 West 55th Street, where they continued to entertain, hosting ever more lavish and crowded parties. Ethel Barrymore remembered attending one of Van Vechten's soirées: "I went there in the evening a young girl and came away in the morning an old woman."

Site of Golden Stair Press

23 Bank Street, between Waverly Place and West 4th Street

The Golden Stair Press was founded by Langston Hughes, Carl Van Vechten, and designer Prentiss Taylor in 1931. The Golden Stair Press published Hughes's *The Negro Mother and other Dramatic Recitations* in its first year.

Carl Van Vechten, 1934.

Site of Stage Door Canteen
216 West 44th Street, between Broadway and Eighth Avenue

Like many major and minor stars in New York, Van Vechten volunteered during World War II at the Stage Door Canteen, a free nightclub organized by the American Theater Wing for soldiers on leave. Lee Shubert donated the site—a former speakeasy in the basement of the 44th Street Theater, and Irving Berlin contributed a piano. The room was enlivened by painted scenery and props donated by stagehands from the Times Square theaters. At the Stage Door Canteen, soldiers on leave could enjoy free entertainment by living greats like Benny Goodman and Count Basie. Marlene Dietrich helped out at the milk bar, and other glamorous actors distributed donuts, cigarettes, candy, and sandwiches to 3,000 servicemen a night. It was here that Van Vechten found his photographic assistant, a Stage Door busboy named Saul Mauriber—the partnership lasted for twenty years. The Stage Door Canteen, demolished in 1945, was immortalized in the 1943 Academy Award nominated film, *Stage Door Canteen*, featuring Harpo Marx and Tallulah Bankhead.

Cornelius Vanderbilt
ENTREPRENEUR 1794–1877

C ornelius Vanderbilt built an incredible personal fortune from nothing as a ferry service owner, cross-continental shipper, and railroad magnate. Born on Staten Island to a farming family of Dutch descent, Vanderbilt grew into a muscle-bound and short-fused young man who refused to farm. He gained a reputation instead as a rogue ferry captain at the helm of *Mouse of the Mountain*. Fearless and shrewd, Vanderbilt spent years outmaneuvering steamboat monopoly lawyers, injunction-wielding police officers, and British gun boats during the 1812 blockade of Manhattan. When the Supreme Court struck down the steamboat monopoly, Vanderbilt emerged as the victor in the free-for-all of open competition. As one of the wealthiest New Yorkers on record, Vanderbilt threw his name and money behind many civic and reform-minded institutions, though he could also be notoriously parsimonious, bullying, and was often dismissive of public health and safety concerns. In love with speed in general, Vanderbilt "trotted" his horses up the unofficial gentlemen's racetrack of Third Avenue, but he was initially barred from elitist institutions like the Yacht Club as a new-money man of low breeding. At his sister-in-law's hugely successful and much-discussed ball of 1883, Vanderbilt dressed as Louis XVI (his forward-looking wife dressed as "The Electric Light").

· ·

Grand Central Terminal
From East 42nd to East 44th Streets and from Vanderbilt to Lexington Avenues
www.grandcentralterminal.com

Vanderbilt christened the station with the optimistic modifiers "Grand" and "Central," both of which were borne out over time. He had muscled in on floundering railroads during the Panic of 1857 and gained control of the Central, Hudson, New Haven, and Harlem lines (all of which converged at his Grand Central Depot). The battles for control of the rails in New York were wild in the Wild West sense, as competitors relied on legislative pressures, underhanded deals, and shootouts between hired gangs. After public complaints about the constant clatter of trains pumping passengers into Grand Central Depot and back out to the provinces, Vanderbilt laid the tracks under Fourth Avenue and bought up most of the land overhead. The strip of nowhere land would become vaunted Park Avenue. On the ceiling of Grand Central is the oak motif, which reflects the Vanderbilt family motto: "from an acorn grows a mighty oak."

Cornelius Vanderbilt, ca. 1844–1860.

Library of Congress Prints and Photographs Division

Staten Island Ferry

Whitehall Terminal
Whitehall Street at South Street
tel. (718) 815-2628, www.nyc.gov/html/dot/html/masstran/ferries/statfery.html

The Staten Island Ferry is free and still offers some of the best views of the Brooklyn Bridge and the Statue of Liberty. The ferry follows the same route young Vanderbilt and his fleet of boats used to transport commuters almost two hundred years ago. Approaching the southern edge of Manhattan on the ferry, it almost comes as a surprise to see that Manhattan is indeed an island.

Moravian Cemetery

2205 Richmond Road
New Dorp, Staten Island

Vanderbilt was born at Port Richmond on Kill van Kull, Staten Island. His great-great-great grandfather, a Dutch farmer, had arrived on the island in 1650. Nearly two centuries later, Cornelius Vanderbilt built a columned mansion on the family farm between Stapleton and Tompkinsville. He had envisioned transforming Staten Island into a resort for wealthy New Yorkers. In 1885, his son, William H. Vanderbilt, commissioned Richard Morris Hunt to design a grand family mausoleum at Moravian Cemetery overlooking New York Harbor. Cornelius was laid to rest here. (The mausoleum is off-limits to the public.) Cornelius's children and grandchildren sustained commercial ties to Staten Island and built extensively on family land. Houses developed by Vanderbilt's grandson, George Washington Vanderbilt, still stand on Vanderbilt Avenue in Clifton.

New York Yacht Club

37 West 44th Street, between Fifth and Sixth Avenues
tel. (212) 382-1000,

The Yacht Club initially rejected Vanderbilt's petition for membership. Many private clubs were torn between the distinction of old money and the abundance of new money. Club members concluded that Vanderbilt was no gentleman; he was only a rough, foul-mouthed boatman with cash. Vanderbilt made himself irresistible by building the *North Star,* the first steam-driven, ocean-safe yacht decked out with the best in Euro-decadence. Vanderbilt was admitted to the Club the following year.

Castle Clinton National Monument

Southern end of Battery Park
tel. (212) 344-7220, www.nps.gov/cacl

Vanderbilt was here in 1834 when tens of thousands of members and supporters of the Whig party gathered to celebrate their partial victory (they had lost the big races, but they had given Tammany Hall a run for its money). Just two years earlier, this area had been the point of frantic departure, as a cholera epidemic sent half of New York (the affluent half) streaming out in a well-appointed panic to outlying areas. In the city, coffins piled up, until there were none left, and then bodies piled up, often in the gutters where they were left to decompose. Many in the upper class rationalized the epidemic (which burned through the poorest neighborhoods first) as God's clearing-out of Irish immigrants, whom they presumed to be idle and sinful. Many politicians played on such racial and religious prejudices to battle Tammany Hall, which was sustained by immigrant votes. The Board of Health scoured the city, burning mountains of clothing and effects of the ill, thickening the air of the city with small fires and a blizzard of lime. Ultimately the epidemic called the attention of the well-off to the plight of the poor, and many relief and charitable institutions started up in the aftermath.

Diana Vreeland

FASHION EDITOR 1903–1989

C lairvoyant and independent in the world of fashion, Diana Vreeland became the arbiter of American style as fashion editor at *Harper's Bazaar,* as editor-in-chief at *Vogue,* and as head of the Costume Institute at the Metropolitan Museum of Art. She was raised in Paris and New York by vibrant, hedonistic parents, who nurtured her hypersensitivity to the details of clothes, accessories, and manners. In her childhood in New York, she took riding lessons from Buffalo Bill Cody. From her first days as a columnist for *Harper's Bazaar,* Vreeland revolutionized fashion by making style about iconoclasm rather than dogged adherence to rules. Upon seeing the mummified victims of Pompeii, Vreeland noted the design of an ancient sandal and

brought it back into fashion the following summer. Her conversation, which was salted with French terms, hyperbole, and rich declaration, set the ongoing editorial tone of fashion magazines. When speaking, she gestured fiercely, from the depths of her early dance training with the Russian Imperial Master of ballet, Michael Folkine. She became *Vogue*'s editor-in-chief in 1963, and her penchant for flamboyant stories that reflected aristocratic, international glamour eventually led to her firing in 1971. She rebounded, however, serving as special consultant to the Metropolitan Museum's Costume Institute until her death.

The Metropolitan Museum of Art

1000 Fifth Avenue at East 82nd Street
tel. (212) 535-7710, www.metmuseum.org

Vreeland guided the prestigious Costume Institute from 1972 until her death in 1989. Founded in 1937, the Costume Institute has tens of thousands of costumes and accessories from the ancient world to modern *haute couture*. Vreeland is still here in spirit, and books by and about Vreeland are for sale in the small gift kiosk. During her tenure, Vreeland exhibited fashions of the Hapsburg era, the clothes of Russian peasantry, and major retrospectives of avant-garde designers. An ingenious purveyor of fantasy in all of her posts, Vreeland insisted on the aesthetic punch of costume presentation, even if it meant mixing eras and regions in the same exhibit.

St. Regis Hotel

2 East 55th Street at Fifth Avenue
tel. (212) 753-4500

Here in 1936, the editor of *Harper's Bazaar*, Carmel Snow, discovered Vreeland. Snow had seen Vreeland on the dance floor and was intrigued by her confidence and her unusual style, a sort of matador chic—bolero, red roses in her hair, theatrical makeup. Snow offered Vreeland her first job as a columnist at *Harper's Bazaar*. Vreeland wrote her irreverent and popular "Why Don't You…" column for a year before being promoted to fashion editor. She would spend the next twenty-five years as the fashion editor, making decrees ("The bikini is the most important invention since the atom bomb") from her bright red office.

Former residence

550 Park Avenue, between East 51st and East 52nd Streets

Vreeland told her friend, the celebrated designer Billy Baldwin, that she wanted her apartment to look like "a garden in hell"—he responded with lush, scarlet fabrics and boulders of soft chintz; hundreds of books, objects, and paintings, including Andy Warhol's portrait of Vreeland as Napoleon and scenes of Venice, a city she loved. Vreeland entertained here often and hosted nearly every celebrity from the 1950s to the 1970s, from Warhol to Gretta Garbo.

Andy Warhol

ARTIST 1927–1987

The son of Czech immigrants, Andrew Warhola emerged from a tormented youth (he suffered from nervous breakdowns, the skin disorder St. Vitus's Dance, and the early death of his father) to work as a draftsman and illustrator in New York City. Warhol succeeded as a commercial illustrator pushing rum and radios long before his unmistakable shock of white hair made the pop art scene. With encouragement from colleagues, Warhol left commercial art to focus on what he called the "Art Business." An admirer of machines and assembly lines, Warhol sapped individuality and sentimentality out of his work. He stamped out mass-produced objects that confused ubiquity and celebrity: the celebrated face of Marilyn Monroe was made ubiquitous in multiple silkscreen prints, while ubiquitous objects like the labels of Campbell's soup cans were elevated to celebrity in fine pop art portraits. A pale robot bent on production, Warhol churned out images of Brillo boxes, soup cans, dollar signs, celebrity portraits. Warhol's Factory produced books, films, the celebrity magazine *Interview*, prints, exclusive parties, posters, and an album cover for the Velvet Underground. Warhol's pop art pieces, preoccupied with the transient in commerce and culture, have outlasted their role as commentary and achieved the patina of classics.

Andy Warhol at "the Factory" on 47th Street and Third Avenue.

© Gretchen Berg/CORBIS

Site of the Factory
158 Madison Avenue, between East 32nd and East 33rd Streets

Andy Warhol founded one of many Factories in this former Con Edison substation. The Factory, as an institution and a destination, became an important waystation for models, painters, writers, celebrities, and misfits. Bob Dylan, Truman Capote, John Lennon, Edie Sedgwick, Lou Reed, Viva, and many others hung out here and at the 47th Street and Third Avenue Factory, famously painted silver and wrapped in foil.

Decker Building
33 Union Square West, between East 16th and East 17th Streets

Warhol ran his Factory here from 1968 to 1974. On June 3, 1968, the mentally disturbed Valerie Solanis, who had worked for the Factory on and off, shot Warhol here. Warhol survived, but never recovered fully.

Chelsea Hotel
222 West 23rd Street, between Seventh and Eighth Avenues
tel. (212) 243-3700, www.hotelchelsea.com

Warhol filmed *Chelsea Girls* here in 1966. He let the camera roll in different rooms, capturing the manic, the depressive, and the eccentric in twelve film shorts, which he pieced together into a single film. *Chelsea Girls* was Warhol's first cinematic hit, after one-shot epics like *Sleep* and *Empire*, and was regarded by many as the Ring Cycle of the art underworld.

Site of Max's Kansas City
213 Park Avenue South, between East 17th and East 18th Streets

In 1966, the back room of this building was the exclusive domain of Warhol and his coterie of fellow artists, friends, freaks, and hangers-on, all of whom gathered around the Round Table. The extras for the 1969 film, *Midnight Cowboy*, were recruited from this back room crowd.

Site of Studio 54
254 West 54th Street, between Broadway and Eighth Avenue

With a pack of fellow celebrities Warhol was a regular at this 1927 theater-turned-discotheque. Forged in New York's gay club scene, disco evolved into a high-profile, sequined, cocaine-fueled lifestyle that collapsed in the early 1980s under the weight of addiction, the onset of the AIDS epidemic, and the ubiquity of discos and dance classes. The hub of disco, drugs, strobe lights, and fashion, Studio 54 shut down in 1980 after its owners were convicted of tax evasion, heralding, for many, the end of an era.

Empire State Building
350 Fifth Avenue, between West 33rd and West 34th Streets
tel. (212) 736-3100, www.esbnyc.com

Warhol made the Empire State Building the subject of his film *Empire* in 1965. Like his earlier lengthy, intentionally "boring" films (eight hours of *Sleep*, for instance), the film was one uninterrupted shot of the building.

Museum of Modern Art (MoMA)
11 West 53rd Street, between Fifth and Sixth Avenues
tel. (212) 708-9400, www.moma.org

MoMA maintains hundreds of Warhol's films shot between 1963 and 1968. The films include portraits of both famous and little known visitors to the Factory, feature films, and others. Many of these, fully restored by MoMA, can be borrowed from the museum's circulating library. In addition to its film collections, MoMA has many other Warhol pieces in its permanent collection, including *Gold Marilyn Monroe* (1962), *Roll of Bills* (1962), *Orange Car Crash Fourteen Times* (1963), and *Self-Portrait* (1966).

Whitney Museum of American Art
945 Madison Avenue at East 75th Street
tel. (800) 944-8639, www.whitney.org

The Whitney and MoMA have collaborated since 1984 on the cataloging and restoration of Warhol's films. Warhol pulled all of his films from the public realm in 1970 and sanctioned the archival efforts of both museums. In 1988, the Whitney's Andy Warol Film Project had its public debut with the exhibition, "The Films of Andy Warhol," simultaneous with MoMA's rerelease of thirteen restored films. The Whitney also has several of Warhol's silkscreens and other works in its collection.

Solomon R. Guggenheim Museum

1071 Fifth Avenue at East 89th Street
tel. (212) 423-3500, www.guggenheim.org

Pieces in the collection include *Orange Disaster #5* (1963) and *Self-Portrait* (1986).

The Metropolitan Museum of Art

1000 Fifth Avenue at East 82nd Street
tel. (212) 535-7710, www.metmuseum.org

The Met has several of Warhol's self-portraits (both photographs and silkscreens), as well as his portraits of other famous figures, including Jackie Kennedy and Mona Lisa.

George Washington, undated.

Library of Congress, Prints and Photographs Division

George Washington

US PRESIDENT 1732–1799

T all, bright, and likeable, George Washington is often described walking around in his boots with a "noble," "soldierly," or "stalwart" air. He was also feared for his hot temper and could crush walnuts with his bare hands. He loved to ride horses and to dance. At six feet four inches, he towered over all the men of his generation. He was an imperfect military leader, an ardent and early defender of his people, and a critic of the Crown. As an individual, he seems almost irretrievable from the fast waters of American political legend: Washington of the intelligent frown, Washington crossing the Delaware, Washington beneath the cherry tree. As president, he perfected the formidable and down-to-earth manner that became the "correct" demeanor for American leaders. Self-consciously a gentleman in the calculated way of early settlers to Virginia, he was nonetheless much loved for his open manner and his directness in speech. Largely self-taught, he disavowed the English emphasis on formal education over life experience, though Washington exhibited a touchy resistance to being treated commonly in matters of rank or money. Moved by the plight of refugees during the French-Indian War, he declared: "I would be a willing offering to savage fury, and die by inches to save a people."

Federal Hall National Memorial

26 Wall Street at Nassau Street
tel. (212) 825-6888, www.nps.gov/feha

In the original building at this site, the fundamental doctrines of the Revolution took shape as the first draft of the Declaration of Rights and Grievances. After the Revolution, the building was rechristened Federal Hall and renovated by the French-American architect Pierre L'Enfant. The nascent government of the United States operated out of Federal Hall and on April 30, 1789, George Washington was inaugurated as the first president here. Observers noted that Washington appeared uncharacteristically and visibly nervous as he delivered his solemn speech, declaring the new republic was "the experiment entrusted to the hands of the American people" and that it was "a novelty in the history of society to see a great people turn a calm and scrutinizing eye upon itself." The current Federal Hall building went up in 1842, and the monumental statue of Washington (by John Quincy Adams Ward) was dedicated in the fall of 1883. The statue of Washington is supposed to occupy the likely spot where Washington took the oath of office in 1789.

St. Paul's Church

Church Street, between Fulton and Vesey Streets
tel. (212) 233-4164, www.saintpaulschapel.org

Washington attended St. Paul's when New York City was the capital of the new republic from 1779 to 1780. His seat, the President's Pew, is intact on the north side of the chapel. Originally roofed with an elaborate canopy, it is now open—a square, wooden "corral" beneath commemorative plaques and a particularly fierce eagle gazing out from an oil painting of the national seal. The interior of the church is light and airy with whitewashed walls and crystal chandeliers from Waterford, Ireland. St. Paul's was the second chapel built by Trinity Church. Dating back to 1764, it is the only pre-Revolutionary municipal building in Manhattan. Other surviving pre-Revolutionary structures were outlying or incidental structures subsumed by the city as it spread north.

After the attacks of September 11, 2001, St. Paul's Church housed rescue and relief workers between shifts—they slept and received medical treatment on the pews during the eight-month operation. The black scuffmarks from their belts and boots are visible throughout the church. St. Paul's has decided to leave them in memory of the struggles and sacrifices of the city's workers and volunteers.

Fraunces Tavern

54 Pearl Street at Broad Street
tel. (212) 968-1776, www.frauncestavern.com

On December 4, 1783, Washington met his officers in the Long Room of Fraunces Tavern to bid them an emotional farewell. Following the retreat of the British, Washington promptly resigned as commander-in-chief to promote democratic process and prevent the creation of a military government.

The winding, pre-grid streets of Lower Manhattan in 1783 were populated with gentlemen wearing powdered wigs, three-cornered hats, velvet breeches, and waistcoats of colorfully iridescent silk. The neighborhood was loud with the rumbling of horse-drawn carriages and the shouts of milkmen and chimney sweeps. Work was done and dinner eaten by oil lamplight; the smell of hickory wood smoke filled the small houses.

Though this is not the original Fraunces Tavern, the current building, which now houses a museum and restaurant, was modeled after the original, and contains memorabilia from the Revolution, including some of Washington's signed military orders.

City Hall
City Hall Park, between Broadway and Park Row

The people of New York used this area as a commons as early as 1686. In 1776, Washington was in attendance here when the Declaration of Independence was read to colonial troops and citizens.

Morris-Jumel Mansion
65 Jumel Terrace at Edgecomb Avenue
tel. (212) 923-8008, www.morrisjumel.org

This ten-acre estate and white-columned mansion, built in 1765, were purchased by the city in 1903 and turned over to the Daughters of the American Revolution to be restored to its original splendor with period furniture. The mansion served as Washington's headquarters during the last five weeks he spent in New York during the Revolution in 1776. Manhattan Island fell to the British on November 16, 1776.

New-York Historical Society
2 West 77th Street at Central Park West
tel. (212) 873-3400, www.nyhistory.org

The New-York Historical Society exhibits some of the desks, lecterns, and chairs used by legislators in the first Congress at Federal Hall. Also on display are two famous George Washington chairs: the mahogany, pine, and poplar armchair in which fifty-seven-year-old Washington awaited his inauguration on the balcony of Federal Hall, and the dark oak 'throne' carved from wood salvaged at George Washington's Cherry Street home (the site of which is now underneath the Manhattan anchorage of the Brooklyn Bridge). Washington's eulogy can be read on period handkerchiefs mourning the death of the first president. His (gigantic) military cot is also on display.

The Metropolitan Museum of Art
1000 Fifth Avenue at East 82nd Street
tel. (212) 535-7710, www.metmuseum.org

In the American Wing are several important depictions of Washington as patriot, hero, and soldier. In many of the portraits, Washington looks like an entirely different man—a case study in how mythic status eclipses the surface particulars of historic figures. Also in this wing of the museum are examples of New York home life from the Colonial and Revolutionary periods—from silk-lined parlors to rustic kitchens.

Caswell-Massey

518 Lexington Avenue at East 48th Street
tel. (212) 755-2254, www.caswellmassey.com

Caswell-Massey is the country's oldest perfumer, and has been creating scents since 1752. In 1780, Washington presented the Marquis de Lafayette with his favorite cologne—Dr. Hunter's No. Six Cologne—in gratitude for aid to the struggling Revolutionary Army. When the Marquis de Lafayette returned to the United States in 1826, he made a point of buying a new supply of No. Six to take back to France. The formula of No. Six remains unchanged.

Van Cortland House

244th Street and Broadway
Van Cortland Park, The Bronx
tel. (718) 543-3344, www.vancortlandthouse.org

Built in 1748, in an area that was then well outside of the city, this house is now the oldest building in the Bronx. Washington first encamped here in the autumn of 1776 in the days leading up to the battle of White Plains. For the duration of the Revolution, enemy lines cut near Van Cortland house, making it a virtual no-man's-land and isolating it from Washington's troops. On the heels of evacuating British troops in November 1783, Washington returned to the house and rested with his troops for several days.

Now under the care of the National Society of Colonial Dames, Van Cortland House has operated as a museum since 1897, and has been restored with seventeenth- and eighteenth-century furniture and objects.

African Burial Ground

290 Broadway, between Duane and Elk Streets
tel. (212) 337-2001, www.africanburialground.com

The fenced-in rectangle of trimmed grass is a memorial to the 20,000 free and enslaved African-Americans believed to have been interred in this area. In the early 1700s, West Indies trade fed the growing appetites for cotton, sugar, and free labor. After a period in which indigenous people, Africans, and dependent women and children of all races were bought and sold, the government codified in law the exclusive enslavement of people of African descent. The legal trade in human beings was conducted at the corner of Wall Street and South Street (then the edge of Manhattan Island). Washington, himself a slave owner, disembarked at the pier at Wall and South Streets on April 23, 1789 to deliver the first inaugural address and to assume the presidency. He arrived in proto-presidential splendor, in a decked-out barge fitted with thirteen oarsmen, symbolic of the thirteen original colonies. By the middle of the eighteenth century, New York had the largest population of slaves north of Virginia. Forbidden by law from burying their dead in Trinity Graveyard, African-Americans, both enslaved and free, conducted traditional African funeral rites in desolate areas then north of the city. During an archaeological excavation, the remains of several hundred African-Americans, buried in the mid-18th century, were unearthed in the block bounded by Broadway, Duane, and Elk Streets. On October 3, 2003, the remains of 419 men, women, and children were returned to the earth in a memorial ceremony.

© Bettmann/CORBIS

Weegee (Arthur Fellig)

PHOTOGRAPHER 1899–1968

W eegee claimed his elbows itched when crime sprang to life in the dark streets of New York. This stout, cigar-smoking insomniac materialized on the scene with his camera before the crowd had absorbed what had happened, and often before the police had arrived. Arthur Fellig emigrated with his family from a town in Ukraine (now within Austria's borders) in 1910 and came of age on the overcrowded Lower East Side. He worked numerous jobs, from day laborer to hole-puncher at the Life Saver factory, before landing a job as a photographer's apprentice. Years later, Weegee became the city's most famous crime photographer from freelancing the nightshift for many newspapers, including the *World-Telegram*, the *Herald Tribune*, the *Sun*, and the *Daily News*. Maneuvering inside the crowd and shooting stealthily in the confusion of a fresh crime scene, Weegee used his unexpected flash to draw frightened, despondent, and curious faces out of the dark air. A relentless and astute self-promoter, he fed public amazement over his sixth sense for finding crime, crowning himself "Weegee the Famous," after the Ouija Board. In fact, he was obsessive: the first photographer to install a police radio in his car, he slept fully clothed with police and fire station alarms at the foot of his bed. His book *Naked*

New York, which documented the underworlds and outcasts of the city, boosted him to fame. At the pinnacle of his success, but eager to retire from the "blood bath" of crime photography, he moved on to Hollywood and celebrity portraits, where further success eluded him.

Former residence

5 Centre Market Place at Grand Street
tel. (212) 925-4881, www.johnjovinogunshop.com

Many Weegee photographs show handcuffed people being dragged up and down the main steps of the domed, palatial former Police Headquarters on Centre Street. These steps are more often under the feet of the elite now that the building has been converted into luxury apartments. Two doormen in dark coats still manage to give the building a slightly foreboding air. Carved lions and spiked, wrought-iron lanterns flank the entrance; statues representing Justice and the outer boroughs stand overhead. From 1934–1947 Weegee lived behind the police headquarters on shadowy Centre Market Place, from which pedestrians can note through the windows the thickness of the walls in the basement—the former jail of the headquarters. Weegee rented a one-room apartment on Centre Market Street above John Jovino, Inc., a police equipment and gun supplier (John Jovino recently relocated to 183 Grand Street). The business, which has been running since 1911, is still marked by a model of a pistol that overhangs the street.

International Center for Photography

1133 Sixth Avenue at West 43rd Street
tel. (212) 857-0000, www.icp.org/weegee

The only museum in New York devoted exclusively to the preservation and exhibition of photography, ICP is home to the largest Weegee archive in the world. Weegee's longtime companion Wilma Wilcox entrusted the archive (more than 14,000 prints and about 1,000 negatives) to ICP after his death. ICP often organizes special exhibitions of Weegee's work.

Lower East Side Tenement Museum

97 Orchard Street at Broome Street
tel. (212) 431-0233, www.tenement.org

During an early stint as a street photographer, Weegee led a pony named "Hypo" through the streets of the Lower East Side, photographing children, whose parents he knew would find a way to buy the pictures. In his autobiography, he wrote: "*The people loved their children and, no matter how poor they might be, they managed to dig up the money for my pictures. I would finish the photographs on the contrastiest paper I could get in order to give the kids nice, white, chalky faces. My customers, who were Italian, Polish, or Jewish, liked their pictures dead white.*"

The best way to get a sense of the Lower East Side of Weegee's day is to visit the Lower East Side Tenement Museum, a typical tenement building occupied from 1863 to 1939 by immigrant families. Individual apartments have been repaired to their original state, filled with photographs, tools, textiles, letters, and objects used in the daily lives of families from different periods of immigration. The Confino family apartment (1913) is contemporaneous with the arrival of the Fellig family.

Mae West

ACTRESS 1893–1980

F amous Brooklynite and actress Mae West was forever grateful for the scandals that boosted her career. West came out of vaudeville as a writer and director of campy, lascivious plays starring herself: a curvaceous blonde with a languid, suggestive way of saying almost everything. Her first play *Sex*, a sympathetically comedic tale of a Canadian prostitute, was winding down, when authorities arrested the entire cast outside the theater. West refused to recant or apologize, served ten days in the workhouse for moral corruption of the youth, and emerged a celebrity with real Broadway clout. Her tsunami success with her next play, *Diamond Lil*, sealed her celebrity and made her a millionaire. Harassed by the House Un-American Activities Committee and the agents of "comstockery," West pressed ahead, fighting censorship with ever-deeper innuendo. In World War II, the Royal Navy christened

Mae West, 1948.

its inflated life-jackets Mae Wests, and the US Army nicknamed its double-turreted tanks Mae Wests.

Jefferson Market Library

425 Sixth Avenue at West 10th Street
tel. (212) 243-4334

In the garden beside what is now Jefferson Market Library once loomed the Women's House of Detention, where West was jailed during her trial. The *Sex* obscenity trial, which excited tabloids and censors equally, was held here. The civil court was located on the second floor of the building, and prisoners were held in cells in the basement, now a reference room. Perfectly composed West consoled the teary-eyed, rosary-clutching leading man of *Sex* after the guilty sentence was read.

Site of Daley's 63rd Street Theater

22 West 63rd Street, between Central Park West and Broadway

In an age when the old theaters were first being bought up, razed, or encased in the shells of larger buildings, West staged her play *Sex* here. According to *The New York Times*, the play offended censors on the basis of its featured "Koochie" dance, strong language, "prolonged kisses," and unscripted suggestive facial expressions. *Sex*, by all accounts a lame but titillating story, had hung on feebly for forty-one weeks and was on the brink of going under, when the police saved the day by providing superb publicity. On February 9, 1927, West was found guilty of "corrupting the morals of the youth."

Roosevelt Island

In the East River, from East 47th Street to East 96th Street

West served her ten-day sentence in the workhouse on Roosevelt Island (then called Welfare Island). At the end of her stay, she donated $1,000 to establish the Mae West Memorial Prison Library, over which the warden promised to exert a "liberal" censorship. Upon her release, she complained only of the "fuzzy" prison underwear she had been required to wear. Questioned by obsessed reporters, the warden relented that she had worn a pair of white stockings (purchased legally in the prison commissary) with her prison uniform, had done some light dusting and "unpretentious" mingling with the other prisoners. West boasted that she had "gathered material for a dozen plays" in the workhouse.

Site of Ritz-Carlton

Madison Avenue at East 54th Street

Fresh from her arrest for corrupting the morals of the youth, West and her producer slyly and gleefully attended the Junior Prom of the Washington Square College of New York University. She visited for a "little while" after two in the morning and was not, as was rumored, elected Prom Girl by the student body.

Royale Theater

242-250 West 45th Street, between Seventh and Eighth Avenues

West had her triumphant run with *Diamond Lil* here.

Teddy's Bar and Grill

96 Berry Street at North Eighth Street
Williamsburg, Brooklyn
tel. (718) 384-9787

West was born in the rooms above the bar, open since 1887, which also served as the watering hole for local Tammany Hall officials and, later, for people drinking their way secretly through the bleak season of Prohibition.

Edith Wharton

WRITER 1862–1937

L ike her close friend Henry James, Edith Wharton spent most of her childhood abroad, and returned to discover what she called the "intolerable ugliness of New York." She disliked the low, dull buildings, the squalid streets "crammed and smug with overblown fashions." She compared Manhattan to Atlantis: doomed. She retreated deep into her father's library, where she read voraciously and composed poetry from the age

Edith Wharton, ca. 1885.

© Bettmann/CORBIS

211

of eleven. In her parents' house, money and Wharton's literary career were two topics never discussed (though her mother paid for the publication of her first book of poems); men and women enjoyed leisurely weekday lunches; and her mother sewed clothes for the poor during Lent. Her parents brought tutors from England to spend Newport summers with the Wharton children. Toward the end of the century, the city emerged from post-Civil War apathy and exhaustion with a new vigor, as leading gentlemen decided to overhaul New York society. Wharton guided the cultural resurgence by her own refined example and with *The Decoration of Houses*, which instructed New Yorkers to show some restraint in their use of fashionable fabrics, furniture, and clothes. She wrote *The Age of Innocence* (for which she won the Pulitzer Prize in 1921), *Ethan Fromme*, and *The House of Mirth*, in which characters struggle against the soft, unbreachable material of Victorian life. She was unique in her ability to thrive socially in a class whose illusions and hypocrisies she detected and reported in print. She married a man with conventional interests and lackluster views. The marriage was long and frustrating for Wharton, who finally divorced her husband in 1913, by which time she had long since settled in France. She returned briefly to the United States to receive an honorary degree from Yale in 1923—the first woman to receive the accolade—and died in France in 1937, survived by her record of vanished Old New York.

Former residence

7 Washington Square North, between Fifth Avenue and University Place

Wharton lived here in 1882; Alexander Hamilton had preceded her as a tenant almost a century earlier. The townhouse has since been consolidated with adjacent townhouses to form the present apartment building, which includes 7 through 13 Washington Square North.

By the time Wharton wrote *The Age of Innocence* in 1920, Washington Square Park no longer represented the cutting edge of New York society. It had become an island inhabited by the old souls of faded nineteenth-century high society, surrounded by the mysterious, mercurial Greenwich Villagers.

In *The Age of Innocence*, Newland Archer strolls through Washington Square Park and reflects upon his parents' world:

"Beyond the small and slippery pyramid which composed Mrs. Archer's world lay the almost unmapped quarter inhabited by artists, musicians and 'people who wrote.' These scattered fragments of humanity had never shown any desire to be amalgamated with the social structure. In spite of odd ways they were said to be, for the most part, quite respectable; but they preferred to keep to themselves. Medora Manson, in her prosperous days, had inaugurated a 'literary salon'; but it had soon died out owing to the reluctance of the literary to frequent it."

Site of former residence

882-884 Park Avenue, between East 78th and East 79th Streets

In 1891, Wharton bought a house at this address (when it was still Fourth Avenue). Ogden Codman, Jr., with whom she would write *The Decoration of Houses* in 1896, renovated the interiors. The Whartons had returned to New York two years earlier after living in a succession of fine houses in Europe, Newport, and Maine.

Former residence

14 West 23rd Street, between Fifth and Sixth Avenues

Wharton was born in this since-renovated brownstone on January 24, 1862.

Site of Wharton's mother's home

28 West 25th Street, between Fifth and Sixth Avenues

On this site stood the house of Wharton's mother. Wharton had breakfast there on the day of her wedding.

St. Sava Serbian Orthodox Cathedral

20 West 26th Street, between Broadway and Sixth Avenue
tel. (212) 242-9240, www.stsavanyc.org

Completed in 1855, this church served as the Trinity Chapel Episcopalian until 1943. Edith Jones married the dud Edward Wharton here in 1885.

Stanford White

ARCHITECT 1853–1906

A t the time of his death, a year in which automobiles were still crashing regularly into horse-drawn carts, Stanford White enjoyed life in the Gilded Age among fellow artists and thinkers. He designed houses for many of the city's wealthiest patrons (Astor, Pulitzer, Vanderbilt, and others) and, with his firm McKim, Mead & White, was responsible for many of the buildings that define turn-of-nineteenth-century Manhattan. In his designs, White converted the authority of the Old Europe into idiosyncratically American forms. His artistic and architectural vision gave New York an authoritative sense of historic depth, one that felt true to New Yorkers. In 1906, White was shot to death by Harry K. Thaw on the roof of Madison Square Garden. Within days of his death, White's professional reputation was eclipsed by scandal: it was revealed that he had installed in his private rooms a red velvet swing, which provided him a steady pendulum of chorus girls and young actresses. One of the young women, the actress Evelyn Nesbit, had gone on to marry the deliriously jealous Thaw.

Site of former residence

22 West 24th Street, between Broadway and Sixth Avenue

Not far from Madison Square Park is the location of White's former private apartment. The press and the gossip mill churned through lurid descriptions of the interior: the red velvet swing, mirror- and velvet-lined rooms, constellations of colored lights, and a paper parasol suspended from the ceiling, which young women reportedly delighted in punching through with their feet as they reached the apex of their swing.

New York Life Insurance Company Building

51 Madison Avenue, between East 26th and East 27th Streets

Now the New York Life Insurance Company Building, this site was once the seat of White's masterpiece, the Madison Square Garden of the 1890s. White's Garden took lavish, classical environs and entertainment to a new height. The building housed a vast restaurant with eighty-eight-foot ceilings and an 8,000-seat concert hall. Stanford White was murdered in the roof garden theater of his own building while watching the musical *Mamzelle Champagne*.

Stanford White, 1895.

Library of Congress Prints and Photographs Division

Jefferson Market Library
425 Sixth Avenue at West 10th Street
tel. (212) 243-4334

The sensational murder trial of Harry K. Thaw took place here when it was a courthouse. The building has since been restored as a branch of the New York Public Library. Exhaustive coverage filled newspaper columns with detailed witness accounts of the shooting and with speculations about White's character. White had arrived late to Madison Square Garden, his architectural masterpiece, to watch *Mamzelle Champagne*—the musical turned out to be extremely dull, even when its star popped from the top of a papier mâché champagne bottle. Thaw, described as a "cigarette fiend," had already attracted attention by pacing through the audience and refusing to remove his overcoat. White was alone at his table when Thaw approached him and fired repeatedly at point-blank range in full view of the performers and audience. Because theatrical pranks abounded at the turn-of-the-nineteenth-century, many witnesses laughed nervously, while the orchestra played on lurchingly under the frantic direction of the producer. Within seconds, blood soaked the white tablecloth, and the crowd scattered in panic. Thaw remained calm and awaited his polite arrest. During the trial, Thaw was championed by Anthony Comstock and the New York Society for the

Suppression of Vice as an avenger of the innumerable young women White had lured to ruin in his sumptuous den. After a few years as an indulged resident of an insane asylum, Thaw was cleared of all charges.

The Players

16 Gramercy Park South, between Park Avenue South and Irving Place
tel. (212) 475-6116, www.theplayersnyc.org

Built in 1845, The Players began as the private home of celebrated actor Edwin Booth (also famous as the brother of President Lincoln's assassin, John Wilkes Booth). Booth converted his private home into a club for people of the theater, who were banned, by low profession, from socializing in the city's established private clubs. White remodeled the building *pro bono* with his firm McKim, Mead & White in 1888. From the street, one can see the two-story columned porch and wrought-iron lanterns, which were added by White during the renovation. According to club lore, White had his last meal at the club before heading to Madison Square Garden and the deadly encounter with Harry K. Thaw. The Players faces lovely Gramercy Park, though the park is owned privately by the residents of the neighborhood and must be enjoyed from outside the gate. The Players remains a private club, though individual tours can be arranged by appointment.

Washington Square Arch

Washington Square North at Fifth Avenue

McKim, Mead & White installed a wood and stucco version of the Washington Square Arch in 1889 to commemorate the centennial of George Washington's inauguration. The arch, constructed several blocks north of where it now stands, was so admired by the public that a permanent, marble version was commissioned (and paid for, in part, through public fundraisers). White designed the new structure, which took its final form in 1895. As builders broke ground for the base of the arch, they hit layers of bones and tombstones, relics of the park's past life as execution and burial grounds. Cars and buses passed through the arch for years, until residents succeeded in having all traffic rerouted around the park. The interior of the arch is closed to the public, but a tightly wound spiral staircase inside the base leads to the top.

Judson Memorial Church

55 Washington Square South at Thompson Street
tel. (212) 477-0351, www.judson.org

Edwin Judson founded this church in 1890 as a spiritual, educational, and political refuge for impoverished immigrants living nearby in Little Italy. The church was funded by wealthy patrons and designed by the firm of McKim, Mead & White. Stanford White drew up the final design for the church, emphasizing the Italianate style of the facade and entry arch. The Bible of Judson's father, a missionary in Burma, is in the cornerstone of the building. Concerts began here in 1948, and in 1956 Judson Memorial Church began exhibiting work by avant-garde artists.

The Metropolitan Museum of Art

1000 Fifth Avenue at East 82nd Street
tel. (212) 535-7710, www.metmuseum.org

An example of McKim, Mead & White interiors can be visited here. An entire entry hall from the Buffalo, New York home of the Metcalfe family, designed by the firm in 1884, is installed in the American Wing. It is one of twenty-five furnished rooms, including a Frank Lloyd Wright living room, that document American architecture and interiors over its three hundred years of development. Also in the museum's collection are sketches of buildings and landscapes by White including *Coutances Cathedral* (circa 1879); *View of the Hudson River from the Catskills* (1870s); and *Sketch of Saint Gaudens's Statue of Deacon Samuel Chapin, Springfield, Massachusetts.*

New-York Historical Society
2 West 77th Street at Central Park West
tel. (212) 873-3400, www.nyhistory.org

The museum houses the architectural files of McKim, Mead & White, which includes White's drawings, photographs, and correspondence.

Walt Whitman

POET 1819–1892

Bard of New York and fanatical walker, Walt Whitman spent most of his life in Brooklyn and Manhattan. While many of his contemporaries saw only the doomed crush of the crowded city and the potential mob, Whitman envisioned a new kind democracy for America. His poetry assigned to every urban gesture, phrase, and transaction a kind of magical principle, a mysteriousness that was human and therefore positive. Like his city, Whitman was confident and fluid in forming and reforming his identity over the years. Already a successful journalist and editor, Whitman reintroduced himself to New York in 1855 as a rumpled, edgy "street rough" on the title page of his epic tribute to the city, *Leaves of Grass*. Though the book and its use of "vulgar" language shocked many critics, others hailed it as the New American Literature that the literary salons had been trying to produce for years. Whitman offered a vision of New York that was neither lonely nor swarming, but made up of individuals bound together in good will. He demonstrated through his life that it was possible to go forth into the city without being swallowed up in the anonymity of the crowd.

Brooklyn Bridge
From Park Row (Manhattan) to Adams Street (Brooklyn)

The Brooklyn Bridge may represent New York more succinctly and beautifully than any other monument. The bridge linked—for the first time—the separate cities of Brooklyn and Manhattan on May 24, 1883. Before the Brooklyn Bridge, when Manhattan could be reached only by boat, Whitman had written famously about his ferry rides across the East River: "I too lived—Brooklyn, of ample hills, was mine; I too walked the streets of Manhattan Island, and bathed in the waters around it." Though bathing in the waters around Manhattan Island is no longer generally practiced (or advisable), the spirit of transition between the two communities can still be experienced as a pedestrian crossing the Brooklyn Bridge. The pedestrian path across the bridge from Manhattan begins on Centre Street in front of the Municipal Building.

Library of Congress, Prints and Photographs Division

The construction of the Brooklyn Bridge was the cultural obsession and pride of New Yorkers; city officials brought visiting dignitaries and international celebrities to the construction site. The bridge was a dangerous and extraordinary engineering feat that almost failed repeatedly. While surveying the future site of the anchorage, the mastermind of the project, John Augustus Roebling, slipped; his foot was crushed between the ferry and platform—he died days later of tetanus. His son, Washington Roebling, a decorated Civil War veteran and an engineer, finished the project. The bridge also crippled the younger Roebling. After each caisson was sunk to the bottom of the East River, pumps forced water out and pressurized air in, so that workmen could descend to the riverbed and begin digging down to bedrock. Roebling, and many of the workmen, fell ill when they returned to the surface—the cause of "caissons disease" (the bends) remained a mystery for the duration of the project. Roebling was forced to survey the construction of the bridge from his Brooklyn Heights apartment. His wife Emily Roebling oversaw much of the work and acted as his representative on the construction site. (She was chosen as the first person to cross the Brooklyn Bridge during the opening ceremony.) When it opened in 1883, Brooklyn Bridge was a spectacular, public display of brand-new electricity and was illuminated at night from the very beginning. Whitman's poem "Crossing Brooklyn Ferry" is inscribed on a fence near the Brooklyn Anchorage of the bridge, in the Fulton Ferry Historic District. The Brooklyn Anchorage is open to the public from early June until early August. The cathedral space under the Bridge fills with farmer's markets, playgrounds, and art. The anchorage was walled off as part of a WPA project in the 1930s, but the City reopened the space as part of the bridge's centennial in 1983.

Site of *Brooklyn Daily Eagle* offices

28 Old Fulton Street at Elizabeth Street
Fulton Ferry Historic District, Brooklyn

This waterfront warehouse, built in 1893, is on the former site of the *Brooklyn Eagle* offices and still contains the facade of the *Brooklyn Eagle* pressroom. A plaque on Old Fulton Street commemorates Whitman's tenure here. Democrats had launched the paper in 1841, and Whitman served as its editor from 1846 to 1848. His editorial stance against the legal extension of slavery into new states eventually forced him to leave the paper. He moved on to edit the radical *Brooklyn Freeman* newspaper. The current building is a study in beautiful sturdiness—fortress-thick walls, deep windows, and low, arched hoods of brick over doorways.

....

Fort Greene Park

From Myrtle Avenue to Dekab Avenue, and from Ashland Avenue to Washington Park
Fort Greene, Brooklyn
www.fortgreenepark.org

The development of Fort Greene Park was launched at the insistence of Whitman while he was serving as editor of the *Brooklyn Daily Eagle* in 1848. In 1867, the park was redesigned by Frederick Law Olmsted. The park slopes upward into a hill towards the water; at the pinnacle of the hill is the Prison Ship Martyr Monument; a grim, fluted column crowning a tiered platform. The monument narrows at the top like a lighthouse and bears a weathered bronze brazier that once held an eternal flame. Between 1776 and 1783, 11,500 Americans died of starvation, dysentery, and abuse aboard British prison ships anchored in Wallabout Bay off the East River near this part of Brooklyn (in the vicinity of the Brooklyn Navy Yard).

....

Fulton Ferry Landing

Foot of Old Fulton Street
Fulton Ferry Historic District, Brooklyn
tel. (212) 742-1969, www.nyc.gov/html/dot/html/masstran/ferries/watertaxi.html

At Old Fulton Street and the water is the Fulton Ferry Landing—verses from Whitman's "Crossing Brooklyn Ferry" can be read in the metal fence by the river.

....

Site of Pfaff's

647 Broadway, between Bleecker and West 3rd Street

The basement of this building was Pfaff's—the place for self-styled, disheveled "bohemian" artists to drink and socialize. Whitman had his own table in the candle-lit cellar bar, and devotees of Edgar Allan Poe, recently deceased, gathered in the low light to pay homage to the master of melancholy. The crowd that gathered under double barrel-vaulted ceiling of Pfaff's helped to produce one of the first counterculture magazines, *The New York Saturday Press*, which published unknown writers, including Mark Twain in 1865. Mainstream newspapers and their readers found edification in the luridly reported bad ends that members of counterculture met—they died young of rabies, pneumonia, drug addiction, suicide, and at the hands of other depraved bohemians. Grisly examples of how "the life" claimed its victims from the ranks of the naïve were used to keep young people from leaving the routines of sanctioned marriages and professions. The building was knocked down in 1870 and replaced by a department store, the facade of which remains at 647 Broadway.

Central Park

From Central Park South (59th Street) to Central Park North (110th Street) and from Fifth Avenue to Central Park West (Eighth Avenue)

In the spring of 1892, Whitman visited Central Park "almost every day." For him, it was the park's best moment—flowering trees, fields of dandelion, and "plentiful gray rocks…cropping out, miles and miles." Whitman recounted a conversation with a young policeman in the park near 90th Street: "There is not so much difficulty as might be supposed from tramps, roughs, or in keeping people 'off the grass.' The worst trouble of the regular Park employee is from malarial fever, chills, and the like." Park police were also often injured in chasing and stopping runaway horse carriages.

World Financial Center Plaza

In Battery Park City, bordered by West Street, the Hudson River, Vesey, and Liberty Streets
tel. (212) 945-2600, www.worldfinancialcenter.com

Incorporated in bronze into the steel fence overlooking the river are fragments of love poems to New York by Frank O'Hara and Walt Whitman.

"City of the sea! City of the wharves and stores—city of the tall facades of marble and iron! Proud and passionate city—mettlesome, mad, extravagant city!"—Walt Whitman

Gertrude Vanderbilt Whitney

PHILANTHROPIST AND SCULPTOR 1875–1942

S culptor Gertrude Whitney founded the Whitney Museum of Art. The granddaughter of Cornelius Vanderbilt, she spent her summer months at the Breakers, the Vanderbilt estate in Newport, Rhode Island, where she was happiest clambering over salt-encrusted rocks, swimming in the ocean, and picking wild berries. In New York, however, she felt burdened by her duty to uphold the family name and her elders considered her sullen and rebellious. She received some formal art training before marrying Harry Payne Whitney, an heir to tobacco and oil fortunes. The Whitneys traveled through Europe at the turn of the nineteenth century and the abundant heroic and romantic statuary of European capitals inspired Whitney to return to sculpture. She established a studio in Greenwich Village, and her largesse provided other Greenwich Village artists with financial support and space in which to work. During World War I, Whitney visited a hospital she had established in the suburbs of Paris. Her encounters with wounded soldiers and with the ravages of the war took Whitney's art in a new direction—large public works that memorialized the physical struggle and sacrifice of men in combat.

Whitney Museum of American Art

945 Madison Avenue at East 75th Street
tel. (800) 944-8639, www.whitney.org

In 1929, Whitney offered to build a new wing onto the Metropolitan Museum of Art to house her 500-piece collection of modern art. The Metropolitan Museum declined, and in 1931 Whitney established the Whitney Studio Club—the first museum to exhibit American art exclusively and the predecessor of the Whitney Museum of American Art. The collection first opened at 8 West 8th Street, moved uptown to West 54th

Street for a period, and has occupied Marcel Breuer's "inverted pyramid" since 1966.

Site of Whitney's studio

19 MacDougal Alley, between Washington Square North and East 8th Street

Whitney set up her own studio in this former horse stable in 1907. She rented additional studio space across the back alley at 8 West 8th Street.

Site of the New York Studio School

8 West 8th Street, between Fifth and Sixth Avenues

Whitney established an exhibition space and studio complex here for young, aspiring artists who had been kept out of conservative, juried shows. The studios provided the successful prototype for the Whitney Museum. The New York Studio School saved the studios from destruction in 1967, and the complex is now a National Historic Landmark.

The Metropolitan Museum of Art

1000 Fifth Avenue at East 82nd Street
tel. (212) 535-7710, www.metmuseum.org

Ornate flotsam from Manhattan's demolished mansions can be found in the atrium of the American Wing. The Vanderbilt mansion, Whitney's childhood home, on Fifth Avenue between 57th and 58th Streets was torn down in the 1920s, though its monumental Augustus Saint-Gaudens mantelpiece has been preserved here. The towering fireplace is reddish marble, mosaic, and dark wood. Two caryatids, Amor and Pax, support the mantle effortlessly, even sleepily, with heads bowed and eyes closed. An inscription in Latin reads: "The house at its threshold gives evidence of the Master's good will. Welcome to the guest who arrives; farewell and helpfulness to him who departs." A great "V" is carved in the wood mantel.

The Conservatory Garden

Fifth Avenue at 105th Street

The Conservatory Garden is a self-contained, lush enclave in Central Park. In May 1939, Whitney donated the elaborate, dark gates that lead into the garden from Fifth Avenue. The gates once guarded the Vanderbilt mansion. The Conservatory Garden is a formal space with tiers of angular hedges and semi-circular raised trellises.

Stuyvesant Square

From East 15th to East 17th Streets, and from Rutherford Place to Perlman Place

Here stands Whitney's statue of Peter Stuyvesant, New Amsterdam's tyrannical first governor. Stuyvesant, whose right leg had been crushed by a cannonball, ringed his false leg with decorative silver bands. Whitney created the sculpture for New York World's Fair of 1939; it was rededicated in this park in 1941 and is one of Whitney's last works.

Washington Heights-Inwood War Memorial

Mitchel Square
Broadway and St. Nicholas Avenue at West 168th Street

In 1922, Whitney completed this grouping of statues: two infantrymen, one kneeling and one standing, support the weight of a third, their wounded comrade. The statue commemorates the men from Washington Heights and Inwood who lost their lives fighting in World War I. The surrounding park is itself a memorial to John Purroy Mitchel (1879–1918), the youngest mayor in New York City's history and a casualty of the war.

Victoria Woodhull

ACTIVIST AND JOURNALIST 1838–1927

V ictoria Woodhull, an adamant and controversial women's rights advocate, established a brokerage firm on Wall Street, used her weekly newspaper to debut the *Communist Manifesto* to American readers, and was the first woman to run for president. In the late nineteenth century, her name was made synonymous with wickedness. The itinerant Woodhull and her sister, Tennessee Claflin, set up shop in New

York as clairvoyants, conveying the messages of the deceased to wealthy clients, including Cornelius Vanderbilt. Grateful Vanderbilt helped the sisters to launch a brokerage firm, and their investments made them a fortune on Wall Street. Woodhull ploughed their new wealth into the publication of a radical newspaper, *Woodhull & Claflin's Weekly*, and into her presidential campaign as a candidate for the People's Party. She advocated universal suffrage, birth control, workers' rights, simplified divorce laws, and the end to the death penalty. She asked Frederick Douglass to be her running mate, though he never accepted the nomination. Her campaign and legal troubles emptied her coffers, and her calls for liberation from "the most terrible curse from which humanity now suffers"(marriage) made her notorious. She was accused of being a witch, a prostitute, and an adulterer. Landlords barred their doors against her family; Anthony Comstock jailed her. Once free, Woodhull left for England, where she lived in exile on Vanderbilt's lush estate. She eventually married an English banker, and paved over her radical past with heavily conservative editorials in the English press.

Plymouth Church

75 Hicks Street, between Orange and Cranberry Streets
tel. (718) 624-4743, www.plymouthchurch.org

Reverend Henry Ward Beecher preached here between 1847 and 1887. Beecher's Sunday sermons were popular, lively events that drew the curious and devout all the way from Manhattan. Beecher promoted free will, the abolition of slavery, and benevolent impulse. He encouraged female congregants to listen to unvoiced yearnings; he and Woodhull were natural ideological kin. When Woodhull was under attack in the press, she beseeched Beecher to silence the false accusations by attesting to her character. In response, he derided her advocacy of "free love," though he was doing some free loving of his own on the side. Woodhull retaliated by exposing Beecher's affair with Elizabeth Tilton, and the so-called "Trial of the Century" was on its way. In 1872, Woodhull was imprisoned by Anthony Comstock for publishing the obscene allegations; the cuckolded man, Theodore Tilton, sided first with Beecher then testified against him, suing for alienation of his wife's affection. Ultimately vindicated by the courts, Woodhull and her sister Tennessee Claflin were nonetheless ruined by legal fees, the government seizure of their brokerage accounts, and the confiscation of their printing press.

Cooper Union

7 East 7th Street at Cooper Square
tel. (212) 353-4100, www.cooper.edu

In March 2, 1871, Woodhull appeared here to address a sympathetic and predominantly female audience on the issue of suffrage. She spoke from the Great Hall stage, which was hung with banners bearing slogans like "Only Criminals, Idiots, and the Insane May be Deprived of the Ballot." She pointed out that, as a citizen and business owner, she paid "every conceivable" form of tax, yet was barred from participating in government in clear contravention of the Constitutional ban on "taxation without representation."

On January 9, 1873, roughly one thousand people filled Cooper Union to hear Woodhull speak here once again. More famous than ever, she had been the object of scandal since publishing accusations of Beecher's adultery in her weekly paper. Anthony Comstock was eager to put her behind bars. Warrant-wielding police officers guarded the perimeter of Cooper Union, scanning the crowds for Woodhull. A *New York Times* article reported that she snuck past them disguised as "an old lady in a pearl colored bonnet, with a veil and a black and white shawl." She entered the hall hunched over, as if frail with age, then tore off her disguise triumphantly at the podium to the exuberant applause of the audience. After speaking "in a violent manner on the crushing out of what she called 'free speech and a free Press'" she was arrested and taken by carriage to Ludlow Street Jail.

Victoria Woodhull, undated.

© Bettmann/CORBIS

Site of Ludlow Street Jail
350 Grand Street, between Ludlow and Essex Streets

The Ludlow Street Jail was built on this site in 1859. Woodhull was jailed here in 1872 after accusing Rev. Henry Ward Beecher of having an affair with one of his parishioners. Authorities locked her in cell number 12 with her first husband, Colonel Blood. In 1877, after a decade of marriage, Woodhull divorced Blood, her second of three husbands. A spiritualist and a veteran of the Civil War, Blood went on to marry for a third time and died in Africa on a gold-mining expedition. Seward Park High School now stands on the site.

Former brokerage firm of Woodhull
44 Broad Street, between Beaver Street and Exchange Place

At this address, with backing from benefactor Vanderbilt, Woodhull and her sister Tennessee Claflin launched their brokerage firm in 1870. It was the first to be owned and managed by women. This address also served as the headquarters for Woodhull's presidential campaign.

Malcolm X

CIVIL RIGHTS LEADER 1925–1965

"New York was heaven to me. And Harlem was seventh heaven!"

C ivil rights leader and black nationalist Malcolm X was born Malcolm Little in Omaha, Nebraska. His father, a staunch supporter of the black nationalist Marcus Garvey, was murdered by white supremacists when Malcolm was six years old. Little graduated at the top of his class in junior high, though he disengaged from school after his white teacher told him that he would never be allowed to become a lawyer, as he hoped. He drifted into a life of crime in Boston and New York. While serving seven years in prison, he joined the Nation of Islam and replaced "Little" with "X" to mark the loss of his family's African name in slavery. He transformed himself from a drug addict into a brilliant autodidact; he studied in the prison library and organized formal debates between fellow prisoners. Malcolm X emerged as the shining disciple of Elijah Muhammad, the founder of the Nation of Islam. His calls for self-defense and the autonomy of the African-American community drew death threats and constant surveillance by the FBI. In 1964, Malcolm X traveled to Mecca as a pilgrim where, for the first time, he witnessed the peaceful integration of worshippers of all ethnicities and complexions. Invigorated spiritually and politically, he split with Elijah Muhammad and he called on African and Arab nations to push the United Nations to make the American government answer for the mistreatment of African-Americans. Back in the United States, Malcolm X evaded numerous assassination attempts, which he reported to the police. They dismissed his reports as publicity stunts. Malcolm X was shot to death as he rose to address a crowd in New York City.

AROUND HARLEM

When he was a teenager, Malcolm X found work as a "sandwich man" on the Yankee Clipper train running between Boston and New York. He spent layover nights in Harlem, first at the YMCA on 135th Street and later in boarding houses and other hotels around the neighborhood. During those weeks of happy transience, he explored all the highs and lows of Harlem. On his first night, he visited many of the places that would become his regular destinations: after Small's Paradise, he went on to the Apollo Theatre, admired the "big, tall, grey" Theresa Hotel across the street, and joined the lindy-hopping crowd at the Roseland Ballroom, while Lionel Hampton played.

Harlem YMCA

180 West 135th Street, between Adam Clayton Powell Jr. Boulevard and Malcolm X Boulevard

When Malcolm X relocated to New York in 1942, he spent his first night here. This branch of the YMCA was the sequel building to the YMCA across the street at 181

West 135th Street (completed in 1919). From its founding in 1851 until 1946, the YMCA maintained a policy of racial segregation, though African-Americans formed their own branches of the YMCA to serve their communities.

In 1936, the name of the 135th Street Branch was officially changed to the Harlem Branch YMCA. It has served as one of Harlem's most important recreational and cultural centers.

Site of Small's Paradise

2294 Adam Clayton Powell Jr. Boulevard at West 135th Street

Malcolm X visited Small's Paradise, a popular Harlem lounge, on his first night in the city.

Malcolm X, 1964.

He was deeply impressed by the sophistication and prestige of the crowd there and became a regular. At the age of seventeen, Small's hired him as a waiter.

Site of Hotel Braddock

Eighth Avenue at West 126th Street

The bar in the Hotel Braddock was another stop on Malcolm X's first night in the city and a favorite place thereafter. Located close to the backstage entrance of the Apollo Theater, the bar filled with celebrities nightly. On his first night in Harlem, Malcolm X saw Billie Holiday, Dizzy Gillespie, and other luminaries at the bar.

Mosque No. 7

106-08 West 127th Street, between Adam Clayton Powell Jr. and Malcolm X Boulevards

Formerly called Temple No. 7, this was where Malcolm X began his ministry for the Nation of Islam in 1954. He estimated that New York membership of the Nation of Islam grew from about four hundred to forty thousand under his leadership. Malcolm X met with people in the affiliated restaurant around the corner, where he fielded constant phone calls from the media and others in the phone booths there.

After Malcolm X's murder, Mosque No. 7 was firebombed in retaliation. It has since been rebuilt.

Theresa Hotel

2090 Adam Clayton Powell Jr. Boulevard, between West 124th and West 125th Streets

In 1963, Malcolm X rented the Carver Ballroom here to announce the creation of his new organization, Muslim Mosque, Inc. He left soon after to make his pilgrimage to Mecca.

Built by a racist lace dealer, the hotel barred African-Americans until 1937. By the time Malcolm X came to New York, it was integrated. In his autobiography, he wrote that the Theresa Hotel was "the finest in New York City where Negroes could then stay, years before the downtown hotels would accept the black man." Malcolm X founded the Organization of Afro-American Unity here in 1964. The Theresa Hotel was also the temporary home of thirty-four-year old Fidel Castro when he visited the United States for the first time in 1960. He took forty rooms on the ninth floor.

Masjid Malcolm Shabazz ("Malcolm X Mosque")

102 West 116th Street at Malcolm X Boulevard

This mosque, now a center of orthodox Islamic study and worship, was named in honor of Malcolm X soon after his death. Formerly Lenox Casino, the building was renovated in 1965 to incorporate traditional Islamic architectural details like the green dome and arched windows.

Former headquarters of the Socialist Workers Party

116 University Place at East 13th Street

This building was the headquarters for the Socialist Workers Party from the 1930s to the 1960s. They hosted many lectures by Malcolm X; he last spoke here in 1964, a few months before his assassination.

Site of 22 West

22 West 135th Street, between Fifth and Lenox Avenues

Malcolm X used the club and restaurant 22 West as a de facto headquarters after his split with the Nation of Islam. As always, he fielded constant phone calls in the restaurant's phone booth and held meetings in one of the booths here.

Audubon Ballroom

166th Street, between Broadway and St. Nicholas Avenue

After his ousting from the Nation of Islam, Malcolm X found a temporary home for his teachings here. He was assassinated while addressing a crowd in the ballroom on February 21, 1965. Three members of the Nation of Islam were convicted of the killing.

The Audubon was built in 1912 as a venue for dance marathons, jazz showcases, and big band performances from the 1930s to the 1950s. The Columbia Presbyterian Hospital Complex has subsumed most of the Audubon Ballroom, though a restored section of the original facade fronts the new research center. The facade has been restored and kept in place as a memorial to Malcolm X. The interior of the building now houses Columbia University's Biomedical Science and Technology Research Center.

Schomburg Center for Research in Black Culture

515 Malcolm X Boulevard, between West 135th and West 136th Streets
tel. (212) 491-2200

In 2003, the estate of Betty Shabazz (the widow of Malcolm X) placed on long-term loan here the letters, photographs, and other memorabilia associated with the life and work of Malcolm X.

Intersections

Site Index

Selected Bibliography

Alland, Alexander Sr. *Jessie Tarbox Beals: First Woman News Photographer*. Camera/Graphic Press, 1978.

Astor, John Jacob. *A Journey in Other Worlds: A Romance of the Future*. D. Appleton, 1894.

Baldwin, James. *Collected Essays*. The Library of America, 1998.

Barnes, Djuna. *New York*. Sun & Moon Press, 1989.

Barnum, P.T. *The Life of P.T. Barnum: Written by Himself*. University of Illinois Press, 2000.

Bernhardt, Sarah. *My Double Life: Memoirs of Sarah Bernhardt*. Heinemann, 1907.

Bishop, Elizabeth. *One Art: Letters*. Edited by Robert Giroux. Farrar, Straus and Giroux, 1994.

Bishop, Elizabeth. *The Complete Poems 1927-1979*. Farrar, Straus and Giroux, 1979.

Bosworth, Patricia. *Diane Arbus: A Biography*. Norton, 1995.

Brady, Kathleen. *Lucille: The Life of Lucille Ball*. Hyperion, 1994.

Bunyan, Patrick. *All Around the Town: Amazing Manhattan Facts and Curiosities*. Fordham University Press, 1999.

Burrows, Edwin G. and Mike Wallace. *Gotham: A History of New York City to 1898*. Oxford University Press: 1999.

Capote, Truman. *A Capote Reader*. Random House, 1987.

Capote, Truman. *A House on the Heights*. The Little Bookroom, 2002.

Coleman, Ray. *Lennon: The Definitive Biography*. McGraw-Hill, 1985.

Cornell, Joseph. *Joseph Cornell*. Solomon R. Guggenheim Museum, 1967.

Cummings, E.E. *Complete Poems 1904-1962*. Edited by George J. Firmage. Norton, 1991.

Day, Dorothy. *The Long Loneliness: The Autobiography of Dorothy Day*. Harper and Row, 1952.

Donald, David Herbert. *Lincoln*. Simon and Schuster, 1995.

Dos Passos, John. *Manhattan Transfer*. R. Bentley, 1980.

Douglas, Ann. *Terrible Honesty: Mongrel Manhattan in the 1920s*. Noonday, Farrar, Straus and Giroux, 1996.

Edmiston, Susan. *Literary New York: A History and a Guide*. Peregrine Smith, 1991.

Eisler, Benita. *O'Keeffe and Stieglitz: An American Romance*. Doubleday, 1991.

Ellis, Joseph P. *Founding Brothers: The Revolutionary Generation*. Vintage, 2002.

Fitzgerald, F. Scott. *This Side of Paradise*. C. Scribner's Sons, 1948.

Gelb, Arthur. *O'Neill*. Harper and Row, 1974.

Gooch, Brad. *City Poet: The Life and Times of Frank O'Hara*. Knopf, 1993.

Gorringe, Henry H. *Egyptian Obelisks*. New York, 1882.

Graham, Martha. *Blood Memory*. Doubleday, 1991.

Guggenheim, Peggy. *Confessions of an Art Addict*. Ecco Press, 1997.

New York Panorama, The Guilds Committee for Federal Writers. Pantheon Books, 1984.

Herring, Phillip. *Djuna: The Life and Work of Djuna Barnes*. Viking, 1995.

Hughes, Langston. *The Collected Poems of Langston Hughes*. Edited by Arnold Rampersad. Knopf, 1994.

Hurston, Zora Neale. *Dust Tracks on a Road: An Autobiography*. Lippincott, 1942.

Hurston, Zora Neale. *I love myself when I am laughing ... and then again when I am looking mean and impressive: A Zora Neale Hurston Reader*. Edited by Alice Walker, Feminist Press, 1979.

Hyams, Joe. *Bogie: The Biography of Humphrey Bogart*. New American Library, 1966.

The Encyclopedia of New York City. Edited by Kenneth Jackson. Yale University Press; New York: New-York Historical Society, 1995.

James, Henry. *The American Essays*. Edited by Leon Edel, Princeton University Press, 1989.

James, Henry. *Washington Square*. Modern Library, 1950.

Kalstone, David. *Becoming a Poet: Elizabeth Bishop with Marianne Moore and Robert Lowell*. Farrar, Straus and Giroux, 1989.

Kayton, Bruce and Pete Seeger. *Radical Walking Tours of New York City*. Seven Stories, 2003.

Koolhaus, Rem. *Delirious New York: A Retroactive Manifesto for Manhattan*. Monacelli Press, 1994.

Kroeger, Brooke, *Nellie Bly: Daredevil, Reporter, Feminist*. Crown, 1994.

Kunkel, Thomas. *Genius in Disguise: Harold Ross of the New Yorker*. Random House, 1995.

Lessard, Suzannah. *Architect of Desire: Beauty and Danger in the Stanford White Family*. Dial, 1996.

Marcus, Leonard. *Margaret Wise Brown: Awakened by the Moon*. Beacon, 1992.

Malcolm X and Alex Haley. *The Autobiography of Malcolm X*. Grove, 1966.

Marx, Harpo and Rowland Barber. *Harpo Speaks… About New York*. The Little Bookroom, 2001.

Melville, Herman. *Moby-Dick*. Bantam Classics, 1981.

Milford, Nancy. *Savage Beauty: The Life of Edna St. Vincent Millay*. Random House, 2001.

Milller, Brett. *Life and the Memory of It*. University of California Press, 1993.

Miller, Terry. *Greenwich Village and How it Got That Way*. Crown, 1990.

Mitchell, Joseph. *Up in the Old Hotel*. Pantheon, 1992.

Morris, Edmund. *The Rise of Theodore Roosevelt*. Random House, 1979.

Mooris, Lloyd. *Incredible New York: High Life and Low Life from 1850 to 1950*. Syracuse University Press, 1996.

Naef, Weston and Alfred Stieglitz. *In Focus: Alfred Stieglitz: Photographs from the J. Paul Getty Museum*. J. Paul Getty Trust, 1995.

Nesbitt, Peter and Michelle Dubois. *Over the Line: The Art and Life of Jacob Lawrence*. University of Washington

Press in association with The Jacob and Gwendolyn Lawrence Foundation, 2000.

O'Connor, Francis. *Jackson Pollock*. Museum of Modern Art, 1967.

Olmsted, Frederick Law. *Creating Central Park, 1857-1861: The Papers of Frederick Law Olmsted*. Edited by Charles E. Beveridge and David Schuyler. Johns Hopkins University Press, 1983.

O'Meally, Robert. *Lady Day: The Many Faces of Billie Holiday*. Arcade, 1991.

Osborne, Charles. *W.H. Auden: The Life of a Poet*. Harcourt, Brace and Jovanovich, 1979.

Paine, Thomas. *Thomas Paine: Collected Writings: Common Sense / The Crisis / Rights of Man / The Age of Reason / Pamphlets, Articles, and Letters*. Library of America, 1995.

Panzer, Mary. *Mathew Brady and the Image of History*. Smithsonian Institution Press, 1997.

Parker, Dorothy. *Portable Dorothy Parker*. Penguin Books, 1991.

Peters, Margot. *The House of Barrymore*. Knopf, 1990.

Placksin, Sally. *American Women in Jazz: 1900 to the Present*. Seaview, 1982.

Poe, Edgar Allan. *The Letters of Edgar Allan Poe*. Edited by John Ward Ostrom. Harvard University Press, 1948.

Powell, Dawn. *Dawn Powell at Her Best*. Steerforth, 1994.

Riis, Jacob. *How the Other Half Lives: Studies Among the Tenements of New York*, Penguin, 1997.

Schwarz, Arturo. *The Complete Works of Marcel Duchamp*. Abrams, 1969.

Silverman, Kenneth. *Houdini!!! The Career of Erich Weiss*. HarperCollins, 1996.

Thomas, Dylan. *The Collected Poems of Dylan Thomas*. New Directions, 1953.

Twain, Mark. *The Oxford Companion to Mark Twain*. Edited by Gregg Camfield. Oxford University Press, 2003.

Van Vechten, Carl. *Sacred and Profane Memories*. Knopf, 1971.

Vreeland, Diana. *D.V.* Edited by George Plimpton and Christopher Hemphill, Da Capo, 1997.

Warhol, Andy and Pat Hackett. *The Andy Warhol Diaries*. Warner Books, 1989.

Warner, Charles Dudley. *Washington Irving* Kennikat, 1968.

Wharton, Edith. *The Age of Innocence*. Norton, 2003.

White, Norval and Elliot Willensky, Elliott. *AIA Guide to New York*. Three Rivers, 2000.

Whitman, Walt. *Leaves of Grass and Other Writings*. Edited by Michael Moon. Norton, 2002.

Notes

ABOUT THE AUTHOR

Julia Holmes has a Master of Fine Arts degree in writing from Columbia University. She lives in New York City.

ACKNOWLEDGMENTS

For their generous guidance and help, the author would like to thank the Museum of the City of New York, the New-York Historical Society, the New York Public Library, the Museum of Chinese in the Americas, and the National Park Service, as well as Mario Pereira, Jeff Alexander, and Molly Kromhout.

NOTE TO THE READER

The photographs of James Baldwin, Tallulah Bankhead, F. Scott Fitzgerald, Emma Goldman, Billie Holiday, Zora Neale Hurston, Jacob Lawrence, Edna St. Vincent Millay, Marianne Moore, Georgia O'Keeffe, Diego Rivera, Alfred Stieglitz, and Carl Van Vechten were taken by Carl Van Vechten, whose profile appears on page 194.